The New York Times

MILD CROSSWORDS

The New York Times

MILD CROSSWORDS

150 VERY EASY PUZZLES
Edited by Will Shortz

ST. MARTIN'S GRIFFIN ⬥ NEW YORK

The New York Times

MILD CROSSWORDS

ACROSS

1 Unwanted e-mail
5 Top spot
9 Stupid jerk
14 Attire for Caesar
15 Get-out-of-jail money
16 Toward the back
17 Writer Waugh
18 "Coffee, Tea ___?" (1960s best seller)
19 Light bulb holders
20 "Vanilla Sky" actress
23 Young 'un
24 "I Like ___"
25 Carryall
29 Dead-on
31 How often Santa checks his list
33 Pie ___ mode
34 "I found it!"
36 Tic-tac-toe win
37 One who's close-mouthed
38 Maiden voyage preceder
43 City near Osaka
44 Live
45 "___ the ramparts . . ."
46 Human's cousin
47 Old-time oath
49 1960s tripper Timothy
53 Best Picture of 1997
55 3 on a sundial
57 Grassy area
58 Ballpark maintenance groups
61 Pulitzer winner ___ Jefferson
64 Unaccompanied
65 Bush's ___ of Evil
66 Be of use
67 Swear
68 Nothing more than
69 Crown sparkler
70 Zany Martha
71 Waterfront walkway

DOWN

1 Paper clip alternative
2 Medieval weapon
3 Meeting plan
4 Nutmeg spice
5 "You can't judge ___ by its cover"
6 Wall-to-wall installation
7 Charades player
8 November event
9 Military action?
10 Fad
11 Skirt stitching
12 Atlas page
13 Hosp. areas
21 Supple
22 Highly ornate
26 "___ Ha'i"
27 "Oh, woe!"
28 Charades, e.g.
30 Wedding reception centerpiece
32 Impressed, and how!
35 Slowly, to a conductor
37 Medical breakthrough
38 It's played with a deck of 32 cards
39 Arizona Indian
40 Aid in crime
41 Delphic
42 Thing from the past
47 Sign up
48 Actor Poitier
50 Soviet leader ___ Kosygin
51 Provide with new cable
52 Late P.L.O. head Arafat
54 Texas A & M athlete
56 Grenoble's river
59 Popular PBS science series
60 Interstate exit
61 Rank below Lt. Col.
62 "___ Maria"
63 Like crunchy carrots

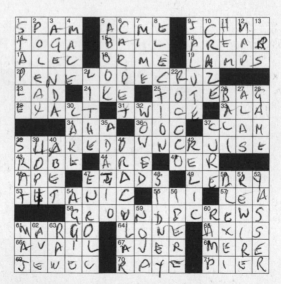

by Allan E. Parrish

2

ACROSS

1 Be sweet on
6 "Quiet!"
9 Boy Scout unit
14 The Bates ___, in "Psycho"
15 Soccer star Hamm
16 Baseball Hall-of-Famer Combs
17 Poolside wear
20 Flat formation
21 Harold Gray's Annie, for one
22 Louse-to-be
23 Mountain debris
25 Gate pivots
27 Bird of 29-Down
30 Smart-mouthed
32 Prefix with asian
33 A, B, C, D or E
35 Marsh plant
39 Giveaway: Var.
41 Place for butts
43 Final authority
44 Copycat's words
46 Auction ending?
47 Race marker
49 Be a buttinsky
51 Disco flasher
54 Put a stop to
56 Jackie's second
57 Available, as a doctor
59 Org. for Annika Sorenstam
63 House wear
66 Kosher
67 Narc's grp.
68 Place for rouge
69 Idyllic places
70 Map rtes.
71 Acts the stool pigeon

DOWN

1 Radio letters
2 1996 Republican standard-bearer
3 Elevator maker
4 Meal
5 Polar helper
6 Campfire treat
7 Maximally cool
8 Truck stop fare
9 Court wear
10 "Awesome!"
11 Sumatra swinger
12 Pal of Kukla and Fran
13 Royal pains
18 Country singer Morgan
19 Contented sighs
24 Ranch wear
26 Russian's refusal
27 Gridiron "zebras"
28 Heavenly glow
29 Mouse, to a 27-Across
31 At the drop of ___
34 Audition tape
36 ___ Scott Decision
37 Celt or Highlander
38 Brontë's Jane
40 Hockey great Phil, familiarly
42 Mogadishu resident
45 Placed in a box, say
48 Late-night Jay
50 Oracle site
51 Fine fur
52 In a tough spot
53 Chain of hills
55 Fitzgerald and others
58 U.S.N. rank below Capt.
60 Hammer's end
61 Cyclist LeMond
62 Questions
64 ___ Tin Tin
65 I.B.M.-compatibles

by Kent Lorentzen

ACROSS

1 Birds' homes
6 Order (around)
10 Quaint cry of shock
14 Not bottled, as beer
15 Choir voice
16 Knot
17 Writer ___ Rogers St. Johns
18 Nay opposers
19 Coin opening
20 Nursery rhyme bakery item
23 Rap's Dr. ___
24 Theater alert
25 More down and out
27 Omaha's home: Abbr.
30 Burden
33 Letters and packages
34 Make, in arithmetic
35 Reception with open arms
39 Was a passenger
41 Play on the radio
42 Supply-and-demand subj.
43 Tidy Lotto prize
48 Mary ___ cosmetics
49 Sweet Spanish dessert
50 Suffix with kitchen
51 Railroad stop: Abbr.
52 Once-fashionable card game
55 PanAm rival
57 Doctors' org.
58 Scarce consolation
64 Pompeii, e.g., today
66 Writer Ephron
67 Anouk of "La Dolce Vita"
68 Capital NNW of Copenhagen
69 Slaughter of the 1940s–'50s Cardinals
70 ___-fatty acid
71 Taking the blue ribbon
72 Fall mo.
73 Elephant groups

DOWN

1 Ark builder
2 Prefix with derm
3 Leave in, as text
4 Bathroom powders
5 Songbird
6 Seabiscuit and Citation, e.g.
7 Barcelona cheers
8 Pierces
9 Flip response to a complaint
10 Naval rank: Abbr.
11 Famous bed tester
12 Love to pieces
13 Keep (from)
21 Mrs. Chaplin
22 Patricia who won an Oscar for "Hud"
26 Backgammon equipment
27 Drug cop
28 Suffix with switch
29 Not the most comfortable place to sleep
31 Russia's ___ Mountains
32 Grin
36 Lawyer's document
37 Palace protector
38 "A Day Without Rain" singer, 2000
40 Singer Fitzgerald
44 Fem. opposite
45 Recites
46 Germany's ___ von Bismarck
47 Educational innovation of the 1960s
52 Tree with pods
53 Entertain
54 By oneself
56 Blazing
59 Let go
60 Play group?
61 Bridge master Sharif
62 Tear
63 "___ of the D'Urbervilles"
65 Word in most of the Commandments

by Kurt Mengel

4

ACROSS

1 Bongo or conga
5 Bellhop's burden
8 Integra maker
13 Diarist Frank
14 Concert halls
16 "Vacancy" sign site
17 Star of 59-Across
20 Got 100 on
21 Extinct bird
22 Brazilian hot spot
23 Director of 59-Across
27 Pampering, briefly
28 Olive __
29 Saragossa's river
30 Circusgoers' sounds
32 Understand
34 "__ Irish Rose"
38 Music featured in 59-Across
42 English assignment
43 Slangy refusal
44 Classic soda brand
45 Tiff
48 PBS funder
50 III, to Jr.
51 Author of 59-Across
56 A.F.L. partner
57 Suffix with Peking
58 "__ #1!"
59 Theme of this puzzle, with "A"
65 Like bell-bottoms, nowadays
66 Claudius's successor
67 Highlander
68 Bus. aides
69 Little bit
70 Fair-hiring org.

DOWN

1 River regulator
2 Genetic stuff
3 Opens, as a gate
4 Hajji's destination
5 Proceed à la Captain Kirk?
6 Nimitz or Halsey: Abbr.
7 Glittering, like a diamond
8 Latin 101 verb
9 It's no bull
10 Wombs
11 Archaeologist's find
12 Free of problems
15 "Have __ and a smile" (old slogan)
18 Wine: Prefix
19 Paint crudely
23 Plumlike fruits
24 Mtn. stat
25 Fiber source
26 Radio personality __ Quivers
27 Repeated words in a famous soliloquy
31 Narc's discovery
33 Hamilton's bill
35 Fundamentally
36 Group values
37 Tibia's locale
39 Doc's needle
40 Half an Orkan farewell
41 Forest name
46 From the top
47 Ex-champ Mike
49 Antiquing agent
51 Capital of Ghana
52 Frasier's brother
53 Whistle blasts
54 Special Forces cap
55 Wipe clean
60 PC component
61 Ring victories, for short
62 Malay Peninsula's Isthmus of __
63 Gloppy stuff
64 List ender

by M. Francis Vuolo

ACROSS

- **1** Layers
- **7** Sound of a lightning bolt
- **10** Cut the hair of
- **14** Main argument
- **15** Frank Sinatra's "___ Fool to Want You"
- **16** Top-notch
- **17** Losses, in accounting
- **18** Charlie Rose's network
- **19** Serving with chop suey
- **20** Jonathan Swift pamphlet about Ireland
- **23** To be given away
- **24** Court
- **25** The whole shebang
- **26** Twisty turn
- **27** See 29-Across
- **29** With 27-Across, get hitched
- **31** Cigarette residue
- **34** Ukr., once
- **35** Flight paths
- **37** Reason for turning down an invitation
- **41** Capulet rival
- **42** Stars and Stripes land: Abbr.
- **43** Ocean
- **44** Guess: Abbr.
- **45** Film director Craven
- **46** Nightwear, for short
- **49** Helios' Roman counterpart
- **51** Calf's mother
- **53** Jai ___
- **54** 2003 teen comedy
- **59** Practice, as skills
- **60** Apply

- **61** Territory
- **62** In addition
- **63** Spy novelist Deighton
- **64** Show clearly
- **65** Spelling contests
- **66** "Acid"
- **67** Caught, as fish

DOWN

- **1** Machine-gun by plane
- **2** One's wife, slangily
- **3** Changes the decor of
- **4** Actor's whisper
- **5** Point at the dinner table?
- **6** Implores
- **7** Nothin'
- **8** Olympian repast
- **9** El ___, Tex.
- **10** Noel

- **11** Clark Kent's gal
- **12** Ancient Peruvian
- **13** Speed away, with "out"
- **21** Number of teeth Goofy has
- **22** Popular discount shoe store
- **27** Tel Aviv native
- **28** Worthless part
- **30** Bandy words
- **32** Capitol Hill V.I.P.: Abbr.
- **33** President after F.D.R.
- **34** Drunkard
- **35** Get better, as wine
- **36** Drs.' group
- **37** Afternoons and evenings, briefly
- **38** Caviar
- **39** Kinda
- **40** Wackos

- **45** Internet start-up?
- **46** Flexible
- **47** Actress Rule
- **48** Like finished contracts
- **50** Nabisco cookies
- **52** Continuously
- **53** Come clean
- **54** Ishmael's captain
- **55** Spy
- **56** Select
- **57** First lady's residence
- **58** Hawk's opposite

Dregs

by Zach Jesse

6

Note: The circled letters will show a "change in the weather."

ACROSS

1 Punching tool
4 Minus
8 Purity units
14 "Quiet down!"
15 Lie next to
16 Supreme Egyptian god
17 Summer weather phenomenon
19 Dreadlocks wearers
20 With little effort
21 Itinerary word
23 Nervous twitches
24 Like an old cigar
25 Repel, as an attack
27 25-Down, e.g.
29 Within view
30 Marina event
35 Drum majors' props
39 Basin accompanier
40 Coeur d'___, Idaho
42 Feminine suffix
43 Arnaz and Ball's studio
45 Eat quickly
47 Pick up
49 Bering, e.g.: Abbr.
50 Dark, heavy type
53 A black key
58 Colombian city
59 Bruised item, maybe
60 Automat, e.g.
61 Ersatz gold
63 Winter weather phenomenon
65 Launderer, at times
66 Sheriff Taylor's son
67 Former New York City mayor Beame

68 Admits, with "up"
69 Not very much
70 Part of CBS: Abbr.

DOWN

1 Hibachi residue
2 Toast choice
3 Tibet's capital
4 Like the Wild West
5 Popular site for collectors
6 Ford Explorer, e.g.: Abbr.
7 Martin of "Roxanne"
8 Martial arts wear
9 "I ___ Rock" (1966 hit)
10 Went back to the top
11 Bit of silliness

12 CD segment
13 Get snippy with
18 Up to, briefly
22 Actor Holm
25 High school subj.
26 Ovine utterance
28 Some prom night drivers
30 Hospital unit
31 Have markers out
32 Loser to D.D.E.
33 Lots and lots and lots
34 A browser browses it, with "the"
36 Lennon's lady
37 Compass heading
38 Six-yr. term holder
41 It smells
44 Topper
46 Like most tires

48 Baseball put-out
50 Ballet rail
51 "Stand and Deliver" star
52 Après-ski drink
54 McHenry and Sumter: Abbr.
55 Olin and Horne
56 Sheikdom of song
57 Pounds on an Underwood
58 Salon creation
60 Director Kazan
62 Jackie Onassis' sister
64 Make a choice

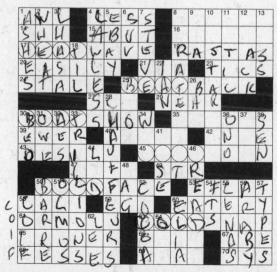

by Eric Berlin

ACROSS

1 Manila envelope closer
6 Computer screen image
10 "Spare tire"
14 Dominican Republic neighbor
15 Italia's capital
16 Interlude
17 Luggage clip-on
18 "Amo, amas, ___ . . ."
19 Prod
20 It made Leary bleary
22 Rizzuto of the 1940s–'50s Yankees
24 Fire, as from a job
25 Unruffled
28 Laid on generously
30 Tot's wheels
32 Hwy. mishap respondent
33 Med school subj.
34 Driveway occupant
36 Becomes a domehead
40 Skirt that shows off legs
41 Pasture
43 Forsaken
44 Fossil fuel blocks
46 Harry Potter's lightning bolt, e.g.
47 Suffix with buck
48 Piercing site
50 Exceed the bounds of
52 Summary holder?
56 With resolute spirit
57 WSW's opposite
58 Party for lei wearers

59 ___ Lanka
60 ___ Jay Lerner of Lerner & Loewe
62 Jolt
64 Jazz's James and Jones
68 Fall's opposite
69 Sea eagle
70 System utilizing grates
71 Editor's mark
72 Space capsule insignia
73 Rulers before Lenin

DOWN

1 Greek X
2 Boy
3 River island
4 Downers?
5 Farm pen
6 Tax deferral means: Abbr.

7 Connectors?
8 Nebraska city
9 Not an emigré
10 Winter ailment
11 Leave in the ___
12 Pond growths
13 Mix
21 Joe that won't keep you up
23 Arm or leg
25 Envelope sticker
26 Bert's Muppet pal
27 Late Princess of Wales
29 Uppers?
31 San ___ Obispo, Calif.
35 Norway's patron saint
37 Peter of "Casablanca"
38 Slobber
39 Like a winter wonderland

42 Wine residue
45 Comedian Mort
49 Sandwich with sauerkraut
51 Least seen
52 Closes in on
53 Dark
54 Pull one's leg
55 Mrs. Bush
61 Volleyball equipment
63 Small coal size
65 Intl. flier, once
66 ___ Lingus
67 Last year's jrs.

by Patrick Merrell

8

ACROSS
1 Cripple
5 Chorus member
9 Old adders
14 Alan of "The Seduction of Joe Tynan"
15 Ballet move
16 Early computer language
17 Light gas
18 Gawk at
19 Type of type
20 Examination, redundantly
23 Increase, with "up"
24 Quick on the uptake
25 Frisk, with "down"
28 "The Way We ___"
31 Perfectos, e.g.
36 Director Kazan
38 Colonel or captain
40 Gymnast Comaneci
41 Pestering, redundantly
44 Uniform shade
45 Student driver, usually
46 Slugger Sammy
47 Gets smart with
49 Try for a part
51 One of 100 in D.C.
52 Conquistador's prize
54 Whisper sweet nothings
56 Angry outburst, redundantly
63 Oscar winner Foster
64 Unable to decide
65 Took off
67 Maine college town

68 "Zounds!"
69 Jacob's twin
70 Von Münchhausen, e.g.
71 Lady of Lisbon
72 Medium-___

DOWN
1 "Hoo-ey!"
2 Baldwin of "Talk Radio"
3 Elvis or Madonna, e.g.
4 Lord's home
5 Skin cream ingredient
6 Longevity at the box office
7 Soft mineral
8 "Il Trovatore," e.g.
9 Driving the getaway car for

10 Island east of Java
11 Z ___ zebra
12 Like lowest-mileage driving
13 Diamonds, slangily
21 Stitch up
22 Bars at the checkout counter: Abbr.
25 Eats like a bird
26 Maui greeting
27 Louise and Turner
29 Carry on
30 Keyboard key
32 Comedian's stock
33 Sonora "so long"
34 Washer cycle
35 "Contact" author Carl
37 Invites
39 Patella's place
42 Get snockered

43 It puts the squeeze on
48 Hindu title
50 Singer McLean
53 Made a choice
55 Put forward
56 Mrs. Dithers
57 Dump problem
58 El ___ (weather factor)
59 Like some pizza orders
60 Gulf land
61 Rick's love in "Casablanca"
62 Something shed
63 Applicant's goal
66 Expected in

by Randall J. Hartman

ACROSS

1 Homebuilder's strip
5 Bruins of the Pac-10
9 Unflashy
14 "Can you hear me? . . . hear me? . . . hear me?"
15 Horse in a '60s sitcom
16 Ralph ___ Emerson
17 "What a shame!"
18 Laser light
19 Go in
20 Overly florid writing
23 Acorn maker
24 Before, to Byron
25 Recharges one's batteries, so to speak
27 Bucky Beaver's toothpaste, in old ads
31 Switchblade
33 Weapons of ___ destruction
37 Pesos
39 Prefix with metric or tonic
40 Author Ferber
41 1951 Alec Guinness film, with "The"
44 City west of Tulsa
45 Night before
46 Go on Social Security, maybe
47 One-and-only
48 Mouth off to
50 September bloom
51 Frisbee, e.g.
53 Some univ. instructors
55 "I knew it!"
58 The 1890s
64 Reaction to the Beatles, once
66 Flying: Prefix
67 Pitch

68 "Git ___ Little Doggies"
69 Section of seats
70 58-Across and others
71 "Death Be Not Proud" poet John
72 North Carolina college
73 Hourly pay

DOWN

1 ___ year (2004, e.g.)
2 Legal rights grp.
3 In that direction, to a whaler
4 The "H" in "M*A*S*H": Abbr.
5 Brownish
6 Thin pancakes
7 "All in the Family" producer Norman
8 Call on the carpet
9 Clean the carpet

10 Brownish
11 Choir voice
12 Notion
13 Social misfit
21 Memorize
22 ___-faire
26 Gets the lead out?
27 Runs in neutral
28 Upright or baby grand
29 Blacksmith's block
30 Had to have
32 Root beer brand
34 Fess up to
35 Sound of slumber
36 Cavalry blade
38 Texas oil city
42 Clear out, as before a hurricane
43 Renter's paper
49 Alternative to mono
52 Likeness
54 Decorate

55 "Diary of ___ Housewife" (1970 film)
56 Angel's headwear
57 Unattributed: Abbr.
59 Bridal wear
60 Grind with the teeth
61 Distinctive quality
62 Quarter-mile race, e.g.
63 In addition
65 Holiday ___

by Gregory E. Paul

ACROSS

1 Sagittarius, with "the"
7 "My gal" et al.
11 Any ship
14 Aplenty
15 Apple product
16 Wee one
17 Goddess of love's love
18 Washroom
20 "___ the season . . ."
21 Roof part
23 Certain refrigerators
24 Broke ground
26 Chicken order
28 Pub stock
29 Showy annual
31 This puzzle has a secret one, starting with the third letter of 4-Down
34 Prefix with classical
36 "___ we forget . . ."
37 Salon stiffener
38 "Unbelievable!"
42 Patient people
44 "Exodus" hero
45 Misses the mark
47 Govt. code crackers
48 What to do to read the secret message (going diagonally down, then diagonally back up the under side)
51 Inputs into a computer
55 Afternoon affairs
56 Say ___ (refuse)
58 Smarmy
59 Throat part
61 Scent

63 "If I Ruled the World" rapper
64 "Is everything all right?"
66 Manage, slangily
68 Dogfaces
69 Scruff
70 Regal fur
71 Plea at sea
72 Took action against
73 Cash in

DOWN

1 First name in mystery
2 Contacts from space
3 Skeleton site
4 Sweetie pie
5 Old railroad name
6 Cut again
7 Llama's head?
8 Docs' grp.
9 Hot issue
10 Con guy
11 "The Flintstones" setting
12 More than a pest
13 Popular ice cream
19 Locker room supply
22 Nobleman above a baron: Abbr.
25 Disavow
27 Greek Mother Earth
30 Booms' opposites
32 ID in a library
33 Overhead trains
35 ___ cloud (cosmic debris)
38 Monopoly token
39 Choral work
40 Portrait, e.g.
41 St. Paul's architect

43 Belafonte song opener
46 Scared a bit
49 "Calm down . . ."
50 Part of E.S.T. Abbr.
52 Small digit
53 "Seinfeld" role
54 Modus operandi
57 Awed one
59 Marks
60 Island get-together
62 Hard to find
65 Reveal, poetically
67 Mil. authority

by Joe Bower and Nancy Salomon

ACROSS

1 People who make you yawn
6 Tibetan monk
10 British fellow
14 Crème de la crème
15 Had payments due
16 Part of a Valentine bouquet
17 Greek marketplace
18 Glenn Miller's "In the ___"
19 Leave out
20 Testifier in a court case
23 Sea eagles
24 "___ will be done . . ."
25 Event with floats
29 Female in a pride
33 Hebrew prophet
34 Be enraptured
36 Animal that beats its chest
37 Pleasant excursion
41 Golf peg
42 Abominates
43 Gillette razor
44 Regards highly
46 Mother of Joseph
48 Wayne film "___ Bravo"
49 Prayer's end
51 Top of a tall building, maybe
59 After-bath powder
60 Former Fed chairman Greenspan
61 Harold who composed "Over the Rainbow"

62 Gait faster than a walk
63 Film part
64 Cotton thread
65 Disastrous marks for a gymnast
66 Gardener's spring purchase
67 Outpouring

DOWN

1 Smile widely
2 Korbut of the 1972 Olympics
3 Very funny person
4 Raison d'___
5 Charred
6 Fictional salesman Willy
7 M.P.'s hunt them
8 Pussy's cry
9 Building wing
10 Actor Hume

11 Where the heart is, they say
12 Sale tag caution
13 Dogs, but rarely hogs
21 Anger
22 Daring bikini
25 Stickum
26 French girlfriends
27 Synonym man
28 Cigarette's end
29 Colleague of Clark at The Daily Planet
30 Our planet
31 Steeple
32 Flower part
34 Film designers' designs
35 Tiny
38 Not our
39 Tea urns
40 Tic-___-toe
45 Builds

46 ___ Speedwagon
47 Chronicles
49 "It is ___ told by an idiot": Macbeth
50 Dug up
51 ___ the Great (10th-century king)
52 Building near a silo
53 ___ gin fizz
54 ___ vera
55 What icicles do
56 Lohengrin's love
57 Boston cager, informally
58 Leg's middle

by Robert Dillman

ACROSS

1 Let out the waist of, e.g.
6 Ark or bark
10 Mexican Mlle.
14 Pet ___
15 Up to it
16 Rattler's posture
17 Supporter of the arts?
18 Title start of a 2003 Al Franken best seller
19 Still pink
20 Fool a onetime child actor?
23 Tiebreakers, briefly
25 Clean-air org.
26 Elite group
27 Cause a sleepy old man to stumble?
32 Car owner's document
33 With respect to
34 Toe the line
35 Black Russian ingredient
37 20's dispensers
41 "See ya!"
42 Orderly grouping
43 Express gratitude to a country singer?
47 Greasy ___
49 Rip-roaring time
50 Frisk, with "down"
51 Tie up a Midwest senator?
56 Wholly absorbed
57 Show opener
58 Like a luxury car
61 Suit to ___
62 Guitarist Atkins
63 Give a wide berth

64 Garden intruder
65 Unabridged dictionary, e.g.
66 The out crowd

DOWN

1 Mock, in a way
2 Grazing locale
3 Bikini atoll, once
4 At any time
5 Take over for, as a pitcher
6 Europe's ___ Peninsula
7 Eastern sashes
8 A Baldwin
9 New-Ager John
10 Dead Sea document
11 Band hand
12 Gets pooped
13 Heads-up
21 Number cruncher, for short

22 Croupier's tool
23 "Beetle Bailey" dog
24 Chicago paper, familiarly, with "the"
28 Panel layer
29 Lehár's "The Merry ___"
30 Publicity, slangily
31 Org. whose members are packing?
35 Chablis, for one
36 ___ Park, Ill.
37 "Exodus" hero
38 Secret exit, perhaps
39 Doll's cry
40 Part of CBS: Abbr.
41 Gives the boot
42 Election loser
43 Rug, so to speak

44 Emceed
45 Set off
46 Fall behind
47 Scarecrow stuffing
48 Chatter idly
52 It's true
53 Bounce back
54 Agenda unit
55 Zero, on a court
59 ___-Atlantic
60 QB's pickups

by Seth A. Abel

ACROSS

1 Chances
5 Wires on a bicycle wheel
11 Tavern
14 In ___ of (substituting for)
15 One of Jerry's pals on "Seinfeld"
16 Down Under bird
17 Bejeweled president?
19 Mo. of Presidents' Day
20 "Much ___ About Nothing"
21 Dine
22 Planet
24 Pale, aging president?
28 Most elderly
31 Hang around for
32 Place to store valuables
33 Hair colorer
34 ___ and hearty
38 Devoted follower
40 Demolisher
42 More's opposite
43 Opening for a tab
45 Zeal
46 Burning up
48 Disinfects
49 Comic president?
53 Wheel turners
54 Tint
55 Historic period
58 Compete (for)
59 Hirsute president?
64 Mont Blanc, e.g.
65 Money earned
66 Communicate by hand
67 Tennis court divider
68 Check receivers
69 Neighborhood

DOWN

1 Gymnast Korbut
2 Stopped working, as an engine
3 Showroom model
4 Total
5 Trigonometric ratio
6 Ancient Greek thinker
7 Paddle
8 Set of tools
9 WSW's reverse
10 Composer Rachmaninoff
11 Obscure
12 Tiny creature
13 "American Idol" winner ___ Studdard
18 Frothy
23 One using lots of soap
24 Object of a dowser's search
25 Reclined
26 Lived
27 Like hen's teeth
28 The White House's ___ Office
29 Delicate fabric
30 Performing twosomes
33 "We love to fly, and it shows" airline
35 Alan of "M*A*S*H"
36 Ponce de ___
37 Goofs
39 Nicholas I or II
41 Appraiser
44 "___ the land of the free . . ."
47 Send again
48 Slides
49 From Jakarta, e.g.
50 Kick out of the country
51 Snoozed
52 Lemon ___ (herb)
55 Kuwaiti ruler
56 Fury
57 "___ and the King of Siam"
60 Santa ___ winds
61 Wintry
62 Shad product
63 Land between Can. and Mex.

by Charles Barasch

14

ACROSS

1 Like some appliances, electrically
5 Field of work
9 Daft
14 Bailiwick
15 Gossip tidbit
16 Wahine's welcome
17 Auto trailblazer
19 Eatery
20 Small sofa
21 "Drat!"
23 Wrap up
24 Ltr. holders
26 First course, often
28 Auto trailblazer
34 Kid-___ (Saturday a.m. fare)
35 "The Thin Man" canine
36 Operation at the Alamo
37 Yalies
39 Slangy denial
42 Protein bean
43 Freeze over
45 Self-identifying word
47 "All Things Considered" network
48 Auto trailblazer
52 Slip on the galley
53 Dead against
54 Little shaver
57 Suffragist Carrie
59 Plays the role of
63 Geologic period
65 What 17-, 28- and 48-Across were, so to speak
67 Alphabet set
68 Director Kazan
69 Equestrian's grip
70 Camera setting
71 Withhold from
72 Hot Springs and others

DOWN

1 Sounds of relief
2 Canadian native
3 Subject of an insurance appraisal
4 OPEC is one
5 Emergency need at sea
6 Skater Midori
7 Dork
8 Ellipsis alternative
9 Villains
10 Poetry-spouting pugilist
11 Muscle quality
12 Ergo
13 Prison exercise area
18 Gossipmonger
22 Here-there connector
25 Young lady of Sp.
27 Trident-shaped letters
28 Radioer's "Good as done!"
29 Toulouse "Toodle-oo"
30 "The Cider House Rules" co-star, 1999
31 Sierra ___
32 Land from which Moses came
33 Bring up
34 Bride hider
38 Spades or clubs
40 Explosive star
41 Refuse admission to
44 Prep mentally
46 Lumberjack's first cut
49 Reviewer of books, for short
50 Place of rapid growth
51 Soda bottle units
54 Fall faller
55 Gibbons and gorillas
56 "Go ahead!"
58 Scrabble piece
60 Trickle
61 Inter ___
62 Workers' ID's
64 Sound in a barn rafter
66 Martini ingredient

by Bob Frank and Nancy Salomon

ACROSS

1 Shade trees
5 Consent (to)
10 Baby bottle contents
14 "See you later!"
15 Senior dances
16 Assert
17 Flimflam
19 Roman cloak
20 ___ of a kind
21 Warp-resistant wood
22 Temptress
23 One who went to tell the king the sky was falling
26 Not just ask
29 Commotions
30 Family data
31 Juicy tropical fruit
33 Watering hole
36 Perform a dance with a shake
40 WNW's opposite
41 Hackneyed
42 Wall Street inits.
43 Wearisome one
44 Archipelago parts
46 Some messing around
49 Narrative
51 The "A" of ABM
52 Just great
55 Royal attendant
56 Mishmash
59 Asia's shrinking ___ Sea
60 County north of San Francisco
61 Where a stream may run
62 Lots of
63 Clay pigeon shoot
64 Final word

DOWN

1 Talk back?
2 Big cat
3 Nutmeg relative
4 Not worth a ___
5 Tack on
6 Bad pun response
7 Having lots of ups and downs
8 Cousin of an ostrich
9 Road curve
10 Morning prayers
11 Off-white
12 Theater section
13 Skating champ Michelle
18 British gun
22 Busybody
23 Dish of leftovers
24 Group of jurors
25 Jittery
26 Florida's Miami-___ County
27 Selves
28 Apportion, with "out"
31 Miser's hoarding
32 Alias
33 ___ terrier
34 Nuisance
35 One side of a vote
37 Jet black
38 "Listen!"
39 Exclusively
43 By the skin of one's teeth
44 Purpose
45 Omit
46 Title colonel in a 1960s sitcom
47 Military chaplain
48 Actress Dickinson
49 Unsolicited e-mail
50 "Gone With the Wind" estate
52 Man cast out of paradise
53 Girl-watch, e.g.
54 Sharp
56 ___ Pinafore
57 Acorn's source
58 Reproductive cells

by Anne Garelick

16

ACROSS
1 Up to, in ads
4 Ozzy Osbourne's music, for short
9 Has a yen
14 Prefix with puncture
15 Big name in refrigerators
16 Good, in Guadalajara
17 Sound of hesitation
18 Desilu head
20 That is
22 Posted
23 Pan pal?
26 Ham, to Noah
29 One who knows all the secrets
30 Deep down
33 Educators' org.
35 Dickens's Heep
36 Jefferson's note
42 Yours, old-style
43 Suffix with expert
44 Spoiled
47 Austere
53 With 36-Down, "Next . . ."
54 Weevil's hatching place
56 Pennsylvania's __ Mountains
59 Usher's locale
60 Michael Jordan, for years
64 Rest and relaxation site
65 Egyptian Christians
66 π, e.g.
67 Often-hectic hosp. areas
68 Minute __
69 Old New Yorker cartoonist William
70 On the __

DOWN
1 Island where Gauguin painted
2 Harborbound, in winter
3 Light flux units
4 Fountain treat
5 Swift bird on foot
6 Center X or O
7 Japanese cartoon art
8 "Deck the Halls" syllables
9 Genesis brother
10 Rubik creation
11 Foremast attachment
12 Big picture?: Abbr.
13 Our sun
19 Cheery song
21 Move among the moguls
24 Former Attorney General
25 Composer Jacques
27 Test type
28 Utmost
31 Airline's home base
32 "__ tu" (Verdi aria)
34 Frazier foe
36 See 53-Across
37 Trachea
38 Que. neighbor
39 Cotillion girl
40 __ prof.
41 Bank take-back
42 Former flying inits.
45 Slip __ (blunder)
46 Bloodmobile visitors
48 Not digital
49 Sacrifice fly stat.
50 Ejected
51 Elite N.F.L.er
52 N.Y. Mets' div.
55 Go __ for (support)
57 Eight: Prefix
58 Wine holder
60 Syringe amts.
61 All the rage
62 Colorado native
63 XXVI doubled

by Alan Arbesfeld

ACROSS

1 Continental currency
5 Give off
9 Assumed name
14 Jazz's Kenton
15 Go (over) carefully
16 Officer's shield
17 Easy wins
19 With 62-Across, a possible title for this puzzle
20 Long sandwich
21 Regarding
23 Word after ready or petty
24 Web addresses, for short
26 List-ending abbr.
28 Young hospital helpers
33 Capone and Capp
34 Always, poetically
35 Predicament
37 Where a car may end up after an accident
40 Have dinner
42 Talent
43 Says "cheese"
45 Part of a baseball uniform
47 Tic-___-toe
48 Credits for doing nice things
52 The writing ___ the wall
53 Choir voice
54 Play parts
57 Fishhook feature
59 Corporate money managers: Abbr.
62 See 19-Across
64 Some USA Today graphics
67 The "V" of VCR
68 "Good grief!"
69 "Uh-huh"
70 Snoozer's sound
71 Old salts
72 Italia's capital

DOWN

1 PC key
2 The Beehive State
3 Yard tool
4 Small winning margin, in baseball
5 Ecol. watchdog
6 Baked beans ingredient
7 Bothers
8 Teacher, at times
9 Middle muscles, for short
10 Legal assistant
11 Brainstorm
12 Mellows, as wine
13 Adam's third
18 Basic dictionary entry
22 Soul singer Redding
25 Caustic substance
27 Rental units: Abbr.
28 Get to the top of
29 Up and about
30 It may be called on the battlefield
31 Singer Bonnie
32 "___ Marner"
33 Computer pop-ups
36 R.N.'s forte
38 Religious site
39 Chops
41 Goldilocks sat in his chair
44 Snooty person
46 Campaigner, in brief
49 All worked up
50 Hankering
51 "That's cheating!"
54 Ones heading for the hills?: Abbr.
55 Nickel or dime
56 Commotion
58 Latvia's capital
60 Approximately
61 Flower stalk
63 Tiller's tool
65 S.&L. offerings
66 Baltic or Bering

by Gail Grabowski

ACROSS

1 One of five Norwegian kings
5 Times in history
9 Longed
14 Bit of mockery
15 Cancel
16 Spoils
17 Breezes through, as a test
18 Chanel competitor
19 Boxer Roberto
20 Story written by 38-Across
23 1960s radical grp.
24 Cities Service competitor
25 And
26 Quaker ___
28 1960s-'70s baseball All-Star ___ Santo
30 It's sometimes hard to make them meet
33 Nicks
35 "___ does what Nintendon't" (old slogan)
37 ___ polloi
38 Writer born March 2, 1904
41 Gooey green substance in the title of a 38-Across story
43 Professional org.
44 It often thickens
46 Thief's "savings"
47 Goes on and on
49 Summer mo.
50 Dueler of 1804
51 Verve
53 Pitcher
55 Took a load off
58 Birthplace of 38-Across
62 Fleeced

63 ___ Minor
64 Service org. since the 1850s
65 Emerged
66 Verve
67 Hammer-wielding deity
68 Fellows
69 "Do it, or ___!"
70 Have the ___ for

DOWN

1 1973 "Love Train" singers, with "the"
2 Ripped (into)
3 Tautology spoken by the title character in 11-Down
4 Jacket accompanier
5 Overage
6 Cheers (for)
7 38-Across and others
8 Eye malady
9 Singer Paula
10 18 holes, say
11 Book written by 38-Across
12 And others, for short
13 Unit of force
21 Eases
22 Dance for two
27 Carbon dating determination
29 Fair-hiring agcy.
31 43-Across members
32 Religious person with a turban
33 Do-or-die time
34 Cookbook writer Rombauer
36 Crazy
39 70-Across, e.g.

40 Former franc part
42 P.O. delivery
45 38-Across's real name, in brief
48 Most clever
50 Miss the start
52 Aconcagua is their tallest peak
54 "Marat/Sade" playwright Peter
56 Fancy tie
57 Romanov V.I.P.'s
58 Kind of carpet
59 Site of a sweat bead
60 Disconcert
61 Fable

by Charles Barasch

ACROSS

1 Fed. food inspectors
5 Raindrop sound
9 Songwriters' grp.
14 Lecherous look
15 Cleveland cagers, briefly
16 Weigher
17 Co-star of 36-Down
19 Jabs
20 It's heard on the grapevine
21 I. M. Pei, for one
23 Red flag, e.g.
24 Lyricist Lorenz ___
25 See 41-Down
29 Online film maker
33 Star of 36-Down
38 Stallone title role
39 Out of port
40 January in Juárez
42 "___ delighted!"
43 Brouhahas
45 Co-star of 36-Down
47 Knock over
49 Fencing blade
50 The "Y" of B.Y.O.B.
52 Barge's route
57 100% incorrect
62 Whooping ___
63 '50s candidate Stevenson
64 Setting for 36-Down
66 ___ breath (flower)
67 "Guilty" or "not guilty"
68 Flex
69 Boffo show
70 Gardener's bagful
71 Counts up

DOWN

1 Part of UHF
2 Capital of South Korea
3 Film director Jonathan
4 Shady spot
5 Alternatives to Macs
6 Syllables in "Deck the Halls"
7 Finished
8 Intimidate, with "out"
9 Person with goals
10 Co-star of 36-Down
11 Wedding reception centerpiece
12 Writer Waugh
13 Exterminator's target
18 Garden products name
22 "Hee ___"
26 ___-inspiring
27 Lois of "Superman"
28 "___ Jacques" (children's song)
30 Naval leader: Abbr.
31 "Dancing Queen" quartet
32 Big name in water faucets
33 Makeshift river conveyance
34 Norway's capital
35 Certain tide
36 TV series that premiered in 1974
37 Cause for a plumber
41 With 25-Across, 50%
44 Molasseslike
46 Muhammad's birthplace
48 Where Switz. is
51 Easy wins
53 Popular Caribbean island
54 Sans clothing
55 Put ___ to (halt)
56 English city NE of Manchester
57 Applies lightly
58 Dutch cheese
59 "Duchess of ___" (Goya work)
60 Cairo's river
61 Elation
65 Mouthful of gum

by Allan E. Parrish

ACROSS

1 Certain iron setting
6 Govt. bill
11 Mars or Milky Way
14 Really, really want
15 Toiled in the galley
16 "I love," to Livy
17 Old "Tonight Show" intro
19 Transcript fig.
20 CPR giver
21 Have a late meal
22 Unlit?
24 Scale of mineral hardness
26 Lions' lairs
29 Tee cry
30 Zeno of ___
31 Atmospheric region with a "hole"
34 Ladies of Spain
36 Word repeated after "Que," in song
37 Draft letters
38 Head honcho
42 Blood-typing letters
45 When repeated, a fish
46 Hose woes
50 Loofah, e.g.
54 Neighbor of Yemen
55 "___ girl!"
56 Hymn start
57 Fodder's place
58 Follower of Zeno
60 U-Haul rental
62 Make public
63 Haw's partner
64 Women's tennis immortal
69 Historic period

70 1940s–'50s slugger Ralph
71 More despicable
72 Thesaurus entry: Abbr.
73 Big name in printers
74 Goes up and down and . . .

DOWN

1 Connived
2 Vibrating effect
3 Made of clay
4 "___ Maria"
5 Many a teen's room
6 Saint-___ (French resort)
7 Japanese drama
8 Hold title to
9 Half a score
10 Breyers competitor

11 Supermarket helpers
12 Current units
13 Lions, at times
18 Self-defense sport
23 Son-gun link
25 Swedish auto
27 Having a snack
28 Snick-a-___
32 Poet's preposition
33 Laddie's love
35 Jazzman Zoot
39 Letterman dental feature
40 Half a train?
41 Son of Seth
42 Makes ashamed
43 9-volt, e.g.
44 Cushioned footrest
47 In a friendly manner
48 1600s stargazer

49 "Z" makers, in comics
51 "Bali ___"
52 Wield authority
53 Dutch seaport
59 Word that can follow the ends of 17-, 31-, 38-, 50- and 64-Across
61 Blue shade
65 Place to put gloss
66 Elected officials
67 Corporate V.I.P.
68 "Flying Down to ___"

by Sarah Keller

ACROSS

1 Did laps in a pool
5 Foolhardy
9 "She loves me . . . she loves me not" flower
14 "Horrors!"
15 "¿Cómo ___ usted?"
16 Blast from the past
17 Spick-and-span
18 Genesis twin
19 F.B.I. worker
20 Achieve initial success
23 Singletons
24 Bullfight cheer
25 Suffix with lion
28 Oar-powered ship
31 Like a fiddle
34 "Scratch and win" game
36 Pub brew
37 Sweep under the rug
38 Estimates
42 Intl. oil group
43 Take to court
44 Use crib notes
45 Cheyenne's locale: Abbr.
46 Kind of underwear
49 Foxy
50 "___ Drives Me Crazy" (Fine Young Cannibals hit)
51 Western tribe
53 Completely mistaken
60 Improperly long sentence
61 Risk-free
62 Number not on a grandfather clock

63 Space shuttle gasket
64 With warts and all
65 Elm or elder
66 ___ Park, Colo.
67 Camper's cover
68 Hankerings

DOWN

1 Spiritual, e.g.
2 Cry on a roller coaster
3 Med. school class
4 E pluribus unum, for instance
5 "___ Madness" (1936 antidrug film)
6 Whence St. Francis
7 Night twinkler
8 Düsseldorf dwelling

9 Within one's power
10 Pond buildup
11 March 15, e.g.
12 Trig term
13 "Are we there ___?"
21 In first place
22 Marisa of "My Cousin Vinny"
25 Arm joint
26 Unrinsed, maybe
27 Fifth-century pope
29 Autumn yard worker
30 Santa's little helper
31 Pink-slips
32 Perfect
33 Short-tempered
35 Nurse's skill, for short

37 "What'd you say?"
39 Gray
40 Feel sorry about
41 Symbol at the head of a musical staff
46 First ___ first
47 Breakfast bread
48 Swear (to)
50 Masonry
52 Nearing retirement age, maybe
53 Yours and mine
54 The "U" in I.C.U.
55 Future atty.'s exam
56 Facilitate
57 Dublin's land
58 Legal claim
59 Goes kaput
60 Salmon eggs

by Gregory E. Paul

ACROSS

1 Spain and Portugal
7 ___ alai
10 Amtrak stop: Abbr.
13 Vietnamese port
14 End abruptly
16 Tense
17 Source of a cry at night
18 Wound
19 ___ Maria
20 Tree-lined road: Abbr.
21 Contribute
22 Uses the HOV lanes, perhaps
24 Butt of jokes
27 Blond shade
29 Krypton or radon
30 Security numbers
33 Groovy
36 ___ apso (dog)
37 It's south of Eur.
38 Sylvester's co-star in "Rocky"
40 Lay turf
41 "As luck would have it . . ."
44 Chemin de ___ (French railway)
45 Med. care provider
46 With a discount of
47 Victoria's Secret item
51 Hush-hush D.C. org.
53 Lena of "The Unbearable Lightness of Being"
54 Guitarist Nugent
55 Seasonal mall employees
59 "Praise be to God!"
61 After-class aides
62 Inclination
63 Even (with)
64 Seattle-to-Las Vegas dir.
65 Rhoda's TV mom
66 Talk show groups

DOWN

1 Person on a poster
2 Undoing
3 Chemical endings
4 Gives off, as heat
5 ___ We Trust
6 Slates
7 Louis-Dreyfus of "Seinfeld"
8 Not yet apprehended
9 Suffix with expert
10 Simply smashing
11 Shrimper's net
12 Courtroom figs.
14 Shore dinner special
15 Some needles
23 Trattoria course
24 Women, casually
25 Dos cubed
26 Military sch.
28 Leave a permanent mark on
31 Bank features
32 Large barrel
33 Run away
34 Is unwell
35 Howls like a dog
39 Brave, for instance
42 Rich, as a voice
43 24-hour
44 Penalized, as a speeder
47 Paint layers
48 "Deutschland über ___"
49 Creator of Pooh and Piglet
50 Nikon rival
52 Place for sweaters?
56 Hit the bottle
57 ___ Sea, east of the Caspian
58 Lith. and Lat., once
60 Wreath

by Eric Berlin

ACROSS

1 Likely
4 Hot dish with beans
9 Bridge maven Charles
14 Justice Sandra ___ O'Connor
15 Appealingly shocking
16 Licorice flavoring
17 Antique auto
19 Frank of rock's Mothers of Invention
20 Vegetable oil component
21 The "S" of CBS
23 Black currant
25 Humiliated
29 Tea server's question
33 Out of one's mind
36 Van Susteren of Fox News
37 Alternative to a nail
38 "That's ___!" (angry denial)
40 Conductor's stick
42 Long-eared hopper
43 Neuters
45 Danger
47 Fashion inits.
48 Cause of an out
51 Refuses
52 Smoothed
56 Drops
60 Baghdad resident
61 ___ Mongolia
64 Small frosted cake
66 Item confiscated at an airport
67 Goofy
68 Wrestler's locale
69 Seasoned sailors

70 Parachute pulls
71 They: Fr.

DOWN

1 ___ committee
2 Newswoman Zahn
3 Varieties
4 Asexual reproduction
5 Where spokes meet
6 Showy flower
7 Showy flower
8 "Beware the ___ . . ."
9 Park shelters
10 Parading . . . or a hint to this puzzle's theme
11 ___ Van Winkle
12 Psychic's claim
13 Educator's org.

18 Japanese soup
22 Punch out, as Morse code
24 Kosovo war participant
26 Not stay on the path
27 Pitchers
28 Wooden pin
30 Bounded
31 Absolute
32 New Zealand native
33 A brig has two
34 ___ male (top dog)
35 Locked book
39 Command to people who are 10-Down
41 "Just do it" sloganeer
44 Gentlemen of España

46 An original tribe of Israel
49 Scatter, as seeds
50 Feudal figure
53 Ashley's country-singing mother
54 Sweet'N Low rival
55 Mud, dust and grime
57 Like "The Lord of the Rings"
58 It's north of Carson City
59 Movie rating unit
61 Approves
62 Spanish article
63 Up to, informally
65 Polit. maverick

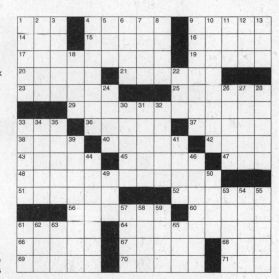

by Joy M. Andrews

24

ACROSS

1 Trunk item
6 Job seeker's success
11 Gridlock
14 Poe's middle name
15 Bisect
16 Mentalist Geller
17 All-freshman team?
19 Zero
20 Ugly Duckling, in reality
21 Reflect (on)
22 Arcade coin
24 So-so
26 Bridle's partner
27 Peter Cottontail?
32 Tonsil neighbor
33 Smallish field
34 Put on TV
37 Boone, to rustics
38 Have a ball?
40 Blue Triangle org.
41 Inventor Whitney
42 Fill-in
43 Heart of France
44 Answer to "Who wrote 'The Highwayman'?"
48 Historical Scottish county
50 Summoned Jeeves
51 M-1, for one
52 Tokyo ties
54 Charlie Chaplin's widow
58 60s muscle car
59 Milliner on the move?
62 Poet's preposition
63 Zoo critter
64 Campfire treat
65 "Shame on you"
66 Supersized
67 Tournament favorites

DOWN

1 __-serif
2 Furrow former
3 Thomas __ Edison
4 Drops from on high
5 Letter accompanier: Abbr.
6 "Yeah, right"
7 Web site sect. for newbies
8 Chimney channel
9 Zsa Zsa's sister
10 Bureaucratic tangle
11 Place for miscellaneous stuff
12 Sharon of Israel
13 Eeyore's creator
18 Oscar winner Jannings
23 Lyrical lines
25 Dr. J's old league: Abbr.
26 Nimble
27 Au naturel
28 Horse course
29 Item in a musician's pocket
30 Arthur Marx, familiarly
31 Columbus Day mo.
35 Hosp. areas
36 Like a compliant cat
38 Banana waste
39 Early hrs.
40 "Dunno"
42 Aspirin alternative
43 Bamboozle
45 Olive in the comics
46 Milk container?
47 Redeem, with "in"
48 Insider's vocabulary
49 Priests' administrations
52 "Rubáiyát" poet
53 Screen door sound
55 Oklahoma Indian
56 One who's unhip
57 Aphrodite's lover
60 __ pro nobis
61 Big jerk

by Lee Glickstein and Nancy Salomon

ACROSS

1 Boeing 747's and 767's
5 The Monkees' "___ Believer"
8 "Am not!" rejoinder
14 Forced out
16 Wash receptacles
17 With 56-Across, lawyer who argued in 19- and 49-Across
18 Pre-Mexican Indians
19 With 49-Across, noted decision made 5/17/54
21 Buying binge
24 Musical talent
25 Eight: Fr.
26 Stuart queen
29 Went after congers
34 Aged
35 On the briny
36 Curious thing
37 Decision reversed by 19- and 49-Across
40 One sailing under a skull and crossbones
41 Locust or larch
42 Spanish aunt
43 Belgian painter James
44 Chief Justice ___ Warren, who wrote the opinion for 19- and 49-Across
45 Rolodex nos.
46 Select, with "for"
48 Stanford-___ test
49 See 19-Across
55 Sitting room
56 See 17-Across
60 Groups of starting players

61 Forebodes
62 Vice President Dick
63 Ave. crossers
64 Mary ___ Lincoln

DOWN

1 Stick (out)
2 Book after Galatians: Abbr.
3 Capote, for short
4 Iced dessert
5 Langston Hughes poem
6 Cat's cry
7 Annex: Abbr.
8 Addis ___, Ethiopia
9 Symbol of sharpness
10 "Cómo ___ usted?"
11 Echelon

12 How a lot of modern music is sold
13 Secret W.W. II agcy.
15 Brute
20 Flying geese formation
21 Quaint establishment
22 Arrive, as by car
23 Passengers
26 "___ sow, so shall . . ."
27 Reno's state: Abbr.
28 U.S./Can./Mex. pact
30 University URL ending
31 Pay attention
32 French star
33 Ruler by birth
35 Houston landmark

36 Pitcher Hershiser
38 ___ Paulo, Brazil
39 Go off track
44 And so forth
45 Soldier's helmet, slangily
47 Short-winded
48 Bruce Springsteen, with "the"
49 ___ of office
50 Gratis
51 Flair
52 Concert equipment
53 Pucker-inducing
54 Angers
55 ___-Man (arcade game)
57 Past
58 Was ahead
59 "Acid"

by Ethan Cooper

ACROSS

1 Wise competitor
5 Quack
10 On vacation
14 Snack sold in a stack
15 Crystal set
16 Lens holders
17 Soccer commentator's cry
18 Shelley's "Adonaïs" is one
19 List-ending abbr.
20 "Aha!"
23 Caper
24 Little one
25 Four-bagger
27 Hosp. workers
28 Top worn with shorts
30 "All in the Family" network
32 Arctic bird
33 Soccer star Hamm
34 ___ correspondent
35 Singer/ songwriter Laura
36 Honky-tonk instruments
40 Mountaintop
41 Aurora's counterpart
42 Wonderment
43 Deli sandwich, for short
44 Corots, Monets and such
45 Sp. Mrs.
46 Qualifiers
49 Red Sea peninsula
51 Cartoon collectible
53 Spokes, e.g.
55 Passable
58 Some drive-thru features, briefly
59 Not as friendly

60 Tennis score after deuce
61 Old-fashioned dance
62 "___ luck!"
63 Evening, in ads
64 Retailer's gds.
65 "Mmm, mmm!"
66 Leave in, to an editor

DOWN

1 River blockage
2 In the vicinity
3 Bakery supplies
4 Longtime Chicago Symphony maestro
5 Air Force One passenger: Abbr.
6 Soft, white mineral

7 Keats's "___ a Nightingale"
8 Bedtime drink
9 Ma with a bow
10 "All systems ___!"
11 How a 43-Across is usually prepared
12 All Olympians, once
13 Designer monogram
21 Play segment
22 Sounds of doubt
26 "King Kong" studio
29 Raring to go
31 Hare's habitat
33 Mystery man
34 Scale amts.
35 Del.-to-Vt. direction
36 Elated

37 Spot and Felix, e.g.
38 Après-ski treat
39 Tony, Oscar or Hugo
40 Middle manager's focus?
44 Balloon filler
45 Most guileful
46 "Hurray for me!"
47 Limited
48 Major paperback publisher
50 Bridal path
52 Gives off
54 Bates and King
56 Pinball stopper
57 Horse-drawn vehicle
58 Pitching ___

by Elizabeth C. Gorski

ACROSS

1 Dreadful, as circumstances
5 One not of high morals
10 Spanish house
14 TV's "American ___"
15 Come back
16 Shakespeare, the Bard of ___
17 1970 Richard Thomas film adapted from a Richard Bradford novel
20 Mao ___-tung
21 Hula shakers
22 To no ___ (uselessly)
23 Outlaws
24 Wall Street business
26 Jumped
29 Long baths
30 Ayatollah's land
31 Kunta ___ of "Roots"
32 Duo
35 1975 Al Pacino film
39 Lamb's mother
40 Landlord payments
41 Shrek, for one
42 Slight hangups
43 Reveries
45 Oilless paint
48 Cure
49 Lily family plants
50 Arias, usually
51 King topper
54 1941 Priscilla Lane film whose title was a #1 song
58 Advance, as money
59 Lollapalooza
60 Bridle strap
61 Football positions

62 "I'm innocent!"
63 Poet ___ St. Vincent Millay

DOWN

1 Earth
2 Midmonth date
3 Was transported
4 Raised railroads
5 Difficult
6 Harvests
7 Intermissions separate them
8 Silent
9 ___-am (sports competition)
10 Sail material
11 Birdlike
12 ___ boom
13 Corner
18 Mongol title
19 Fouler
23 Wedding reception staple

24 Type assortments
25 "I can't believe ___ . . ." (old ad catchphrase)
26 Lateral part
27 Ship's front
28 Fury
29 Sorts (through)
31 Australian hopper, for short
32 "Gladiator" garment
33 Fish bait
34 Halves of a 32-Across
36 James of "Gunsmoke"
37 Wine vintage
38 Christmas song
42 Zips (along)
43 X out
44 Cause for umbrellas
45 Billiards furniture

46 Actress Burstyn
47 Knoll
48 Yawn-inducing
50 Yards rushing, e.g.
51 Elderly
52 Goatee site
53 Sicilian volcano
55 Son of, in Arabic names
56 Recent: Prefix
57 Fury

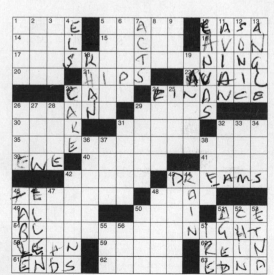

by Frederick J. Healy

ACROSS

1 Doze (off)
4 Following
9 Infield fly
14 Pub offering
15 "Death, Be Not Proud" poet
16 "Maria ___," 1940s hit
17 At leisure: Abbr.
18 Pact made at The Hague?
20 Legacy sharer
22 Directors Spike and Ang
23 Co., in France
24 Talks wildly
26 One more
28 Emulated O. Henry?
31 Many eras
32 Distress signal
33 ___ to go
37 Six-time U.S. Open tennis champ
40 Fool
42 Dweeb
43 Longing
45 Onetime neighbor of Israel: Abbr.
47 Neckline style
48 Where chocolate candy is made?
52 Procession
55 Sensation
56 Mancinelli opera "___ e Leandro"
57 They're welcome on the back
59 Epoch of 50 million years ago
62 Part of a shirtmaker's education?
65 Female rabbit
66 Place to moor
67 Stan's foil, in old films

68 Not well
69 Reluctant
70 Interminably
71 Taboos

DOWN

1 D.E.A. agent
2 Butter alternative
3 Removes from power
4 Summing
5 Quarters
6 Explosive
7 Abbr. at the bottom of a business letter
8 Consider again
9 Kind of ad
10 Corrida cry
11 Miss ___ of the comics
12 Loosen
13 Reimburser

19 Pavarotti, notably
21 ___ de Cologne
25 Portico in Athens
27 Beginner
28 Work in the garden
29 Wander
30 Promulgate
34 Gets elected
35 ___-do-well
36 Joel of "Cabaret"
38 Estrangement
39 God's way, in religion
41 Umpire's call
44 Mystery writer's award
46 Arrived quickly
49 Mounts
50 Was too sweet
51 Middle X or O
52 Rhodes of Rhodesia

53 College town on the Penobscot River
54 University of Missouri locale
58 W.W. II battle town
60 ___ contendere
61 Fish caught in pots
63 Tennis call
64 Suffix with mod-

by Richard Chisholm

ACROSS

1 Gun-toting gal
5 ___ vu
9 Put forth, as a theory
14 Singer Brickell
15 Greek counterpart of 27-Down
16 Wonderland girl
17 Mediocre
18 "___, vidi, vici" (Caesar's boast)
19 Ohio birthplace of William McKinley
20 Bridge
23 Widespread
24 April 15 deadline agcy.
25 Fond du ___, Wis.
28 Take the witness stand
31 Classic muscle car
34 Caribbean resort island
36 "___ we having fun yet?"
37 Conclude, with "up"
38 Bridge
42 Spew
43 Washington's ___ Stadium
44 Below
45 Young fellow
46 Feature of Texaco's logo, once
49 Period in history
50 Sawbuck
51 Periods in history
53 Bridge
61 Ancient Greek marketplace
62 Prayer's end
63 Govern
64 Laser printer powder
65 Left, at sea
66 Vicinity
67 War horse
68 Some Father's Day callers
69 Sign of boredom

DOWN

1 Flat-topped hill
2 Reason to say "pee-yew!"
3 "Schindler's ___"
4 Sainted ninth-century pope
5 Concoct
6 Puts up, as a tower
7 Mitchell who sang "Big Yellow Taxi"
8 India's locale
9 Kitchen closet
10 Miscellanies
11 Building next to a barn
12 Noted rapper/actor
13 Radio host John
21 Deadly
22 Prisoner who'll never get out
25 Sports jacket feature
26 Inviting smell
27 Roman counterpart of 15-Across
29 Bulletin board stickers
30 Savings for old age: Abbr.
31 Exam mark
32 Worker with circus lions
33 "La Bohème," e.g.
35 Except that
37 Chicago-based Superstation
39 Where the action is
40 TV's "Mayberry ___"
41 German engraver Albrecht
46 Offer on a "Wanted" poster
47 Alehouse
48 C.I.A. operatives
50 Number of points for a field goal
52 Deodorant type
53 Stetsons, e.g.
54 Gershwin's "___ Rhythm"
55 Sold, to an auctioneer
56 Puppy sounds
57 1847 Melville novel
58 Mysterious quality
59 Whole bunch
60 Actor Connery

by Gregory E. Paul

30

ACROSS

1 Sir, in India
6 Gounod production
11 Word with toll or roll
14 ___ acid
15 Cartoonist Kelly and others
16 Singer on half the 1984 album "Milk and Honey"
17 Hard-to-please labor protester?
19 Bird's beak
20 ¢¢¢
21 Unc's wife
23 Busta Rhymes rhymes
27 Like some of the Sahara
28 Flies off the handle
29 West Indian native
30 Mar. 17 figure, from 58-Across
31 Hooch
33 Punch in the stomach response
36 Shirts and blouses
37 Beetle Bailey's commander
38 ___'acte (intermission)
39 With 4-Down, modern printing fluid
40 Farm fence features
41 Prefix with -gon
42 A paramedic may look for one
44 Employ
45 Popular Ford
47 Skilled in reasoning
49 Eve's downfall
50 Lose at the bank?
51 Race unit
52 Cheap promotional trip?
58 See 30-Across

59 1973 #1 Rolling Stones hit
60 Bench site
61 Long-distance letters
62 Sailors' stories
63 Like a beach

DOWN

1 Doofus
2 Parisian pal
3 Drunk's utterance
4 See 39-Across
5 Political protest of sorts
6 Because of, with "to"
7 Successful negotiation results
8 The "E" of B.P.O.E.
9 Way to go: Abbr.
10 "Steps in Time" autobiographer
11 Pretty woman's hat?
12 Singer Bryant
13 ___ Smith, first female jockey to win a major race
18 Cross and Parker products
22 Where: Lat.
23 Musical breaks
24 ___-Detoo ("Star Wars" droid)
25 Plaything that yips?
26 Vacation spots
27 Loll
29 Gear teeth
31 Au naturel
32 Globe
34 Holy Roman emperor, 962–73
35 Swiss money
37 Talk back
38 Creepy: Var.
40 Toronto ballplayer
41 Multicar accidents
43 www.yahoo.com, e.g.

44 Pilgrimage to Mecca
45 Actress Shire
46 Besides, with "from"
47 Actor Alan
48 "The Highwayman" poet Alfred
50 Bridge builder, e.g.: Abbr.
53 Italian article
54 Actress Vardalos
55 "The Wizard of Oz" locale: Abbr.
56 Bitter ___
57 Slinky or boomerang

by Roy Leban

ACROSS

1 Pitches four balls to
6 Cain's brother
10 Insurrectionist Turner and others
14 Not reacting chemically
15 Muse of history
16 Monogram part: Abbr.
17 Pilfer
18 Kitchen gadget that turns
20 "Faster!"
22 No great __
23 Iced tea flavoring
26 Full complement of fingers
27 Sob
30 Before, in poetry
31 Classic gas brand
34 Composer Rachmaninoff
36 Midsection muscles, for short
37 "Faster!"
40 Knight's title
41 Rat or squirrel
42 Dye containers
43 Western Indian
44 Linear, for short
45 Rope-a-dope boxer
47 Fixes
49 1960s–'70s space program
52 "Faster!"
57 Cramped space
59 Rich cake
60 Primer dog
61 Sharif of film
62 Gives an audience to
63 Band with the 1988 #1 hit "Need You Tonight"
64 Monthly payment
65 Birds by sea cliffs

DOWN

1 Bit of smoke
2 Contrarians
3 Bloodsucker
4 Volcano that famously erupted in 1883
5 Acts of the Apostles writer
6 Bank holdings: Abbr.
7 Dull
8 Mozart's "a"
9 Circle
10 Daughter of a sister, perhaps
11 Ben Stiller's mother
12 Bit of business attire
13 Narrow water passage: Abbr.
19 Washed-out
21 Money for retirement
24 What a satellite may be in
25 Digs with twigs?
27 Kennel club info
28 "Son of __!"
29 Had a cow
31 __ salts
32 Luxury hotel accommodations
33 Safe
35 Mahler's "Das Lied von der __"
38 Snowman of song
39 Villain
46 Can't stand
48 Amounts in red numbers
49 Notify
50 Ship's navigation system
51 Weird
53 Norse thunder god
54 Terse directive to a chauffeur
55 Panache
56 "__ of the D'Urbervilles"
57 Popular TV police drama
58 WB competitor, formerly

by M. Francis Vuolo

ACROSS

1 Home to Honolulu
5 Sticky stuff
9 Mends, as socks
14 "The Good Earth" mother
15 Good lot size
16 "The Waste Land" poet
17 Where to find a hammer, anvil and stirrup
19 Oro y ___ (Montana's motto)
20 Charlie Rose's network
21 An Arkin
22 Ease up
23 It may be found in front of a saloon
26 Tone-___ (rapper)
27 Strong hand cleaner
31 "Doe, ___ . . ." ("The Sound of Music" lyric)
34 Former Queens stadium
36 6 on a phone
37 Picture-filled item often seen in a living room
41 "C'___ la vie"
42 Missing the deadline
43 Bonkers
44 Hopelessness
47 What 20-Across lacks
48 Foyer
54 Former White House pooch
57 Private eyes
58 Romance
59 Seed coverings
60 International business mantra
62 Carnival show
63 Lends a hand
64 Valuable rocks
65 Odist to a nightingale
66 McCartney played it in the Beatles
67 Top ratings

DOWN

1 That certain "something"
2 It may be airtight
3 Verb with thou
4 Sturm ___ Drang
5 Irish dialect
6 Continental divide?
7 Big ape
8 ___ capita
9 Unseat
10 Apportions
11 Inlets
12 Post-it
13 Ollie's partner in old comedy
18 Capital of Punjab province
22 Faithful
24 Staff leader?
25 First-year West Pointer
28 Melville romance
29 Before long
30 Snaillike
31 Passed with flying colors
32 Teaspoonful, maybe
33 Young newts
34 Football legend Bart
35 Where a rabbit may be hidden
38 10-point type
39 First-born
40 Twaddle
45 Small shot
46 Liqueur flavorers
47 Admission
49 Courtyards
50 Must-haves
51 Vigilant
52 Waterproof wool used for coats
53 Silt deposit
54 Word that can follow the end of 17-, 23-, 37-, 48- or 60-Across
55 "Dies ___" (liturgical poem)
56 Old Italian coin
60 Groovy
61 Twaddle

by Sarah Keller

33

ACROSS

1 Poi source
5 "The Thin Man" dog
9 Rum-soaked cakes
14 Stench
15 Where an honoree may sit
16 Friend, south of the border
17 Rocket scientist's employer
18 Prefix with potent
19 Alpine song
20 Not much
23 ___ glance (quickly)
24 Center of activity
25 Grammys, e.g.
29 Tip for a ballerina
31 Aide: Abbr.
35 Funnel-shaped
36 Craze
38 Hurry
39 Activities that generate no money
42 Surgery spots, for short
43 Indians of New York
44 Jack who ate no fat
45 Seeded loaves
47 Dog-tag wearers, briefly
48 Choirs may stand on them
49 Overly
51 Loser to D.D.E. twice
52 Boatswains, e.g.
59 R-rated, say
61 Poker payment
62 Confess
63 Tutu material
64 Rude look
65 Peru's capital

66 Back tooth
67 Slips
68 Fizzless, as a soft drink

DOWN

1 Cargo weights
2 Sandler of "Big Daddy"
3 Painter Bonheur
4 Face-to-face exam
5 Takes as one's own
6 Pago Pago's land
7 Salon application
8 Where Nepal is
9 Louisiana waterway
10 Microscopic organism
11 Bridge declarations
12 Questionnaire datum
13 Note after fa
21 Scottish beau
22 "A League of ___ Own" (1992 comedy)
25 Cast member
26 "What, me ___?"
27 Liqueur flavorer
28 Speed (up)
29 Blackmailer's evidence
30 Burden
32 English county
33 Ravi Shankar's instrument
34 Checkups
36 1052, in a proclamation
37 St. Francis' birthplace
40 Lingo
41 Raises

46 "A Streetcar Named Desire" woman
48 Directs (to)
50 Stream bank cavorter
51 "___ you" ("You go first")
52 Clout
53 Connecticut campus
54 Unique individual
55 Ranch newborn
56 Diabolical
57 Capital south of Venezia
58 Whack
59 Bank amenity, for short
60 Pair

by Joy C. Frank

ACROSS

1 ___ the Red
5 Fragrant blossom
10 "Right on!"
14 Woodworking groove
15 Excitedly
16 Stack
17 He wrote "Utopia" in an ancient language
19 Yard sale tag
20 Partner of "ifs" and "ands"
21 Arterial trunks
23 Do a favor
26 Be charitable
28 Tilted
29 Oxidize
30 A.A.A. suggestion: Abbr.
33 Office stamp
34 Better halves
35 Disney Store item
36 "How Sweet ___"
37 Mocks
38 Something that shouldn't be left hanging
39 Twilight time to a poet
40 More immense
41 Rear
42 TV prog. with a different host each week
43 Cupid's counterpart
44 Author Lee
45 Inner circle member
47 Keats and others
48 Hogan dweller
50 Seed cover
51 Oscar winner Guinness
52 Blind poet who often wrote in an ancient language
58 Desertlike
59 Gladden
60 Dust Bowl refugee
61 Pianist Dame Myra
62 Dravidian language
63 ___ contendere

DOWN

1 Summer hrs. in N.J.
2 Cheer
3 Life-changing statement
4 Farm vehicles
5 Endured
6 Many P.C.'s
7 London lav
8 Vacuum's lack
9 Purifies
10 Not close
11 He taught an ancient language in film
12 Old London Magazine essayist
13 Celebrated Prohibition-era lawman
18 Tool with a cross handle
22 Feedbag feed
23 "Golden" things
24 Vanquished
25 What 17- and 52-Across and 11-Down all were
26 Curtain
27 North Carolina's ___ Banks
31 Some china
32 Church V.I.P.'s
34 Myopic cartoon character
37 Certain Boeing
38 Church music maker
40 Muslim pilgrimage
41 Arm bones
44 Spam producer
46 Adds punch to, as punch
48 Bygone auto
49 Toward shelter
50 Not pro
53 Commercial suffix with Motor
54 Biblical ark passenger
55 Ref's decision
56 3-in-One product
57 "The Matrix" role

by Gene Newman

ACROSS

1 Tree that people carve their initials in
6 Pepper's partner
10 Author Dinesen
14 Stevenson of 1950s politics
15 Dunkable cookie
16 Plot parcel
17 "Dee-licious!"
19 Alum
20 Carson's predecessor on "The Tonight Show"
21 Surgeon's outfit
23 Play parts
26 Goes to sleep, with "off"
29 Skirt lines
30 Bangkok native
31 Like snow after a blizzard, perhaps
33 Corrosions
35 Eyelid problem
36 Spanish aunt
39 Crying
42 Evangeline or Anna Karenina, e.g.
44 What candles sometimes represent
45 "Very funny!"
47 Animal nose
48 Show biz parent
52 Go left or right
53 Petri dish filler
54 Where the Himalayas are
55 Not in port
56 Main arteries
58 Den
60 High spirits
61 "Dee-licious!"
67 Fanny
68 Certain woodwind
69 Pitcher Martinez

70 Painting and sculpting, e.g.
71 Yards advanced
72 Animal in a roundup

DOWN

1 San Francisco/Oakland separator
2 School's Web site address ender
3 Shade tree
4 Where a tent is pitched
5 "Howdy!"
6 Grow sick of
7 Quarterback's asset
8 Moon lander, for short
9 Santa's sackful
10 "Amen!"
11 "Dee-licious!"

12 Saudis and Iraqis
13 Classic sneakers
18 American, abroad
22 Bar "where everybody knows your name"
23 Skylit lobbies
24 Newswoman Connie
25 "Dee-licious!"
27 ___ Moines
28 Genesis son
32 Color, as an Easter egg
34 African desert
37 Get used (to)
38 MetLife competitor
40 Scandal sheet
41 Where the Mets could once be met
43 Perfectly precise

46 Mornings, briefly
49 Spuds
50 Some Texas tycoons
51 "Just the facts, ___"
53 One who hears "You've got mail"
56 Taj Mahal site
57 Urban haze
59 Little devils
62 Entrepreneur's deg.
63 "Who, me?"
64 "___ to Joy"
65 Mine find
66 "Le Coq ___"

by Nancy Salomon and Kyle Mahowald

ACROSS

1 Sharp-eyed raptor
6 Kid's getaway
10 Military level
14 Lamebrain
15 Off base illegally
16 "Garfield" dog
17 "The Godfather" actor's reputation?
19 Umpteen
20 UFO fliers
21 Novelist Zane
22 River under London Bridge, once
24 Alfalfa, Spanky and others
26 Tibia's place
27 Christian pop singer Grant
28 Camera-friendly events
32 Cheap jewelry
35 Rapunzel's abundance
36 Off-key, in a way
37 Garage occupant
38 "It ain't over till it's over" speaker
39 Gawk at
40 Beach sidler
41 New York City's ___ River
42 Comprehend
43 Arrange in columns
45 Old French coin
46 Rolling in the dough
47 Stops talking suddenly
51 Pants measure
54 Soccer success
55 Expert
56 Fan club's honoree
57 U2 singer's journey?
60 Indian tourist site
61 River to the Caspian
62 Lecture jottings
63 Posterior
64 Kittens' cries
65 Dress to kill, with "up"

DOWN

1 Fireplace glower
2 Line from the heart
3 Wimbledon court surface
4 Actor Chaney
5 Final stage, in chess
6 Yuletide sweets
7 On vacation
8 S.U.V. "chauffeur," maybe
9 Overabundance
10 Actor Ray's discussion group?
11 First mate?
12 "The Whole ___ Yards"
13 Florida islets
18 Air France destination
23 Chart topper
25 Roman statesman's thieving foe?
26 Tank top, e.g.
28 Analyze, as a sentence
29 Gymnast Korbut
30 Buddies
31 Put one's foot down?
32 Hostilities ender
33 Subtle glow
34 Attempt
35 Shrubby tract
38 Lauderdale loafer
42 Cooperate (with)
44 Soused
45 Pole or Bulgarian
47 Puts on ice
48 Petty quarrels
49 More than suggests
50 Metrical verse
51 Tall tale teller
52 Upper hand
53 Writer Ephron
54 Chew like a rat
58 Vein contents
59 "___ rang?"

by Lynn Lempel

ACROSS

1 Tow
5 From County Clare, e.g.
10 ___ pet (onetime fad item)
14 "The Thin Man" pooch
15 Off-limits
16 "Crazy" bird
17 Manual transmission
19 "What've you been ___?"
20 Politely
21 High-spirited horse
23 Swap
24 From one side to the other
26 Shade of beige
28 Warwick who sang "Walk On By"
32 Tree branch
36 Makes a row in a garden, say
38 "Hasta la vista!"
39 Operatic solo
40 Academy Award
42 Fighting, often with "again"
43 Goes off on a mad tangent
45 With 22-Down, Korea's location
46 Bone-dry
47 Moose or mouse
49 Perlman of "Cheers"
51 Upstate New York city famous for silverware
53 Twinkie's filling
58 Versatile legume
61 Entraps
62 Jai ___
63 Lakeshore rental, perhaps
66 Lass
67 Between, en français
68 Taking a break from work
69 One of two wives of Henry VIII
70 Hem again
71 Loch ___ monster

DOWN

1 Lacks, quickly
2 Up and about
3 Ancient city NW of Carthage
4 Tied, as shoes
5 ___-bitsy
6 Shout from the bleachers
7 There: Lat.
8 Until now
9 Souped-up car
10 Standard drink mixers
11 Arizona tribe
12 Tiny amount
13 Shortly
18 Swiss artist Paul ___
22 See 45-Across
24 Came up
25 What a TV host reads from
27 Funnywoman Margaret
29 Evening, in ads
30 Dark film genre, informally
31 Villa d'___
32 "___ Croft Tomb Raider" (2001 film)
33 Tehran's land
34 Prefix with skirt or series
35 Transportation for the Dynamic Duo
37 Bird's name in "Peter and the Wolf"
41 Numbered rd.
44 Of sound mind
48 Frog, at times
50 Unappealing skin condition
52 Idiotic
54 1990s Israeli P.M.
55 Wear away
56 Breakfast, lunch and dinner
57 Kefauver of 1950s politics
58 The "Star Wars" trilogy, for one
59 Actress Lena
60 Folksy tale
61 Whole bunch
64 Alcoholic's woe
65 Rapper Dr. ___

by Jeffrey Harris

38

ACROSS

1 New stable arrival
5 Wrigley team
9 Beginning
14 Old Dodge model
15 Pronto!
16 Captain Nemo's creator
17 Jared of "Panic Room"
18 "A ___ formality!"
19 Chip away at
20 Winter accessory
23 Up to, in ads
24 Coll., e.g.
25 However, informally
28 Caffeine source for many
33 Learn about
35 The whole shebang
36 Forest canine
38 Sailing hazards
41 Geo. W. Bush has one
42 Artfully dodge
43 Simple door fastener
46 Price word
47 Black-and-orange songbird
48 Polite drivers, at merges
51 Columbia Univ. locale
52 Something to shuck
54 ___ de Cologne
55 What the ends of 20-, 36- and 43-Across suggest
61 Language of India
64 Actress Malone
65 Tea time, perhaps
66 French farewell
67 Wide-eyed
68 Book after II Chronicles
69 1692 witch trials city
70 Fine-tune
71 For fear that

DOWN

1 Arlo Guthrie's genre
2 Spilled salt, say
3 Pro's foe
4 Ray of "GoodFellas"
5 The Kennedy years, figuratively
6 Played for a sap
7 3 Musketeers units
8 Eyeglasses, informally
9 "Yoo-hoo!"
10 Soft ball material
11 Sellout indicator
12 Cut short
13 Pigskin prop
21 Part of three-in-a-row
22 Yearn (for)
25 Minstrel show group
26 Player in extra-point attempts
27 Job seekers' good news
28 Graphite element
29 Legendary Mrs. who owned a cow
30 Frock wearer
31 Arm or leg
32 Perth ___, N.J.
34 Piercing tool
37 Java neighbor
39 To's partner
40 Element #34
44 First wife of Jacob
45 Like many MTV viewers
49 Slip behind
50 Camper's bag
53 Indian prince
55 ___ fixe (obsession)
56 Toy block maker
57 Get ___ the ground floor
58 Gooey stuff
59 Sharer's word
60 "Dang!"
61 Is afflicted with
62 Actress Lupino
63 Zip

by Nancy Kavanaugh

ACROSS

1 Child by marriage
8 Downtown Chicago
15 Percentage listed in an I.R.S. booklet
16 "Good shot!"
17 Woman who's "carrying"
19 Anger, with "up"
20 Summer: Fr.
21 Coin opening
22 Lottery player's exultant cry
23 Obstreperous
26 Wash
27 Put on board, as cargo
28 ___ constrictor
29 Bits of land in la Méditerranée
30 Ogled
31 Yankee Stadium locale, with "the"
33 Role
34 "Vive ___!" (old French cheer)
35 Trail
39 Uncles' mates
40 Shakespearean king
44 On the ocean
45 Schubert's Symphony No. 8 ___ Minor
46 Wheel turner
47 Pie pans
48 Patronizes a library
51 Italian resort on the Adriatic
52 Founded: Abbr.
53 Bill Clinton's relig. affiliation
54 New-___ (devotee of crystals and incense)
55 Traditional end of summer ·
60 Lenders, often
61 International alliance
62 Summed
63 Appetizer

DOWN

1 Germless
2 What a plane rolls along
3 Go off, as a bomb
4 Dressed up in a fussy way
5 Anatomical pouch
6 Playful aquatic animal
7 "Pretty amazing!"
8 Boom producer, for short
9 "She Done ___ Wrong"
10 Environmental prefix
11 Accidentally reveal
12 "Sexy!"
13 Bogey, in golf
14 Most cheeky
18 Maternity ward arrival
24 Start of a forbiddance
25 Vertical line on a graph
31 Former British P.M. Tony
32 Get together with old classmates, say
35 Kneecap
36 "Let me repeat . . ."
37 Covered place to sleep
38 Committed, as an act
40 Staples Center player, for short
41 Requiring immediate attention
42 Somewhat firm, as pasta
43 Organize differently, as troops
49 1920s vice president Charles
50 Paid out
56 Wand
57 R&B band ___ Hill
58 Nile viper
59 Greek letter

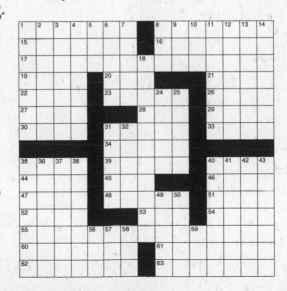

by Michael Shteyman

ACROSS

1 Kind of boom
6 Celeste who won an Oscar for "Gentleman's Agreement"
10 Ticks off
14 "Love Story" author Segal
15 Tribe defeated by the Iroquois
16 Webster who had a way with words
17 Point between Hawaii and Guam
19 Center of a cathedral
20 Mine find
21 Chem. or biol.
22 Narrowed
24 Snapple rival
26 Mary __ Moore
27 "Oklahoma!" aunt
29 Eye holder
33 Knock out of the sky
36 Pick a card
38 Actress Foch and others
39 "Pumping __"
40 Divans
42 Civil rights activist Parks
43 Money substitute
45 The end __ era
46 "Good buddy"
47 Dorothy's home in "The Wizard of Oz"
49 Poker player's declaration
51 Doubting Thomas
53 Spanish dish
57 Silt, e.g.
60 Stick in the water?

61 Crest alternative
62 Jacob's twin
63 Hock shop receipt
66 Ado
67 Gen. Robt. __
68 "There __ free lunches"
69 Reporter Clark
70 Some loaves
71 Limb holder?

DOWN

1 Attach, as a patch
2 "__ Ben Jonson" (literary epitaph)
3 Alternatives to Reeboks
4 Rocks at the bar
5 Sculpt
6 Prefix with port or pad
7 __ pro nobis
8 Like a dryer trap
9 Some awards
10 Group of confidants
11 Surf's sound
12 Gutter location
13 Place for a mower
18 Heats just short of boiling
23 Unskilled laborer
25 Place for sets and lets
26 Word that can precede the last word of 17- and 63-Across and 10- and 25-Down
28 Suffix with switch
30 Door opener
31 Facilitate
32 Russian leader before 1917
33 Tiddlywink, e.g.
34 Shamu, for one
35 Slightly tattered

37 Female W.W. II grp.
41 Attack verbally
44 Settles up
48 Concealed shooter
50 Rodeo rope
52 "Boot" in the Mediterranean
54 Los Angeles player
55 Property claims
56 Response to "Are not!"
57 Office necessity
58 Villa d'__
59 What an analgesic stops
60 Addition column
64 Minute
65 __-Magnon

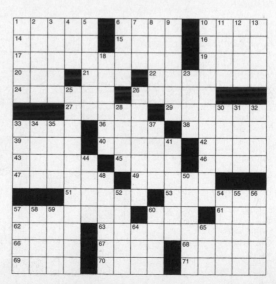

by Sarah Keller

ACROSS

1 Raindrop sound
5 Sgt., e.g.
8 Present for a teacher
13 Kelly of morning TV
14 Marlboro alternative
15 Shine
16 Son of Isaac
17 Metal that Superman can't see through
18 On again, as a candle
19 Fashionable London locale
21 Ardor
22 Big containers
23 Filmmaker Spike
24 GM sports car
27 Whitewater part of a stream
30 Fireplace accessory
32 UK record label
33 Cast member
36 Hits head-on
37 Get help of a sort on "Who Wants to Be a Millionaire"
41 Wriggling fishes
42 Place
43 Tit for ___
44 Teems
47 Zoo denizens
49 Something "on the books"
50 Motorists' grp.
51 Skier's transport
52 Quick job for a barber
54 Sweater
58 To no ___ (purposelessly)
60 Classic artist's subject
61 Sandwich spread, for short

62 Oscar who wrote "The Picture of Dorian Gray"
63 Popular shirt label
64 Certain stock index
65 Los Angeles cager
66 Craggy hill
67 Agile

DOWN

1 Make ready, for short
2 Elvis's daughter ___ Marie
3 Milky gem
4 1960s–'70s pontiff
5 December songs
6 Fuel from a mine
7 Bygone
8 Consented
9 Bit of begging

10 Educational assistance since 1972
11 China's Chou En-___
12 Expert in resuscitation, in brief
14 Coffee gathering
20 Angry with
21 ___ state (blissful self-awareness)
23 Lash of old westerns
25 Frisky feline
26 Beginnings
27 Statute removal
28 Itsy-bitsy creature
29 Bedtime gab
31 Anger
34 Actress Allen of "Enough"
35 Cheerios grain
38 Baton Rouge sch.

39 Tried a little of this, a little of that
40 Rarely-met goal
45 Hammer user
46 Hoover ___
48 Scents
51 Henry VIII's family name
53 Travel on horseback
54 Mario who wrote "The Godfather"
55 Seductress
56 Witness
57 Classic theater name
58 Leatherworker's tool
59 By way of
60 Annual hoops contest, for short

by Jay Giess

42

ACROSS

1 Dispensable candy
4 On pins and needles
8 Meeting
14 "The Name of the Rose" writer
15 Chaucer offering
16 1966 Mary Martin musical
17 Dog with an upturned tail
19 Big-time brat
20 Slugger Sammy
21 Glasgow gal
23 Master's worker
24 Gambler's marker
26 Choice word
29 Give one's word
35 Beantown team, briefly
36 Press release?
37 Santa ___, Calif.
38 Holder of two tablets
39 Mingling with
42 Camera type, briefly
43 Taoism founder Lao-___
44 Horror film staple
45 Site of a racing win or a tie
47 Traditional elocution exercise
51 Beheaded Boleyn
52 Den denizen
53 Injure seriously
56 Limp watch painter
58 Sci-fi sightings
62 Take stock of
65 Intellectual
67 Fire escape, e.g.
68 Turkish honorific
69 Clean air grp.

70 Be obsequious
71 One of the "Little Women"
72 Letters for a psychic

DOWN

1 They're above the abs
2 It might be off the wall
3 Animal keepers
4 And so on: Abbr.
5 Veronica Lake film "The Blue ___"
6 What a poor winner does
7 They have boughs for bows
8 Peach part
9 Words from Wordsworth
10 Go downhill
11 Put a traveling mike on
12 Reason for nose-pinching
13 Klingon on the Enterprise
18 Odd fellow
22 Baseball commissioner Bud
25 Honeycomb shape
27 Periscope part
28 "The Bartered Bride" composer
29 Trunk with a chest
30 Out of kilter
31 Dog tag datum
32 Explorer ___ da Gama
33 Not at full power
34 Job for a dermatologist
35 Ordeal for Rover, perhaps

40 Like a trim lawn
41 Globular
46 Second-stringer
48 "Anything you want"
49 Make beholden
50 Scale reading
53 Halloween accessory
54 Concerning
55 Middle of Caesar's boast
57 "Moby-Dick" captain
59 Unbind
60 "My bad!"
61 Give and take
63 Sign of a sellout
64 Opposite NNE
66 "I told you so!"

by Nancy Salomon and Harvey Estes

ACROSS

1 Go to sea
5 Feet above sea level: Abbr.
9 Boston's airport
14 Stubborn animal
15 Ear part
16 Ex-Mrs. Trump
17 Fitzgerald who sang "I'm Making Believe"
18 University V.I.P.
19 Car parker
20 Decreed
23 ___ foil
24 Before, in verse
25 Fleming of 007 fame
26 Bad mark
28 Discontinued
29 Lacking muscle
33 Writer Welty
35 Throng
36 Document of legal representation
40 Liqueur flavoring
41 Armadas
42 Nary a soul
43 Injection units, for short
44 Relaxed
48 Tree swinger
49 Joanne of "Sylvia," 1965
50 1959 hit song about "a man named Charlie"
51 Children's game
56 Easy gallops
57 Bad place to drop a heavy box
58 Landed (on)
59 Florida city
60 Advantage
61 Ready for picking
62 Like sea air

63 Flagmaker Betsy
64 1930s boxer Max

DOWN

1 Refines, as metal
2 How some café is served
3 "Fighting" Big Ten team
4 Starring role
5 Fabled New World city
6 "Camelot" composer
7 Israel's Abba
8 Open the windows in
9 Jazz up
10 Running track
11 Festive party
12 Again
13 ___ King Cole

21 Shy
22 "This ___ better be good!"
27 Honkers
28 Rigorous exams
29 On the downslide
30 Sea eagle
31 Lemon or lime drink
32 C minor, for one
34 Unbalanced
35 Spa feature
36 Criticize, as a movie
37 Plastic ___ Band
38 Victory
39 Fragrant flowers
43 Overseer of co. books
45 Earhart who disappeared over the Pacific
46 Skunk feature

47 It immediately follows Passiontide
48 Examine, as ore
49 Bottom of the barrel
51 ___-Cola
52 Iridescent stone
53 Skin
54 One slow on the uptake
55 Cutting remark
56 The "L" of L.A.

by A. J. Santora

ACROSS

1 Unconsciousness
5 Govt. security
10 Tell all
14 Eve's mate
15 North of talk radio
16 Leave in the dust
17 Player of Ginger
19 A few chips in the pot, maybe
20 Kind of scene in a movie
21 Other, to Ortega
22 Inspirations
23 Player of the title role in 37-Across
26 [Woe is me!]
30 Social historian Jacob
31 Charles Lamb, pseudonymously
32 Desist
34 Ewe's cry
37 Classic sitcom that debuted on 9/26/1964
41 ___ sauce
42 Blue-haired lady of TV cartoons
43 Ye ___ Shoppe
44 7-Eleven, e.g.
45 Adorable "bears"
47 Player of Thurston Howell III
50 Half-man/ half-goat creatures
52 ___-majesté
53 Org. that helps with motel discounts
56 Remark while putting chips in the pot
57 Player of the Skipper
60 Mexican fast food

61 Mob
62 "I smell ___!"
63 Slow-boil
64 Got up
65 Hunky-___

DOWN

1 See 3-Down
2 "Garfield" dog
3 With 1-Down, tailless pets
4 Doctor's org.
5 Overly
6 Squib on a book jacket
7 Ancient Greek class reading
8 Fleur-de-___
9 Name that's a homophone of 8-Down
10 Shivs
11 Society avoider
12 Nick and Nora's pooch
13 Spelling contests
18 Gray wolf
22 Harvard, Yale, Princeton, etc., for short
24 Rub out
25 Not yet final, at law
26 Importunes
27 Mixture
28 Greasy
29 Actor Linden or Holbrook
32 Magna ___
33 Essay writer's class: Abbr.
34 Shiny on top?
35 "Three Men ___ Baby"
36 Summer drinks
38 Some prayer leaders

39 Dress
40 Actor Chaney
44 Boat on 37-Across
45 Shoved
46 Lost
47 Result of squeezing, maybe
48 Mild cigar
49 Japanese form of fencing
50 Partner of starts
51 Latin 101 verb
53 Prefix with nautical
54 Slightly open
55 Creative
57 Responses to a masseur
58 Home stretch?
59 Irish fellow

by Andrea Carla Michaels

45

ACROSS

1 Leaf's support
5 Knife
9 Wood for chests
14 Like a lemon
15 Medal of honor recipient
16 "Stayin' __" (disco hit)
17 Prison sentence
18 Therefore
19 Without a stitch on
20 Eventually
23 The "M" in MSG
24 Calif.'s northern neighbor
25 Ewe's mate
28 Main school team
31 Valedictorian's pride, for short
34 Make amends (for)
36 Ubiquitous bug
37 QB Tarkenton
38 Daring bet
42 Whom Ingrid played in "Casablanca"
43 Pea container
44 Many a John Wayne film
45 Spanish cheer
46 Most sore
49 Tricky
50 Title car in a 1964 pop hit
51 Have to have
53 Availability extremes
59 Alaskan islander
60 Lifeguard's watch
61 "__ honest with you . . ."
63 The vowel sound in "dude"
64 That girl, in Paris
65 Problem with a fishing line
66 Excited, with "up"
67 Funnyman Foxx
68 Stringed toy

DOWN

1 Jet decommissioned in '03
2 They may get stepped on
3 Continental "dollar"
4 1983 role reversal film
5 The Ramones' "__ Is a Punk Rocker"
6 Extreme fear
7 Jason's ship, in myth
8 Unmannered fellow
9 Bird in a cage
10 Gladden
11 Dutch embankment
12 Swear to
13 Bloodshot
21 "The Catcher in the Rye," e.g.
22 Game with a drawing
25 The "R" of NPR
26 Polynesian island
27 Cat's quarry
29 Noted New York restaurateur
30 A home away from home
31 Southern breakfast dish
32 Discussion group
33 Incensed
35 Hoops grp.
37 Home loan agcy.
39 Disney's __ Center
40 "That feels good!"
41 Carving on a pole
46 Offered for breeding, as a thoroughbred
47 Wrap up
48 Made airtight
50 Measuring tool
52 Scatterbrained
53 Ice sheet
54 Start of a counting-out rhyme
55 0 on a phone: Abbr.
56 Play part
57 Talking on a cell phone during a movie, e.g.
58 Online auction house
59 Chemical base: Abbr.
62 Swellheadedness

by Gregory E. Paul

ACROSS

1 ___-serve
5 Desert flora
10 Fresh kid
14 Jacob's twin
15 Venusian, e.g.
16 Suffix with Cine-
17 T ___ tiger
18 Muscle injuries
19 Lyric poems
20 Protest formally
23 Not well
24 Silver ___ (cloud seed)
25 Before now
28 Cry out loud
30 Moon or sun, poetically
31 Diet plate serving
36 Falco of "The Sopranos"
37 Battery type
38 Siberian city
41 Cockpit gauge figure
46 ___ Ronald Reagan
47 In the style of
48 Go astray
49 Moral standards
53 A smartypants may have a big one
55 Cohabitate
62 Juan's emphatic assent
63 Actress Verdugo
64 Ocean motion
65 Penny-___ (trivial)
66 Aired again
67 Caesarean rebuke
68 Time to go once around the sun
69 Peter, Paul or Mary
70 Invitation letters

DOWN

1 One seen playing with a beachball
2 Logo along U.S. highways, once
3 Placed
4 Mold and mildew, for two
5 Former Sears mailing
6 A Baldwin
7 "See ya!"
8 Semester, e.g.
9 Fill with confidence
10 Like a sombrero's brim
11 Pie chart lines
12 Make better
13 "Take a sip"
21 Lanchester of film
22 Stud site
25 Air force hero
26 1977 George Burns title role
27 Ear-related
29 Trivial amount, slangily
30 Tara name
32 Mad Hatter's drink
33 Salary max
34 Message from a desert isle, perhaps
35 Cousins of an ostrich
39 ___ Lanka
40 Barbie's ex-beau
42 Simoleon
43 Publishers
44 Swanky
45 Herb in stuffing
49 Op-ed piece, e.g.
50 Quaker's "yours"
51 "___ la vista!"
52 Not so cordial
54 Riverbank romper
56 Courtroom statement
57 Actress Hatcher
58 ___ even keel
59 Half of a batting average calculation
60 1999 Ron Howard comedy
61 Do another hitch

by Nancy Kavanaugh

ACROSS

1 Used a broom
6 Opened just a crack
10 Doesn't guzzle
14 Place for a barbecue
15 "Uh-uh"
16 Threaded fastener
17 Proverb
18 Managed, with "out"
19 ___ avis (unusual one)
20 Bathroom fixture sales representative?
23 Way to the top of a mountain
26 Stave off
27 Hanging sculpture in Alabama?
32 Alleviated
33 Words said on the way out the door
34 E.M.T.'s skill
37 Pub drinks
38 Gasps for air
39 "Scram!"
40 Dashed
41 Sunday newspaper color feature
42 Continue downhill without pedaling
43 Warsaw refinement?
45 G-rated
48 Accustoms
49 Majestic summer time?
54 Solar emissions
55 Really big show
56 Lubricated
60 Victim of a prank
61 Choir voice
62 State fund-raiser
63 Retired fliers, for short
64 Spinks or Trotsky
65 Company in a 2001–02 scandal

DOWN

1 Hot springs locale
2 Bankroll
3 When a plane should get in: Abbr.
4 Dirty places
5 Initial progress on a tough problem
6 From a fresh angle
7 Wisecrack
8 Copycat
9 Cincinnati team
10 Endeavored
11 Dumbstruck
12 Less adulterated
13 Sudden jump
21 Be behind in payments
22 50/50 share
23 Besmirch
24 Down Under critter
25 "A Doll's House" playwright
28 Dolphins' venue
29 Onetime Dodges
30 Mess up
31 Contingencies
34 Committee head
35 Search party
36 Some I.R.A.'s, informally
38 One in the legislative biz
39 "Eureka!" cause
41 Swindles
42 TV cabinet
43 Purposes of commas
44 Little, in Lille
45 Deck of 52
46 Hawaiian feasts
47 "Aïda" setting
50 Bluish green
51 Car rod
52 "What've you been ___?"
53 Hired thug
57 Epistle: Abbr.
58 W.W. II arena
59 Underworld boss

by Seth A. Abel

48

ACROSS
1 Spills the beans
6 Got along
11 Epitome of simplicity
14 Accountants may run one
15 Entanglement
17 Said with a sneer
18 Garb for Tarzan
19 Eskimo building material
20 Bill of Rights defender, in brief
22 ___ voce (quietly)
23 "Maybellene" singer
27 Cries like a wolf
28 ___ Constitution
29 Three-legged piece
31 Stir up
34 Certain seat request
36 Suffix with fictional
39 Grimm brothers fairy tale
43 Popular fuel additive
44 Reveal
45 Openly mourned
46 Send (to)
48 Menu phrase
50 Lots and lots
52 Indirect
58 Inamoratas
60 Horn sound
61 Bearded animal
62 The starts of 18-, 23-, 39- and 52-Across
65 Spiral
67 Crystal-clear
68 Rugged ridge
69 Every other hurricane
70 Like music
71 Stallions' interests

DOWN
1 Underlying
2 Something for friends to "do"
3 A fond farewell
4 Wish
5 Butchers' offerings
6 Girl: Fr.
7 ___ propre
8 Baseball stat.
9 Sea eagle
10 Diagnosers
11 Similar
12 Itty-___
13 Some salmon
16 Boston newspaper
21 "CSI" network
24 Cosby's "I Spy" co-star
25 Amber or copal
26 Everyone, in the South
30 Toy train purchase
31 Trains: Abbr.
32 Passé
33 Not follow the book
34 Houston pro
35 "What was ___ think?"
37 Rush (along)
38 Tolkien creature
40 Jolly old ___ (Santa)
41 Lothario's look
42 Gun barrel cleaner
47 Other side
48 Big fuss
49 Philadelphia landmark hotel
50 French peaks
51 Religious parchment
53 Unadulterated
54 Pried (into)
55 Eyeballer
56 Conglomerate
57 Frequent Astaire wear
59 Genesis brother
63 Sebastian who once ran the world's fastest mile
64 Dos Passos work
66 Century 21 competitor

by James R. Leeds

ACROSS

1 The "D" of D.J.
5 Huge hit
10 Nile reptiles
14 Great Salt Lake's state
15 Cosmetician Lauder
16 Junk e-mail
17 "The Price Is Right" phrase
19 Trig function
20 Eugene O'Neill's "___ for the Misbegotten"
21 Some necklines do this
23 Flatters, with "up"
26 Egypt's capital
27 2004 Olympics city
28 Made a cashless transaction
31 Accomplisher
32 Up, on a map
33 Chicago-to-Atlanta dir.
34 Factory-emissions testing grp.
35 "The Weakest Link" phrase
37 Photo ___ (picture-taking times)
38 Cotton ___
39 Bassoon's smaller cousins
40 Et ___ (and others)
41 Protective wear for airborne toxins
43 Wonder to behold
45 Nursery supplies
46 "___ Gump"
47 Oreo fillings
49 Wonderland cake message

50 Looooong sandwich
51 "Family Feud" phrase
56 Wading bird
57 Painting stand
58 Cafeteria carrier
59 Space shuttle launcher
60 Attire
61 "The ___ the limit"

DOWN

1 French nobleman
2 "How was ___ know?"
3 ___ Adams, patriot with a beer named after him
4 One peeking at answers on a test
5 Spanish gents
6 1980s PC's ran on it

7 Lots and lots
8 Finish, with "up"
9 All-female get-together
10 State confidently to
11 "Wheel of Fortune" phrase
12 Sign of hunger
13 "Peter Pan" pirate
18 Future indicator
22 Like a ballerina's body
23 No-goodnik
24 Paradise
25 "Jeopardy!" phrase
26 Atkins diet concerns, briefly
28 ___ well (is a good sign)

29 Glimpses
30 Make potable, as sea water
32 Partner of crannies
35 Flip out
36 Fanatical
40 Handcuffs
42 Brunch cocktail
43 Roadside stops
44 The Cadets, in college sports
46 Ones you just adore
47 Goatee's locale
48 Singer McEntire
49 Gaelic tongue
52 Former Mideast grp.
53 Noah's craft
54 Palindromic cheer
55 Part of CBS: Abbr.

by Jim Hyres

50

ACROSS
1 Asian nannies
6 Ending with land or sea
11 Legal org.
14 Josh ___, who directed and co-produced "South Pacific"
15 Inventor Howe
16 Right this minute
17 Skylit areas
18 Pipsqueaks
19 Genetic material
20 Items on some necklaces
22 Actor Estrada
23 Colorful tropical fish
24 Lacking vigor
26 Swing on an axis
29 Minor railroad stop
32 The first or fifth letter of George
34 DeMille films
35 Overly
36 Simulate, as an old battle
39 "Where ___?"
42 Goethe classic
43 Early evening hour
45 1998 Sandra Bullock film
50 Bronx Bomber
51 Comfortable with
52 Life of Riley
54 Parts of bridles
55 Words that can precede the starts of 20-, 29- and 45-Across
61 Grand ___ (wine words)
62 Mob scenes
63 Column style
64 Feel sick

65 Gas in a layer
66 Flash of light
67 Free TV spot: Abbr.
68 Obsolete VCR's
69 Brief brawl

DOWN
1 [sigh]
2 Closet invader
3 Taj Mahal site
4 Cafeteria headwear
5 Adder, e.g.
6 Williams of tennis
7 Hint
8 "___ it the truth!"
9 Pitiful
10 Tricky curve
11 Dissident Sakharov
12 Mackerellike fish

13 Rise and shine
21 Wrecker's job
22 Young newts
25 What Sgt. Friday sought
26 It's not breaking the sound barrier anymore
27 London facility
28 ET's ride
30 Busybody
31 Place for sweaters?
33 Transplant, of a sort
37 Praise posthumously
38 "___ Beso" (1962 hit)
39 Gardner of Hollywood
40 Stag attendees
41 Sign, as a deal
42 A.T.F. agents, e.g.

44 Mask opening
45 Lug nuts' cover
46 Husband of Isis
47 "Downtown" singer Clark
48 Acts the coquette
49 Used a bench
53 Drinks from a flask
56 Radish or carrot
57 European erupter
58 "What's ___ for me?"
59 Salon job
60 Prefix with plasm
62 Stick up

by Nancy Kavanaugh

ACROSS

1 How ham may be served in a sandwich
6 Popular kitchen wrap
11 Tiny bit, as of hair cream
14 Oscar Mayer product
15 Skip to the altar
16 Billy Joel's "___ to Extremes"
17 The Bard
19 Judges administer it
20 Hammed it up
21 Thick urban air condition
23 City where "Ulysses" is set
26 Item carried by a dog walker
28 Columbus sch.
29 "Mona Lisa" features that "follow" the viewer
32 Years, to Cicero
33 Large bays
35 PIN points
37 Concept
40 Shopping ___
41 Theme of this puzzle
42 Shopping ___
43 ___ Romeo (Italian car)
44 Former G.M. car
45 Birth-related
46 Ancient South American
48 Meditative exercises
50 Spanish "that"
51 Lions and tigers and bears
54 Stage comments to the audience
56 Alternative
57 Safes

60 Turncoat
61 Very scary
66 Spanish cheer
67 Synthetic fiber
68 Continental money
69 Neither's partner
70 Mexican money
71 Gaucho's rope

DOWN

1 Delivery room docs, for short
2 "I don't think so"
3 Major TV brand
4 Bumpkin
5 Foes
6 Equinox mo.
7 Out of the wind, at sea
8 All of them lead to Rome, they say
9 Tax mo.
10 Liam of "Schindler's List"
11 Run-down
12 Staring
13 Shady garden spot
18 Major TV brand
22 One of the friends on "Friends"
23 Bedrock belief
24 Commonplace
25 Waver of a red cape
27 Throw, as dice
30 Count's counterpart
31 Pore over
34 Projecting rim on a pipe
36 Japanese soup
38 Wipe out
39 World book
41 Pillow filler
45 Not as nice

47 Drive-in restaurant server
49 Grand party
51 Element with the symbol B
52 Author Calvino
53 Lesser of two ___
55 It's debatable
58 Suffix with buck
59 Big coffee holders
62 With 64-Down, reply to "Am too!"
63 Tax adviser's recommendation, for short
64 See 62-Down
65 Fed. property overseer

by Steve Kahn

ACROSS

1 Fall (over)
5 Stadium walkways
10 At a distance
14 Wall Street letters
15 10 out of 10, e.g.
16 Western tie
17 Gambling actor?
19 Savvy about
20 Most miniature
21 Waiting room sound, maybe
22 Aloof
23 Keep ___ (persist)
25 Queue before Q
28 Gambling baseballer?
34 Pile up
36 Hydrox alternative
37 Avoiding the draft?
38 "___ Ha'i"
39 Hardhearted
40 Mrs. Dithers, in "Blondie"
41 Getting ___ years
42 Have dog breath?
43 Jerry or Jerry Lee
44 Gambling singer?
47 Take-home
48 "Queen for ___" (old TV show)
49 "Go ahead, shoot!"
51 Muscat, for one
54 Tallinn native
59 Anise-flavored liqueur
60 Gambling politician?
62 Stink
63 Hearing-related

64 Teetotalers' org.
65 Campbell of "Party of Five"
66 Feel blindly
67 Cold-shoulder

DOWN

1 Shoelace problem
2 Brontë heroine
3 In ___ (actually)
4 Téa of film
5 Steakhouse offering
6 Sidewalk stand beverages
7 5-Down, e.g.
8 Follow with a camera
9 ___-mo
10 180° turn
11 Henry Winkler role, with "the"
12 Sask. neighbor

13 Piece next to a knight
18 Barbershop boo-boos
21 1,002, in old Rome
23 Some of them are secret
24 "Iliad" locale
25 Fat cat
26 Muscat native
27 Michael of "Monty Python"
29 ___ public
30 Maine college town
31 Taken wing
32 Bone-chilling
33 You'll get a rise out of it
35 Asian city-state
39 Humane grp.
43 Popular disinfectant

45 Work of praise
46 Fight it out
50 Has memorized
51 "Tell me more"
52 Like some awakenings
53 Sea of ___ (Black Sea arm)
54 Eliel's architect son
55 Quick pic
56 Cast wearer's problem
57 Westernmost Aleutian
58 It may be proper
60 What "it" plays
61 Capek play

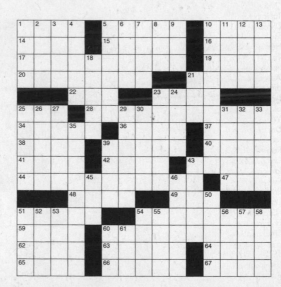

by Adam Cohen

ACROSS

1 "So long!"
5 Burden
9 Museo in, Madrid
14 Death notice
15 It follows song or slug
16 Pine exudation
17 Gets together in person
20 "Blondie" or "Beetle Bailey"
21 Tennis champ Steffi
22 Vegetable that rolls
23 Narrow street
26 Jannings of old movies
28 Confronts, with "with"
34 "___ Baba and the 40 Thieves"
35 "Kiss me" miss
36 Tangle
37 Dietary no-no for Mrs. Sprat
39 Holds on to
42 Tiny weight
43 Former Argentine dictator
45 Actress Patricia of "The Subject Was Roses"
47 Drunkard's woe, for short
48 Returns a gaze
52 Ugandan tyrant Idi ___
53 Rules, shortly
54 Pres. Lincoln
57 Urges (on)
59 "Gesundheit!" preceder
63 Strolls, as with a sweetheart
67 1950s candidate Stevenson
68 B or B+, say

69 Nobelist Wiesel
70 Irish poet who wrote "The Lake Isle of Innisfree"
71 Lambs' mothers
72 Soaks

DOWN

1 Big gobblers
2 Aid and ___
3 Layer
4 Famous Hun
5 Not at work
6 Teachers' org.
7 Grp. that patrols shores
8 Sound system
9 Opposite of losses
10 Ump
11 "Quickly!"
12 Backgammon equipment
13 Prime draft status
18 Not spare the rod
19 Domesticate
24 Bismarck's state: Abbr.
25 Toward sunrise, in Mexico
27 Yearn (for)
28 Precipitation at about 32°
29 Crown
30 Itsy-bitsy
31 Late
32 Speak from a soapbox
33 Stately shade trees
34 Austrian peaks
38 Comic Dunn formerly of "S.N.L."
40 Person of equal rank
41 Fill up

44 Unbeatable foe
46 Boston airport
49 ['Tis a pity!]
50 Capture, as one's attention
51 Shun
54 Not home
55 Requested
56 Fitzgerald, the First Lady of Jazz
58 Precipitation below 32°
60 Robust
61 "Don't bet ___!"
62 Lyric verses
64 Krazy ___
65 Mother deer
66 They're checked at checkpoints, in brief

by Kurt Mengel and Jan-Michele Gianette

ACROSS

1 "Hold on there!"
5 Tiled art
11 Suffix with glob
14 Help for the stumped
15 Not rejecting out of hand
16 Stetson, for one
17 Particular
18 Nonsense
20 Fun time, slangily
21 Does superbly, as a stand-up comic
22 The March King
23 1988 Olympics site
25 L'Oreal competitor
26 Nonsense
30 ___ left field
31 Cast-of-thousands films
32 It may be 20%
35 Iowa State city
36 Zoo behemoth
37 Dairy Queen order
38 It begins in Mar.
39 Handed out
40 Knight stick?
41 Nonsense
43 Book boo-boos
46 Latish bedtime
47 Ready to fall out, as pages from a book
48 '60s "V" sign
51 Relax, with "out"
53 Nonsense
55 Chess player's cry
56 Conditions
57 Crater Lake's state
58 Composer ___ Carlo Menotti
59 Bottom line

60 "Maybe later"
61 1070, in old Rome

DOWN

1 Taylor or Tyler, politically
2 Go 0-for-20, say
3 Bicycle or kayak, usually
4 20's dispenser
5 Alexander Calder creation
6 October birthstone
7 Broker's advice, at times
8 Added stipulations
9 Suffix in many ore names
10 Waist constrictors

11 Self-mover's rental
12 The end of one's rope?
13 Hawke of film
19 Hawk's opposite
21 Former baseball commissioner Bowie ___
24 Elevator pioneer
25 Puerto ___
26 Burlesque show props
27 Program for sobering up
28 Diner accident
29 Kunta ___ ("Roots" role)
32 In vain
33 Paycheck deduction
34 Have a look-see
36 C&W's McEntire

37 Lion tamer's workplace
39 Spoiled rotten, maybe
40 "Fatal Attraction" director Adrian
41 [I'm shocked!]
42 Museum guide
43 Like Santa's helpers
44 Pocahontas's husband
45 Cut of beef
48 Limerick writer, say
49 Fidgeting
50 Natural emollient
52 Boomers' kids
54 "___ y plata" (Montana's motto)
55 "The Wizard of Oz" studio

by Brendan Emmett Quigley

ACROSS

1 Strait-laced
5 It can make you sick
9 Raise a glass to
14 Mrs. Chaplin
15 Charles Lamb's nom de plume
16 Stan's sidekick in old comedy
17 Gulf sultanate
18 After-bath powder
19 Mexican coins
20 "Get rid of your inhibitions!"
23 Phoned
24 Lennon's lady
25 Mil. stores
26 Hard ___ rock
28 Very, in Vichy
31 Indy racer sponsor
33 Baseball scores
35 Without much thought
37 Cuban line dance
41 "Dance the night away!"
44 Big mug
45 18-wheeler
46 Lacking slack
47 Sgt., for one
49 Easy marks
51 Mad Hatter's drink
52 Univ., e.g.
55 Downs' opposite
57 Hairdo
59 "Party hearty!"
65 Label with a name on it
66 Stench
67 Drop from the eye
68 Home of Arizona State
69 "___ my lips!"
70 Glowing review
71 Sauna feature
72 Concludes
73 Gave a thumbs-up

DOWN

1 Betting group
2 The Eternal City
3 Spellbound
4 Craze
5 "Control yourself!"
6 Israeli airline
7 Small stream
8 Very virile
9 A-one
10 Designer Cassini
11 Journalist Joseph
12 Language of the Omahas
13 Midterms, e.g.
21 Cable TV choice
22 Partner of a ques.
26 Synagogue chests
27 Office wear
29 "Grand" ice cream brand
30 Tart fruits
32 Frost or Burns
34 Where pores are
36 City WSW of Phoenix
38 Compulsive cleaner
39 Stickum
40 "The Thin Man" dog
42 Diamond in the rough, e.g.
43 Parachutists' lifelines
48 Select, with "for"
50 Female pig
52 Barbecue rods
53 West Pointer
54 Blackjack request
56 Seashell site
58 Foreword, for short
60 California wine valley
61 Steinbeck's "East of ___"
62 Little hopper
63 Roof's edge
64 ___ Scott decision, 1857

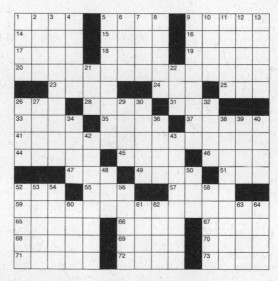

by Kendall Twigg and Nancy Salomon

ACROSS

1 Gangster's blade
5 Datebook entry: Abbr.
9 Brief news report
14 Prefix with -batic
15 Detective's discovery
16 Explode
17 Flying irritant
18 Runners
20 Pleasingly drawn
22 E.R. personnel
23 Tuscan home of St. Catherine
24 Last herb in a Simon & Garfunkel title
26 Clay, after 1964
29 Wildebeest
31 Cinderella's accompaniers to the ball
33 Caveat emptor phrase
36 Loll in a tub
38 Skewered food
39 Place for a bagel and a schmear
40 Binge
42 State bird of Hawaii
43 Area at a river's mouth
45 Having time on one's hands
46 Alum
47 Zoo baby
49 Islands welcome
51 Plastic __ Band
52 Half of a 1960s pop quartet
54 Cattle breed
58 Bobby of hockey
59 Desperate final effort
61 Where elections are decided

65 Marc Antony's love, for short
66 Chemist Pasteur
67 Finished second
68 Château __-Brion wine
69 Fathered
70 LAX listings: Abbr.
71 Wriggly biters

DOWN

1 Short stories they're not
2 Rousseau or Matisse
3 Furious
4 Booth, e.g.
5 Bank statement no.
6 Braid of hair
7 Obsolescent election item
8 A Kennedy

9 Rustic . . . and proud of it
10 Notable times
11 Scene-ending cry
12 Gibbon or orangutan
13 Scoreboard nos.
19 "__ la Douce"
21 __ Gabriel
25 Rube
26 Yellow shade
27 Hotelier Helmsley
28 Under the covers
30 Beginning of many ship names
32 Potential problem with 7-Down
33 Enlarge, as one's lead
34 Greet, as a new year
35 Volunteer's statement
37 Kind of den

41 Long fish
44 It's often shared in theaters
48 Complain
50 Have a bite
53 Mexican restaurant bowlful
55 Inaugural balls
56 Deplete
57 Dalmatian features
58 Perennial battleground state
60 Retired Atl. fliers
61 Priestly garb
62 Bath water tester
63 Harbor craft
64 Grand __ Opry

by Patrick Merrell

ACROSS

1 Wildcat
5 "Hey . . . over here!"
9 Look without blinking
14 Smile proudly
15 Canyon sound
16 Artist's stand
17 Not crazy
18 Wander
19 The Little Mermaid
20 Pass along some football plays?
23 "The loneliest number"
24 Owl sound
25 Rots
29 Alexander ___, secretary of state under Reagan
30 Listening device
33 Texas battle site, with "the"
34 Does tailoring
35 McDonald's arches, e.g.
36 Begin to use wrestling feats?
39 Salt Lake City collegians
40 Sculls
41 Wall climbers
42 Club ___ (resort)
43 It turns at a pig roast
44 Dangerous African fly
45 Recipe direction
46 Tic-___-toe
47 Make time for aerobics classes?
54 Being from beyond Earth
55 Toward shelter
56 Not nerdy

58 Rain-snow mixture
59 Calendar span
60 Tackle box item
61 Jeans and khakis
62 Lushes
63 Side squared, for a square

DOWN

1 Dieters' units: Abbr.
2 "Right on!"
3 Mom's mom
4 Marvel Comics group
5 Eva and Juan
6 British biscuit
7 Old Iranian ruler
8 Weapons on the warpath
9 Veteran sailor
10 Cards for the clairvoyant
11 "Oh, that'll ever happen!"
12 Coral ridge
13 Building annexes
21 "___ want to dance?"
22 Cacophony
25 Informational unit
26 Overjoy
27 Like thick, dry mud
28 Iowa State's home
29 Valentine symbol
30 Namely
31 Moorehead of "Bewitched"
32 Sheriff's crew
34 Railing sites
35 Valentine subject
37 Stop by briefly

38 1970s–'80s musical craze
43 Periods on jobs
44 "Any ___?"
45 Trapshooting
46 Pick up the tab
47 Winged stinger
48 Earthen pot
49 It means nothing to the French
50 Bread spread
51 Sch. where Bill Walton played
52 What a band may have planned
53 Achy
57 Meadow

by Damon J. Gulczynski

58

ACROSS
1 Cyber-junk mail
5 Nose-in-the-air type
9 "And thereby hangs __"
14 To boot
15 Suffix with soft or china
16 Movado competitor
17 Jib or spanker
18 Eyebrow shape
19 Let up
20 Invoice surprises
23 Carol starter
24 Aussie jumper
25 Beanball target
28 One with answers
33 Guitarist Eddy
37 Antlers point
39 Comic Rudner
40 James Bond, e.g.
43 "__ Kampf"
44 Mimicker
45 Avian mimickers
46 To the rear
48 Slangy prefix meaning "mechanical"
50 Abbr. after an attorney's name
52 Buries
57 Hunter concealer
61 "Ulysses" author
63 Pupil controller
64 Captain of the Nautilus
65 "__ Day's Night" (Beatles film)
66 Demolish
67 Small combo
68 Miser's fixation
69 Airport postings, for short
70 "The __ Baltimore" (Lanford Wilson play)

DOWN
1 Skater Cohen
2 Tartan pattern
3 Stage digression
4 Chocolatiers' equipment
5 "Old Folks at Home" river
6 Drug buster
7 Philharmonic grp.
8 Joy on "The View"
9 Catherine of __
10 "Hamlet" soliloquy starter
11 "Sad to say . . ."
12 Court do-over
13 Program file extension
21 It'll knock you out
22 Al of "Today"
26 At the peak of
27 Navy Seal, e.g.
29 Bacchanalian blast
30 Austria's capital, to Austrians
31 Sicilian spouter
32 "Phooey!"
33 Russian legislature
34 French singles
35 Mine opening
36 Hawaii's state bird
38 Emperor who presided over a great fire
41 Reply to a childish taunt
42 In the company of
47 Pain reliever, e.g.
49 Skewed views
51 Paper purchase
53 Tither's amount
54 Month after diciembre
55 Send as payment
56 Barfly's seat
57 Printer's color
58 Plot measure
59 Beer bust locale
60 Four-time-wed Minnelli
61 Wing it, musically
62 Cry of revelation

by Robert Dillman

ACROSS

1 Frozen treats
5 Soothing cream
9 Cursed
14 Chef's serving
15 Seller of his
   birthright, in
   Gen. 25
16 Hizzoner
17 ___'acte
18 Flexible,
   electrically
19 One with an
   amorous eye
20 Hidden
   advantage
23 "___ Doone"
   (romance)
24 Run-of-the-mill:
   Abbr.
25 Gentle ___ lamb
28 Lion, by
   tradition
33 Maybes
36 Den
37 Run for the ___
   (Kentucky
   Derby)
38 Shingle site
40 Lady's title
43 Singer Horne
44 Farm measures
46 Dutch cheese
48 Yo-yo or Gobot
49 1950s–'60s
   game show
53 Neighbor of Syr.
54 Second letter
   after epsilon
55 Dough leavener
59 Start of a
   nursery rhyme
63 Actress Kim
66 Hobbling
67 Israel's Abba
68 Nitrous ___
   (laughing gas)
69 Shade trees
70 New Jersey
   hoopsters
71 Light sleeper

72 Affirmative votes
73 Understanding
   words

DOWN

1 Perfect
2 ___ de Mayo
   (Mexican
   holiday)
3 Fragrant
   compound
4 Psychiatrist,
   slangily
5 Regular
   drumming
6 Author Sholem
7 Put on board
8 Not quite all
9 Burn without a
   flame
10 What a worker
   earns
11 Popeye's
   Olive ___

12 Fish eggs
13 Mess up
21 It's on the tip of
   one's finger
22 Globe
25 Winning smile,
   they say
26 Dictation taker
27 Test
   mineralogically
29 "Platoon" setting
30 Actress Scala
31 Opposite of
   chaos
32 Netscape's
   owner
33 Baghdad
   resident
34 Concentrate
35 More achy
39 Lawyer's charge
41 Letters on a
   toothpaste tube
42 Irate

45 Athletic shoe
47 "___ help you?"
50 Agcy. that
   promotes fair
   competition
51 Markswoman
   Annie
52 Sana'a native
56 French clerics
57 List of candidates
58 Not relaxed
59 Green gem
60 Hay bundle
61 Jane Austen
   heroine
62 Loch ___
63 Sign of approval
64 Losing tic-tac-toe
   line
65 Namely: Abbr.

by Alison Donald

60

ACROSS

1 Rating a blue ribbon
5 Unceasingly
10 Sign over, as rights
14 Florence's river
15 Gossip's tidbit
16 W.W. II general Bradley
17 "Uh-uh!"
20 "The Natural" role Roy ___
21 Some parents
22 Sergeant once played by Phil Silvers
23 Unlocks, poetically
25 Doctor's charge
26 "Uh-uh!"
31 Mideast grp.
34 Higher on the Mohs scale
35 Basketball's ___ Ming
36 Words to an old chap
37 Fact-filled volume
39 Cultural programs they're not
41 Newshawk's source, often
42 Tacit approval
44 Food or air
45 Hook shape
46 "Uh-uh!"
48 "Now I see!"
49 Pro foe
50 "So long, mon ami"
53 Farmer's sci.
54 Mall stand
59 "Uh-uh!"
62 Bit attachment
63 Muralist Rivera
64 Within reason
65 Singer James or Jones

66 First name in cosmetics
67 Part of many "shoppe" names

DOWN

1 Sen. Evan of Indiana
2 Suffix with switch
3 Give the cold shoulder
4 Pyramid, maybe
5 "Chicago Hope" sets, for short
6 Pumpkin pie spice
7 Diplomat's post
8 Answers from a 49-Across
9 Hoopster Erving's nickname
10 Newswoman Roberts
11 Early Oscar winner ___ Jannings
12 Like a damp cellar
13 Hence
18 Ashe Stadium event
19 Outdated wedding-vow word
24 Voracious fish
25 One making arrangements
26 Jonah's swallower
27 Patriot Nathan and others
28 "Aunt ___ Cope Book"
29 Bismarck's state: Abbr.
30 ___ Tuesday (Mardi Gras)
31 "Nonsense!"

32 Andy Kaufman's role on "Taxi"
33 Yiddish "Egad!"
36 Analogist's words
38 Iowa college
40 Golf's Sorenstam
43 Where Friday was once seen on Thursday
46 Hoodlum
47 Cause to see red
48 Big name in health care
50 River of Bern
51 South Beach ___
52 "What's ___ for me?"
53 Black cuckoos
55 ___ facto
56 Fire ___ (gem)
57 E-mail command
58 Tot's perch
60 Lines from Shelley
61 Clod chopper

by Stella Daily and Bruce Venzke

ACROSS

1 The "A" in I.R.A.: Abbr.
5 Chili con ___
10 Do newspaper work
14 End of a fishing line
15 Sewing machine inventor Howe
16 Financial page inits.
17 Charles Lindbergh's feat across the Atlantic
19 Nameless, for short
20 Prehistoric
21 Marked down
22 "Friends, ___, countrymen"
24 Antlered deer
25 The City of Witches
26 Thin, as oatmeal
29 Game show player
32 See eye to eye
33 "It takes two" to do this
34 When repeated, a ballroom dance
35 Explore the seven seas
36 Emphatic ending with yes
37 Tennis score after deuce
38 Uncle: Sp.
39 External
40 Three sheets to the wind
41 Oratorio performers
43 Fake ducks
44 Martini garnish
45 Golf shirt
46 Present to Goodwill, e.g.
48 Is no more, informally

49 "That's it!"
52 At the drop of ___
53 Paul Scott tetralogy, with "The"
56 Formal ceremony
57 Rainbow ___
58 Dory or ferry
59 Cousin of a frog
60 Eye sores
61 Memorial Day weekend event, briefly

DOWN

1 Mock words of understanding
2 In the 40's, say
3 In the 20's, say
4 Certain boxing win, for short
5 Stalk vegetable
6 Desirable party group
7 Fixes illegally
8 "I'd rather not"
9 Alienate
10 Tooth cover
11 Batman and Robin
12 The Rolling Stones' "Time ___ My Side"
13 Hamilton bills
18 Marooned person's signal
23 Skillet lubricant
24 Rear of a sole
25 Less loony
26 "___ not, want not"
27 Once more
28 One of six Bach compositions
29 "Gay" city
30 Polished, as shoes
31 "Patton" vehicles

33 Sir or madam
36 Undermines
37 Sacramento's ___ Arena
39 Leave out
40 Atlanta-based airline
42 Pleased as punch
43 Krispy Kreme products
45 Excite, as curiosity
46 Bull's-eye hitter
47 The Buckeye State
48 "A thing of beauty is ___ forever"
49 Oodles
50 Noggin
51 Trial fig.
54 The "A" in MoMA
55 Baseball stat

by Gregory E. Paul

ACROSS

1 Thin-waisted flier
5 Lad's partner
9 Game player's cry
14 Teen People cover subject
15 Ashe Stadium org.
16 Congested, say
17 "__ Lisa"
18 Genesis brother
19 Bobby of the Black Panthers
20 Posters of a pop music icon?
23 Pie chart piece
24 Eastern "way"
25 Supermodel Carol
28 Weekend ice cream treat?
32 Shooter ammo
35 Ring
36 Relaxed
37 Baby in wool?
39 Pug or boxer
41 Ready for business
42 View
45 Tide type
48 Give it a shot
49 Vintner?
52 England's Isle of __
53 J.F.K. Library architect
54 Greets the dawn
58 What makes a bivalve move?
61 Of the Vatican
64 Small combo
65 Moolah
66 Staring intently
67 "Zounds!"
68 Actor Estrada
69 Apartment sign
70 Trevi Fountain locale
71 Crummy grades

DOWN

1 Wusses
2 Be nuts about
3 __ boom
4 Botanists' concerns
5 Swiss tourist destination
6 "Rush!"
7 To-do
8 Sensibleness
9 Stage a prison break
10 Ticks off
11 Hoops grp.
12 "My __ Sal"
13 Word on a dollar
21 Quite a feat
22 Inits. on Mars
25 Trim to fit, perhaps
26 Light-show light
27 Itsy-bitsy
29 The old man
30 Dateless, say
31 Prefix with classical
32 Take second
33 Flow chart site
34 Sufficiently
38 __ Paese cheese
40 Hair goo
43 Montague rival
44 Uno + dos
46 Apple pie order?
47 Llama land
50 Sob __
51 Put on the line
55 Close shave
56 "Dallas" matriarch
57 Goes after
58 Rat's challenge
59 By logic, then . . .
60 Neeson of "Kinsey"
61 Soft touch
62 Going back in time
63 Buddy

by Kurt Mengel

ACROSS

1 Spats
6 Poker variety
10 Theda ___ of the silents
14 18-and-over
15 Sit for a shot
16 Catchall abbr.
17 Auto racer Andretti
18 Humorist Bombeck
19 K–12, in education
20 "If looks could kill" look
23 Dog sled driver
26 Former telecommunications giant: Abbr.
27 ___ Luis Obispo
28 Bickering
29 Racetrack fence
32 Courtroom pledge
34 Coarse file
35 Helping hand
36 Big inits. in trucks
37 Welcome that's not so welcoming
43 Vienna's land: Abbr.
44 Fitting
45 Meditation method
46 Hoodwinks
48 Close angrily
49 The "O" in S.R.O.
50 George W., to George
51 Shirt or sweater
53 Tickles the fancy
55 Snub
59 Merle Haggard's "___ From Muskogee"
60 Ponder
61 Not live

65 Just dandy
66 Away from land
67 Light on one's feet
68 Serve supper to
69 Geeky sort
70 Open the door to

DOWN

1 Tartan cap
2 Boise's state: Abbr.
3 Mink, for one
4 Pilot's pre-takeoff filing
5 Mink, for one
6 On ___ (without a contract)
7 Pop singer Amos
8 Label on a street-corner box
9 Handed out cards

10 Symbol of redness
11 "Finally!"
12 Gung-ho
13 Non-earthling
21 Lines up
22 Jazz dance
23 Artist Chagall
24 Great Salt Lake state
25 Mexican's assent
30 Ventilate
31 Standard of perfection
33 "Stop behaving like a child!"
36 Start to fume
38 Hungers (for)
39 Number cruncher, for short
40 Charged particles
41 Gawk at, as on the beach

42 Thumbs-down votes
46 Gingersnap, e.g.
47 Connected to the Internet
48 Marital partner
50 Speak derisively
52 "What now?!"
54 Rock music genre
56 Monopoly card
57 Exploitative type
58 Show the way
62 Peach center
63 Samuel's mentor
64 Comfy room

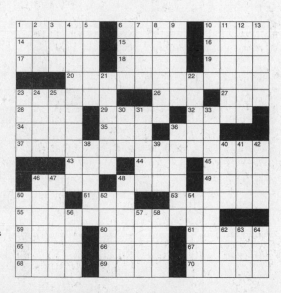

by Kendall Twigg and Nancy Salomon

ACROSS

1 Protrudes
5 Stay to the finish
9 Harness racer
14 Straddling
15 Whale of a movie?
16 Be wild about
17 Hourly pay
18 Try to persuade
19 "The Thinker" sculptor
20 Title of a certain astronomy lecture
23 ___ de France
24 Auction unit
25 Fraternal group
29 Custard dessert
31 Part-goat god
34 Funny Sherman
35 Call it a day
36 Fill beyond full
37 With 48-Across, practical advice for attending the lecture
40 Tolkien tree creatures
41 Bagpiper's wear
42 Augusta's home
43 Bandleader Brown
44 Gullible sorts
45 Astaire or Rogers
46 Roadie's load
47 In great shape
48 See 37-Across
56 Yule tune
57 Orange component
58 On the road
60 For all to see
61 Leap for Lipinski
62 Veg out
63 Withdraws gradually

64 Apportion, with "out"
65 Had down cold

DOWN

1 Paleontologist's discovery
2 EnergySolutions Arena N.B.A. team
3 Like some pizza orders
4 Gush forth
5 Townies
6 Lost a lap?
7 "Vamoose!"
8 Hailer's cry
9 Person of the cloth
10 Vote to accept
11 Musical finale
12 ___ the Red
13 Director Clair
21 1992 Joe Pesci title role

22 Party offering
25 Silents star Normand
26 Unescorted
27 Vegas coin-ops
28 Producers of 46-Downs
29 Rolls up, as a flag
30 Shopper's aid
31 Lose one's cool
32 Make amends
33 Fresher
35 Groucho remark
36 Mikita of hockey
38 Cousin of a giraffe
39 Valuable violin
44 Refines, as ore
45 Endearing facial feature
46 Squirrel's stash
47 Boneless cut

48 Flat-bottomed boat
49 Do roadwork
50 Neck of the woods
51 Many cyber-ads
52 Richness
53 Spill the beans
54 Actor McGregor
55 Stun
59 Bow wood

by Joan Yanofsky

ACROSS

1 Beginner
5 Ceiling support
9 Brass instruments
14 Crowd noise
15 The Bruins of the Pac-10
16 Take by force
17 Just twiddling one's thumbs
18 Diagram
19 Juliet's beloved
20 Navel
23 Louisville Slugger
24 French president's residence
25 Critical
27 "Oh my goodness!"
30 Hippie happening
33 One of the Bushes
36 Not completely dissolved, as a drink mix
38 Online auction house
39 Collect
41 "Dear" letter recipient
42 Guitar bars
43 Pickle flavoring
44 Copier of a manuscript
46 Wide shoe specification
47 Mama Cass ___
49 Dirties
51 TV host Winfrey
53 Shines
57 F.B.I. employee: Abbr.
59 The Midwest, agriculturally speaking
62 Bar mitzvah officiator

64 Fitzgerald of scat
65 It ebbs and flows
66 Approximately
67 "Whatcha ___?"
68 Dublin's land, in poetry
69 School readings
70 Gulp from a bottle
71 Mexican sandwich

DOWN

1 Arapaho or Apache
2 Alpine song
3 Come from behind
4 Ultimatum words
5 Hobgoblin
6 Off-white
7 Landed (on)

8 Fox comedy series
9 Seek help from
10 Bob Hope tour grp.
11 Big stinger
12 ___ code (long-distance need)
13 Parking place
21 Safecrackers
22 Slick
26 Profess
28 Frisbee, e.g.
29 Mixes
31 "Must've been something ___"
32 Nasdaq rival
33 Green gem
34 Silents star Jannings
35 Vote depository
37 Threesome
40 Lingerie item

42 Guy
44 Christmas tree topper
45 Cosmic explosion
48 Satellite paths
50 Last six lines of a sonnet
52 Obeys
54 Director Kurosawa
55 Doc
56 Meeting transcriber
57 Smell ___ (be leery)
58 Kotter of "Welcome Back, Kotter"
60 Strike ___ blow
61 552, in old Rome
63 Except

by Barry C. Silk

66

ACROSS

1 Moulin Rouge dance
7 "That's hardly proper"
13 Shoulder adornment
15 Riviera resort
16 Fellow traveler
17 One of a Yule trio
18 Tees off
19 Inscribed stones
21 Onetime Ford model
22 Be more patient than
24 Consumer protection org.
27 "Mornings at Seven" playwright Paul
28 Brooklyn or the Bronx, informally
29 Dissenting votes
32 Ham or hamburger
33 Baby talk
35 Bar, at the bar
37 Matchsticks game
39 Strike caller
40 Overly stylish
42 Boot camp fare
44 Just manage, with "out"
45 Superman sans cape
46 Further amend
48 Droop
49 Leaf bisectors
50 Tony winner Caldwell
53 One of the Gorgons
54 Come down hard
55 From east of Europe
58 CN Tower city
61 Faint
62 Visitors to a justice of the peace
63 Part of a drum kit
64 Political pundit Myers

DOWN

1 Beany's cartoon pal
2 To the left, at sea
3 Appointed
4 Junkyard dogs
5 C.S.A. state
6 Composer Rorem
7 On the heels of
8 Not hard yet
9 "___ bien!"
10 President pro ___
11 Actress Thurman
12 Whole bunch
14 Antinuclear agreement
15 Use cusswords
20 Title of this puzzle
22 Pizazz
23 Play for a sap
24 "The Maltese Falcon" actor, informally
25 Babbling water
26 Trailblazer Daniel
28 ___ vivant
29 Makes out
30 Milo of "Barbarella"
31 Hurt bad
34 Kicks out
36 World Series mo.
38 Help settle
41 Metal in surgical tools
43 Sis or bro
47 Something drawn out
49 Copycat's words
50 Spaced (out)
51 More than eccentric
52 Irregularly notched
53 Crow's-nest spot
54 Bishop of Rome
55 Fitting
56 ___ Paulo
57 Doctrine
59 Moth-eaten
60 Shad delicacy

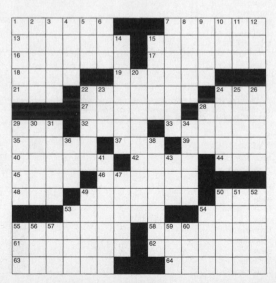

by David Diefendorf

ACROSS

1 Drug buster, for short
5 Apartments
10 Arizona city
14 Mishmash
15 Scoundrel
16 Kuwaiti leader
17 Group voting the same way
18 Car from Japan
19 It may be carried with a guitar
20 Unexpectedly
23 Dismal, in poetry
24 Not just anger
28 "___ out!" (ump's call)
29 Mine finds
33 Grassy Argentine plains
34 Gap and Toys 'R' Us, e.g.
36 Verb not in the king's English
37 Unexpectedly
41 Pro ___ (proportionally)
42 Followed smoothly
43 Natural to a creature
46 Rocker David Lee ___
47 Sup
50 "Saturday Night Fever" group, with "the"
52 "Where the deer and the antelope play"
54 Unexpectedly
58 Shoot (by)
61 Decree
62 Family rooms
63 Detest
64 Delay leaving
65 Stow cargo
66 Reason to put a clothespin on your nose
67 Earl of ___, favorite of Queen Elizabeth I
68 Pitching stats, for short

DOWN

1 Opposite of everyone
2 That certain something
3 Violent troublemaker
4 Beverage with a marshmallow
5 Pledges' group, for short
6 ___ Ness monster
7 Flulike symptoms
8 Supercharged engine
9 Close tightly
10 Parking ticket issuer
11 Flightless Australian bird
12 Break a Commandment
13 "___ you there?"
21 Foam
22 Actress Hagen
25 Neat as ___
26 Jets or Sharks, in "West Side Story"
27 Not an exact fig.
30 Howard of "Happy Days"
31 Archer of myth
32 Waste conduit
34 Telescope user
35 Palm starch
37 Decrease gradually
38 "Can ___ true?"
39 Same old same old
40 Kind of jacket
41 "Spare" item at a barbecue
44 Snakelike fish
45 Erase
47 Make lovable
48 Slate
49 Present and future
51 Ice cream concoctions
53 Confuse
55 Some evergreens
56 Land unit
57 River to the underworld
58 Group with the rock opera "Tommy," with "the"
59 Owned
60 Judge Lance of the O. J. Simpson case

by Sarah Keller

68

ACROSS
1 The "one" in a one-two
4 White Rabbit's words
10 Médoc or muscatel
14 ___ Lingus
15 From Genève, par exemple
16 Emcee Trebek
17 Actress Peeples
18 A A
20 Columnist Maureen
22 They follow Aprils
23 The Joads, e.g., in "The Grapes of Wrath"
24 State capital since 1959
26 ___-a-brac
27 B B
33 Nasal partitions
36 Punxsutawney groundhog
37 Old Roman road
38 Sharer's word
39 Uses again, as Tupperware
42 Fairway position
43 "Mila 18" author
45 58-Down digs
46 With cunning
48 E E
51 Ste. Jeanne ___
52 And others
56 Accused's response
58 Defunct gridders' org.
61 Race of about 6.2 mi.
62 L L
65 Massachusetts' Cape ___
66 Aweather's opposite
67 Alchemist's potion
68 Carnival city

69 Duck's place
70 "Duck Soup" performers
71 Just hired

DOWN
1 Band-Aid co.
2 Kindergarten quintet
3 Muscleman's quality
4 Words before and after "rose"
5 10-Down dress
6 ___ fire (started burning something)
7 Pale as a ghost
8 General ___ chicken
9 Auction conclusion?
10 Hawaiian surfing mecca
11 In an unlawful way
12 Hawaii's state bird
13 Alimony senders, maybe
19 Eve's opposite
21 It may be something of great interest
25 Winged
26 Masquerader's event
28 ___ salts
29 Col. Potter of "M*A*S*H," to pals
30 Home of the N.B.A.'s Heat
31 Buzz's moonmate
32 ___ Poupon mustard
33 "Du jour" item
34 International money

35 Used a crowbar on
40 Cabinet dept. since 1979
41 Army N.C.O.
44 Ready for the post office
47 Hurdle for an aspiring J.D.
49 Canadian tribe
50 World traveler Bly
53 Pick up
54 Many a navel
55 "That's not news!"
56 End of filming
57 Angelic topper
58 The Bruins' sch.
59 Evening, in Paris
60 Comic Redd
63 Dream state, for short
64 High school yearbook sect.

by Martin Schneider

ACROSS

1 God of love
5 Diehard
9 Give the heave-ho
14 Audition goal
15 Pet on "The Flintstones"
16 Bravery
17 Start of a Yogi Berra quote
19 Online periodical, briefly
20 "This is only ___"
21 Ear part
23 Off the wall
24 Susan who wrote "Illness as Metaphor"
26 Peruvian beast
28 End of 17-Across
33 Russian leader of old
36 Knock the socks off of
37 African fly
38 ___ Lilly & Co.
39 Alternative to dial-up Internet: Abbr.
40 "Quiet!"
41 Cheerios ingredient
42 The "r" of "πr²"
44 When a plane is due to take off: Abbr.
45 B&B's
46 Start of a Yogi Berra quote
49 Mild cigar
50 New Haven collegians
54 Prefix with bytes or bucks
57 Out of control
59 Spice of life
60 Spend, as energy
62 End of 46-Across
64 Ditch digger's tool

65 Plant's start
66 Slightly
67 Play (around)
68 Bookie's quote
69 Telescope part

DOWN

1 Diva performances
2 "Live Free or Die," for New Hampshire
3 Mary-Kate and Ashley ___ (celebrity twins)
4 Antares, e.g.
5 Modifying word: Abbr.
6 Small container for liquids
7 Entail
8 Two-base hit
9 Christmas ___
10 The 1920s
11 Pen name for Charles Lamb
12 It's south of Mass.
13 Deuce topper
18 And others: Abbr.
22 Environmentalists' celebration
25 Boxer's weak spot
27 Beat to a pulp
29 Harry Potter's messenger bird Hedwig, e.g.
30 Lots and lots
31 "No man ___ island . . ."
32 New Jersey hoopsters
33 Actress Garr
34 Venetian blind part
35 Gives a hand

39 Old-fashioned showdown
40 TV classic "The ___ Erwin Show"
43 What bouncers check
44 Went from apes to humans
45 Prohibited
47 Melodious
48 Volcano flow
51 Seeing red
52 Big name in bottled water
53 Mails
54 Net material
55 Giant fair
56 Cyclist's choice
58 Monopoly card
61 Golf peg
63 Hwys.

by Kyle Mahowald

70

ACROSS

1 Headquartered
6 "Zounds!"
10 Links numbers
14 "Goodnight" girl of song
15 Six Flags attraction
16 Pull a sulky, perhaps
17 She appeared in "Thelma & Louise" with 24-Across
19 Top of the heap
20 Say "cheese," say
21 Cut and paste
23 Bard's "always"
24 She appeared in "The Witches of Eastwick" with 53-Across
27 Wide of the plate
29 Hospital fluids
30 G.I.'s mail drop
31 Opposite of sud
33 Aggressive, personalitywise
37 Sticks up
39 An absence of musical skill
42 Layered do
43 Quarterback's ploy
45 Writer Harte
47 Iron or gold source
48 Bonny one
51 Unrestricted, as mutual funds
53 He appeared in "A Few Good Men" with 63-Across
57 Big bird
58 Bounce back
59 Storage spot
61 Ankara native
63 Actor famously connected to many other actors
66 Canadian gas brand
67 Sign from above
68 Not straight
69 Marsh plant
70 Woods plant
71 Not o'er

DOWN

1 Megaproportioned
2 Mars, to the Greeks
3 Appears
4 "Annales" poet Quintus ___
5 Buys and sells
6 Mound stat
7 "What ___?!"
8 Nike rival
9 Hanker for
10 School org.
11 Rainbow-shaped
12 Star-crossed lover of fiction
13 Violinist Isaac
18 Exactly right
22 Lip-puckering
25 "Quo Vadis" emperor
26 Second half of a vote
27 Propels a shell
28 Well-versed in
32 Society girl
34 Tyre's ancient land
35 Be worthy of
36 Got mellower
38 Polio vaccine developer
40 Suffix with buck
41 Map out again
44 Classic Welles role
46 Antinuclear treaty
49 Fed up with
50 Hatch a plot
52 Represent with symbols
53 Shortstop Derek
54 Elicit a chuckle from
55 Say "@#$%!"
56 Hang like a hummingbird
60 Stallion-to-be
62 Down for the count
64 Overnight spot
65 Ultimate degree

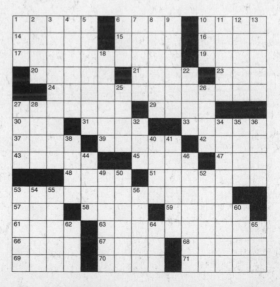

by Kurt Mengel

ACROSS

1 Hatch plots
7 Busy activity
11 Little devil
14 Broadway musical based on Dickens
15 In the thick of
16 Lao-tzu principle
17 Gets noticed, as an actor?
19 Mustache site
20 Paradises
21 ___ Kong, China
22 Hawkeye player on "M*A*S*H"
23 "The Nutcracker" attire
25 Resentful
27 Cable film channel
30 Gets noticed, as an acrobat?
33 Newspaperman William Randolph ___
35 Book before Job
36 "It was ___ mistake!"
37 Tiny hill builder
38 Tizzy
41 Noisy insect
44 Harmonize
46 Gets noticed, as a chef?
49 "Harper Valley ___"
50 Napping
51 Count ___, villain in Lemony Snicket books
53 Neighbor of Niger
54 Get ___ a good thing
57 Telegraph pioneer
61 Do-it-yourselfer's purchase
62 Gets noticed, as an artist?

64 Sign after Cancer
65 Period after dark, in ads
66 Shabby
67 Go wrong
68 Ever and ___
69 Causing goosebumps

DOWN

1 Not all
2 Dressed
3 Nature walk
4 Super Bowl or the Oscars, e.g.
5 Boo-boos
6 Mesozoic, for one
7 Mexican serving
8 Mysterious sign
9 Nutcake
10 Poetic tribute
11 "We'll find it"
12 Whom a dragon threatens in a fairy tale
13 Certain 1960s paintings
18 Synagogue
22 Swear (to)
24 When repeated, "For shame!"
26 Suffix with devil
27 "Now I see!"
28 Gibson who directed "The Passion of the Christ"
29 Texas Instruments product
31 Horne and Olin
32 Grounded jet, for short
34 Reared
37 Org. for tooth doctors
39 Bankbook abbr.

40 Drink with one lump or two
42 Middle grade
43 Headache queller
44 Have headaches, say
45 Trolley
46 Witch's laugh
47 More grayish
48 Truck scale units
52 Blacksmith's workplace
55 Defense grp. since 1949
56 Actor Wilson of "Shanghai Noon"
58 Monotonous learning
59 Give this for that
60 Nervously irritable
62 Paternity identifier
63 Bowlike line

by Levi Denham

72

ACROSS

1 Banned orchard spray
5 Obey
9 Problem with eyeliner
14 "Smooth Operator" singer
15 With the bow, in music
16 Small songbirds
17 Welcome forecast for Santa
18 Undecided
19 Chopin's Mazurka in __
20 Double-H of magic
23 "Old MacDonald" refrain
24 Not precise
28 Rwandan people
32 Kind of counter
33 Double-H of film
37 __ list
38 Author Umberto
39 Nocturnal lizards
42 Sparks's home: Abbr.
43 Birth place
45 Double-H of politics
47 "Seinfeld" role
50 Sawyer of morning TV
51 Secret pros
53 Game where you might hear "7 come 11"
57 Double-H of literature
61 Holy war
64 Prefix with distant
65 Emphatic type: Abbr.
66 To no __ (unsuccessfully)
67 Imperfect gravy feature
68 Works of Michelangelo
69 Cinema vérité, e.g.
70 Test areas
71 Forest growth

DOWN

1 "Steady __ goes"
2 Molokai porch
3 Like a lot
4 Put another way
5 Biblical verb
6 Suffix with smack
7 Neutral shade
8 Title boy of old comics
9 Al Jolson standard
10 Handyman
11 Migratory fish
12 Santa __
13 Letter run
21 Babies
22 Gerund suffix
25 A long, amateurish piano recital, maybe
26 Gave up
27 Cache
29 It's definite
30 Quite
31 Signed
33 Lumberjack
34 Cause of an intestinal problem
35 Willy of "Death of a Salesman"
36 "Beloved" writer Morrison
40 Popular laundry detergent
41 Matched, after "in"
44 Outcome of merciless teasing?
46 "Yoo-hoo!"
48 Christmas tree dropping
49 Miscalculate
52 Bloodhound's sense
54 Jetsons' dog
55 High school exams, for short
56 Two-time U.S. Open tennis champ
58 Water color
59 Without feeling
60 Cheese __
61 English sports car, informally
62 "__ Got the World on a String"
63 Solo in space

by Elizabeth C. Gorski

ACROSS

1 Swear to
5 "What's the ___ that can happen?"
10 Nose (out)
14 Ending with hard or soft
15 Baker who sang "Sweet Love," 1986
16 Shed one's skin
17 Many a homecoming attendee
18 Work over, as a ship
19 Fat of the lamb
20 "Draw one," in diner slang
23 Wildebeest
24 English dog
25 Straight from the garden
27 Rewrites
30 Broken arms may go in them
33 Foul callers
36 Irrelevant, as a point
38 Jump for joy
39 A barber has to work around it
40 Faculty member
42 Burn ___ crisp
43 First-class
45 Radio tuner
46 Glimpse
47 Gym shoes, for short
49 "Golden Boy" playwright Clifford
51 Clothesline alternative
53 Wrestler
57 Companion for Tarzan
59 "Sun kiss," in diner slang
62 Holds close
64 Oak-to-be
65 Gaming table fee
66 Hence
67 ___ four (teacake)
68 Marsh plant
69 Clutter
70 Perfect places
71 Luke Skywalker's mentor

DOWN

1 ___ plane (military craft)
2 Comparison shopper's quest
3 Blow one's top
4 Channel surfers' gadgets
5 Violation of the Geneva Convention
6 "___'Clock Jump" (1930s hit)
7 Jazz phrase
8 Not flexible
9 Idaho produce, informally
10 Ambulance inits.
11 "Life preservers," in diner slang
12 Secluded valley
13 "___, Brute?"
21 Gave dinner
22 Moray catcher
26 Half a dozen
28 Land hopper
29 Prefix with logical
31 Ladleful of unappetizing food
32 Command to Fido
33 Foes of Dems.
34 Make, as money
35 "Flop two," in diner slang
37 Sen. Cochran of Mississippi
40 Capital where the yen is capital
41 Periodic table listings
44 Deface
46 Ocean inlet
48 South-of-the-border shawl
50 ___ Mahal
52 Went like the wind
54 Sal of "Rebel Without a Cause"
55 Played on stage
56 "I ___ vacation!"
57 Throat-clearing sound
58 Unadulterated
60 Written reminder
61 Smile
63 "Send help!"

by Gregory E. Paul

74

ACROSS

1 Philosopher William of ___
6 Kid around with
10 Helgenberger of "CSI"
14 "Naughty you!"
15 Wheel shaft
16 Radio "good buddy"
17 All smiles
18 Quilters' parties
19 "Elephant Boy" boy
20 Crops up
22 Hatchling's home
24 Actor Herbert of "Pink Panther" films
25 One way to stand
26 Purge
28 Dense fog
30 Cheese in a ball
32 Lee's uniform color
34 Shrewd
35 Kosher ___
36 Amount left after expenses
37 Feted with sherry, say
38 Woman associated with seven other answers in this puzzle
41 Loathe
43 "You've got mail" co.
44 Houlihan portrayer
48 Way up or down
49 B'way hit signs
50 Mambo king Puente
51 Kodak inventor
53 "What's up, ___?"
55 Bro. or sis.

56 Utmost
57 Chop ___
59 Observant ones
61 Clump of hair
63 Good buy
65 ___ home (out)
66 In alignment
67 Poet Pound
68 Poetry Muse
69 Joad family's home state: Abbr.
70 Part of a Fifth Ave. address
71 A bit stupid

DOWN

1 Circular in form
2 Acting out of a phrase
3 London or Lisbon
4 Sound boosters
5 Mob figure Lansky
6 Sharp left or right

7 Yoked team
8 Ready to turn in
9 "Steppenwolf" author
10 TV hosts, briefly
11 Mother-of-pearl source
12 Hoopster's grab
13 In a cranky mood
21 Milano Mr.
23 Not spoken
27 Prepared to shoot in a shootout
29 Least crazy
31 Bad, as a tennis shot
33 Doing battle
37 W.W. I president
39 Benchmarks
40 Where the boyz are
41 Founder of modern Turkey
42 Given to blushing

45 Bug
46 Say over
47 "War and Peace" author
48 Directed at
49 Tormented by pollen, say
52 Poet W. H. ___
54 Funnel-shaped
58 Ball material
60 Corrida charger
62 Tetley product
64 Nonprofessional

by John Underwood

ACROSS

1 Trophies and such
7 Give at no charge, as a hotel room
11 Hypodermic units, for short
14 Magical drink
15 Cousin of a bassoon
16 "Roses ___ red . . ."
17 1981 Mel Gibson film, with "The"
19 Fellows
20 Go in
21 Basic beliefs
23 Gorbachev was its last leader: Abbr.
26 404 in old Rome
28 Niagara source
29 ___ de mer
30 The Ocean State
33 ___ donna
35 They split when they're smashed
36 Motorcycle attachment
39 English pool game
43 Sign up for more issues
45 Scoundrel
46 Arrived like Michael in an old song?
51 Decimal base
52 Spoken
53 Singer Turner
54 Penny
55 Actress Roberts and others
58 Electrical pioneer
60 Explosive initials
61 Had the passenger seat

66 Winning 1-Across can make this grow
67 Blue-green
68 Fancy home
69 Room with an easy chair
70 Master thespians they're not
71 Like a professional haircut

DOWN

1 Mo. before May
2 Court
3 ___ disadvantage (handicapped)
4 Equestrian
5 Sad
6 Grab
7 Bullfight
8 Kimono sash
9 Not worth debating
10 French father
11 Kodak, e.g.
12 Lowlife
13 Felt
18 Make a change in the decor
22 "Full" or "half" wrestling hold
23 Diamond V.I.P.'s
24 Delhi dress
25 Moved on ice
27 Dog docs
30 Zoomed
31 Charged particle
32 Cig
34 Just
37 Commercial suffix with Tropic
38 Remainder
40 Smith who sang "God Bless America"

41 Not odd
42 Landlord's due
44 Bleaches
46 Went bad
47 Juice source
48 Malicious
49 Change for a five
50 Epidermal eruptions
54 Feline
56 Part of McDonald's logo
57 Bean type
59 Disoriented
62 Hoover ___
63 Lass
64 Western tribe
65 Actor Beatty

by David Pringle

ACROSS

1 Nasty habits
6 Homes for hermanos y hermanas
11 "Dracula" creature
14 Blaze of glory
15 African wader
16 Emissions watchdog: Abbr.
17 See 29-Across
19 Dollop
20 Redder, as a tomato
21 Empire State Building style
23 Butcher's cut
25 Bigheads
27 Repeat performance?
28 Semicircle
29 Beginning of a daffy-nition of 17-Across
32 Winter warmer
34 Discover
35 Paid respect to
38 A cheap way to fly
42 Kisses in Castile
44 W.W. II conference site
45 Daffy-nition, part 2
50 For example
51 No in Nuremberg
52 Cambodian currency
53 Eight: Prefix
54 Ballroom dance
57 Chutzpah
59 U.S./Eur. divider
60 End of the daffy-nition
64 Runner Sebastian
65 Old sporty Toyota
66 Pertaining to an arm bone
67 You can get a bang out of it
68 Data processing command
69 ___ coil (electrical device)

DOWN

1 American Legion member
2 Rocks at the bar
3 Like much office work
4 Option at a fast-food restaurant
5 "That's enough!"
6 Pay with plastic
7 Feel bad
8 Results of dives
9 Mimic
10 Separate into whites and darks, e.g.
11 Beautify
12 Military helicopter
13 No-nos
18 High-schooler
22 Durbin of Hollywood
23 Young woman
24 Killer whale
26 Barn bird
29 Many a time
30 Cereal grain
31 Area of land
33 Classical Flemish painter
36 Inexact fig.
37 Lintel support
39 Perceives
40 Troublemaker
41 Something to swing on a string
43 ___ Lanka
45 Not broken up
46 Formulator of the law of universal gravitation
47 Shrinking ___
48 Desire strongly
49 A Baldwin brother
53 Little egg
55 Copy, as a film
56 Former New York City archbishop
58 Drubbing
61 Golf's ___ Elder
62 Mule of song
63 Large time piece?

by Sarah Keller

ACROSS

1 Jazz style
6 Reclusive actress Greta
11 Sandwich initials
14 Tehran native
15 Perfect
16 Karel Capek play
17 Rooming house offering
19 Whiz
20 Tints
21 Tasteless
23 Large monkeys
27 Happy-face symbols
29 Peter of "Lawrence of Arabia"
30 Cuban dance music: Var.
31 Make up (for)
32 Rent
33 ___ King Cole
36 "___ Lama Ding Dong" (1961 nonsense hit)
37 Nullifies
38 Author Ferber
39 Mrs., in Madrid
40 Like the weather around lighthouses, often
41 Open, as a package
42 Ed of "The Honeymooners"
44 Carve
45 Golf attendants
47 Prayer book
48 Country bumpkins
49 Et ___ (and others)
50 Part of a college e-mail address
51 Like a native
58 Bro's sibling
59 Tape deck button
60 Ham it up
61 Asian holiday
62 Cosmetician Lauder
63 Dork

DOWN

1 Baby's mealtime garment
2 Afore
3 Naughty
4 ___ case-by-case basis
5 Tiny puncture
6 Scoffs
7 Fusses
8 Stephen of "The Crying Game"
9 Drinker's place
10 Antiquated
11 Drilling tool
12 Like a rabbit's foot, supposedly
13 Deuce toppers
18 Sand hill
22 Priest's robe
23 Wild swine
24 ___ of roses
25 Economic cycle
26 Mrs. Chaplin
27 Disreputable
28 Rumple
30 King's time on the throne
32 Apple's apple and Chevron's chevron
34 Win by ___
35 Levy imposer
37 Cast a ballot
38 Letter accompanier: Abbr.
40 Toy loved by dogs
41 Without assistance
43 Wordsworth creation
44 "The proof ___ the pudding"
45 Toothpaste brand
46 War hero Murphy
47 Dish
49 Suffix with accept
52 Breakfast drinks, briefly
53 No longer working: Abbr.
54 Mercedes competitor
55 Fish eggs
56 Summer on the Seine
57 Belle of a ball

by Alison Donald

ACROSS

1 "Qué ___?"
5 1970s White House name
11 Revolutionary Guevara
14 Often
15 There are eight in a cup
16 ___ Luthor, of "Superman"
17 Evangelist and friend of presidents
19 ___ pro nobis
20 1956 Elvis hit that went to #2
21 Sun. talk
22 Mil. weapon that can cross an ocean
23 Some short plays
25 Nosh
27 French composer Erik
29 Turned sharply
32 Diplomat's asset
35 "Tickle me" guy
37 Parenthetical comment
38 Part of H.R.H.
39 Word that can follow the ends of 17- and 62-Across and 11- and 34-Down
41 Break a commandment
42 On ___ (winning)
44 Vaccines
45 Understands
46 "Forget about it!"
48 Art supporter
50 Words of agreement
52 German thoroughfare
56 Huck Finn's transport
58 Digital readout, for short
60 Walk nonchalantly
61 ___ Baba
62 Takes no chances
64 Word with pool or port
65 Go back to a favorite book
66 Pitcher
67 Language suffix
68 Antsy
69 Some cameras, for short

DOWN

1 Picasso or Casals
2 "March comes in like ___ . . ."
3 Figure out
4 As a minimum
5 Energetic one
6 Part of E.U.: Abbr.
7 Genetic molecules
8 Flu symptoms
9 Becomes aware of
10 Mil. award
11 How bidding proceeds in bridge
12 Basil or oregano
13 Midterm, e.g.
18 Gym site, for short
22 Prepares, as Champagne
24 ___ Marner
26 Banned apple spray
28 Show host
30 Get to work on Time
31 TV rooms
32 Holier ___ thou
33 Prefix with space
34 Dangerous thing to be caught in
36 Gumbo vegetables
39 Dressed
40 First and Second Avenues area, in Manhattan
43 Ransack
45 Spectacles
47 Common allergen
49 Part of Q.E.D.
51 Words of compassion
53 Wrap
54 Morley of "60 Minutes"
55 Observers
56 Preakness, for one
57 "Woe is me!"
59 Not natural
62 In favor of
63 Droop

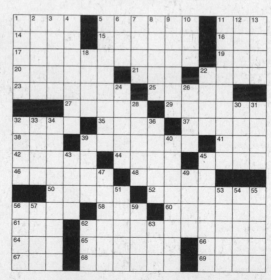

by Richard Chisholm

ACROSS

1 Ones filling out 1040's, for short
5 Dangers
10 Fed. workplace watchdog
14 Nimble
15 Irish-born actor Milo
16 San ___ Obispo, Calif.
17 ___ avis
18 Téa of "Hollywood Ending"
19 Greek war god
20 Longtime ABC daytime drama
23 Thought things over
24 "C'est si ___"
25 Little white lie
28 Classic children's nursery song
33 BB's and bullets
34 Rowed
35 Lays down the lawn
39 Made a statement on a stack of Bibles?
42 "___ of the D'Urbervilles"
43 Hatred
45 Best buds
47 1970 Jack Nicholson film
53 Folk singer DiFranco
54 Genetic info
55 "It's ___ nothing"
57 1952 George Axelord Broadway farce, with "The"
62 Gangster's blade
64 Butcher's offerings
65 Slowish

66 Finish a drive?
67 Capri and Wight
68 City near Provo
69 "You said it, brother!"
70 "This is ___ . . ." (radio announcement)
71 Memo

DOWN

1 PC storage accessory
2 Treat for an elephant
3 Once more
4 More hackneyed
5 Massage intensely
6 "Yes, it's clear now"
7 Attempt to score
8 Obi-Wan ___ of "Star Wars"

9 Poetic command before "O Ship of State!"
10 Former king of Norway
11 Guaranteed to succeed
12 Hurry
13 Nitwit
21 Bright thought
22 Prefix with European
26 Summer coolers
27 Mattress holders
29 Letters on an ambulance
30 Audi rival
31 Nutso
32 Welcome ___
35 Davenport
36 Father of Thor
37 Creating dissension
38 Seek damages

40 Hip-hop
41 Nickname for a 59-Down student
44 ___ Griffin, 1960s–'80s talk show host
46 Scorch
48 Deficiency of red blood cells
49 Most reasonable
50 Attachable, as sunglasses
51 Matador charger
52 Bulb holder
56 Moon to June
58 Smooth
59 College where an athlete might wear a "Y"
60 Summers on the Riviera
61 Helper: Abbr.
62 Health resort
63 ___ and cheese

by Sarah Keller

ACROSS

1 Document burial place
5 Marilyn Monroe mark
9 Full range
14 Like ideal cactus climate
15 E-garbage
16 Degrade
17 Something to play in Kinshasa?
19 Increased, as the score
20 "Come in!"
21 Baby bug
23 Moo goo ___ pan
24 Fresh talk
26 From time immemorial
28 Eye part
31 Regained consciousness
33 Like "fuzz" for "police"
34 Rock band equipment
35 High do
38 Beaujolais, e.g.
39 Letters that make you feel important?
42 Unbridged area
43 Cribbage markers
45 Alternative to gin or vodka
46 TV viewer's aid
48 Away, but not completely off-duty
50 Sidestepped
51 French-born satirist Hilaire
53 Author Dinesen
54 Meyers of "Kate & Allie"
55 Live's partner
58 "Phooey!"
62 ___ de Mayo
64 Intermediary (or a title for this puzzle)
66 Rivers' destination
67 Cry from the pews
68 Start of a magician's cry
69 Foul
70 Cincinnati team
71 Freeway exit

DOWN

1 Place for a smile
2 Wrinkle remover
3 Buildup on a suit jacket
4 Sidles through a doorway
5 Chow mein additive
6 October birthstones
7 Tibetan priest
8 Reason to call 911: Abbr.
9 Bodywork place
10 Lawyers' org.
11 The Lord's tropical fruit?
12 Run-of-the-mill
13 Not very hot
18 Grove fruit
22 Some Anne Rice characters
25 Bless the food
27 J.F.K. posting, for short
28 Request of an invitee, briefly
29 Nobelist Wiesel
30 Romantic ballroom queues?
31 Bedouin's mount
32 Doctor's org.
36 Hourly charge
37 Guest column
40 Olive ___
41 Acerbic pianist Oscar
44 John Belushi was originally on it: Abbr.
47 Start a battle
49 Any of the original 13
51 Breakfast strip
52 Author Jong
53 Laid up
56 Thickening agent
57 Vatican's home
59 ___ Hart, sitcom title character
60 Presidential time
61 Go bananas
63 Friskies eater
65 Nav. rank

by Lee Glickstein and Nancy Salomon

ACROSS

1 "Show Boat" author Ferber
5 Sheep cries
9 Sense much used in a bakery
14 Stick-to-itiveness
15 Pac-10 member
16 Shire of "Rocky"
17 Strong wind
18 Metric weight
19 Back street
20 Forecast maker
23 Leader known for his "little red book"
24 Quantity: Abbr.
25 Lucy of "Charlie's Angels," 2000
28 Slugger called the Sultan of Swat
31 Commendation
36 Gaelic tongue
38 Crystal ball user
40 Sea duck
41 "Melrose Place" actress
44 Loos who wrote "Gentlemen Prefer Blondes"
45 Wire screen
46 Fill up
47 Episodes of "Friends" and "Seinfeld," now
49 Within a stone's throw
51 Acid, in the '60s
52 700, on monuments
54 Actor Stephen
56 Motorcyclist's wear, often
63 Final authority
64 Extol
65 Former Baathist state
67 "You're ___ talk!"
68 "Do you come here often?," e.g.
69 Scrabble piece

70 Accelerator or brake
71 Pindar writings
72 Scored 100 on

DOWN

1 Fabergé collectible
2 Shout at a shootout
3 River with Blue and White tributaries
4 Special forces unit
5 Crazy, slangily
6 Farm division
7 Having wings
8 Brazilian dance
9 TV series with Klingons and Romulans
10 Having XY chromosomes
11 Scat queen Fitzgerald

12 Place
13 Place
21 Road topper
22 "Steee-rike!" caller
25 Franz who composed "The Merry Widow"
26 In an old song, the "I'll see you in my dreams" girl
27 Carrier that acquired Piedmont
29 Period in office
30 Beauty of Troy
32 Is sick
33 Perfect
34 Theater reservations
35 Missed the mark
37 "___, Brute?"
39 Switch-hitter known as Charlie Hustle
42 Screwdriver or wrench
43 Pantomime game

48 Educ. site
50 ___ room
53 Yo-Yo Ma's instrument
55 Japanese dog
56 Swim meet division
57 Gazed at
58 "The Thin Man" dog
59 Police action
60 Father's Day month
61 Guitarist Clapton
62 Story
63 Soak (up)
66 Mathematical proof letters

by Randall J. Hartman

ACROSS

1 Morocco's capital
6 "Oh, my stars!"
10 Recipe amt.
14 They're not PC
15 Inner: Prefix
16 Pro ___ (one way to divide things)
17 African language family
18 Close
19 They can be refined
20 Ford explorer?
23 Jock: Abbr.
26 Sailor's affirmative
27 Mississippi city where Elvis was born
28 Hospital's ___ center
30 Positioned
32 Far Eastern bread
33 "The Hours" role for which Nicole Kidman won an Oscar
36 Genre for Aretha Franklin
37 Dashboard inits.
38 Pupil's locale
41 Billiards great
46 Org. with a complex code
48 ". . . ___ the whole thing!"
49 Rejoinder to "Am too!"
50 With grace
52 Computer monitor: Abbr.
53 Bout enders, for short
54 Ambassadors and such, or an appropriate title for this puzzle
58 Ambience
59 Det. Tiger or N.Y. Yankee
60 Blow one's lid
64 Kind of mile: Abbr.

65 Cry out
66 Where the Decalogue was received
67 Shade trees
68 Talk back to
69 Ability

DOWN

1 Josh
2 Physician's org.
3 Roll-on brand
4 When Hamlet sees the ghost
5 Literally, "harbor wave"
6 One often seen in a turban
7 Fit for drafting
8 Ollie's partner
9 Friend of Hamlet
10 Jamboree group
11 Longtime Massachusetts congressman

12 Writer Shelby
13 Give, as a gene
21 Actress Cannon
22 Sport in which Israel won its first Olympic medal
23 Off-roaders, for short
24 ZZ Top, musically
25 Reckless
29 Trademarked fruit name
30 Discontinuance
31 Seuss's "Horton Hears ___"
34 "___ a man with seven wives"
35 Popular cereal or magazine
39 Langston Hughes poem
40 Discontinued fliers, quickly
42 River past Luxor
43 Rejects

44 Protective covering
45 Unaffected
46 Demented
47 Initiation, for one
51 French political divisions
52 Marine ___
55 Nolo contendere, e.g.
56 Unagi, in a sushi bar
57 Best-selling author Larson
61 Prefix with cycle
62 Chum
63 Up to, informally

by Kevan Choset

ACROSS

1 Jane Austen novel
5 Chopper blade
10 Friend
13 Meat cuts behind the ribs
15 Give the slip
16 Pharmaceutical giant ___ Lilly
17 Poker instruction
19 ___ v. Wade (1973 Supreme Court decision)
20 Elapsed time
21 Slowly merged (into)
23 Filling maker: Abbr.
24 Saudi export
25 "The final frontier"
27 Slots instruction
31 Burn with hot liquid
34 His and ___
35 Cousin of an ostrich
36 "Piece of cake!"
37 Diamond weight
39 Mojave-like
40 Mornings, for short
41 Boot bottom
42 Devoutness
43 Roulette instruction
47 Paris divider
48 Versatile truck, informally
49 ___ King Cole
52 Carafe size
54 Step-up
56 Critic ___ Louise Huxtable
57 Craps instruction
60 Chess pieces
61 Clear the blackboard
62 Breed of red cattle
63 Mammal that sleeps upside-down
64 Shut out
65 New Jersey five

DOWN

1 Castilian hero
2 Pitcher's place
3 Pitchers' gloves
4 Prelude to a deal
5 Carmaker's woe
6 Racetrack
7 Road goo
8 Strange
9 Closes again, as an envelope
10 Keep working hard
11 ___ vera
12 Told a whopper
14 Hide from view
18 Like Darth Vader
22 11-pointer in blackjack
25 Queens ball park
26 Sassy
27 Work at, as a trade
28 Pitched
29 Send forth
30 New York's Giuliani
31 The world has seven of them
32 Where soldiers stay overnight
33 Helper
37 Harry ___, Columbia Pictures co-founder
38 Sheltered, nautically
39 Be under the weather
41 How 007 does not like martinis
42 Squinted
44 Formerly known as
45 Orion, with "the"
46 Leave one's mark on
49 Unsophisticated
50 High-class tie
51 Parenting challenges
52 Ewe's baby
53 "I had no ___!"
54 Rick's love in "Casablanca"
55 Paradise lost
58 It's north of Calif.
59 Research room

by Gordon Seaberg

84

ACROSS

1 The Beatles or the Stones
5 Penny
9 When repeated, a city in Washington
14 Inter ___
15 Penny, maybe, in poker
16 With 3-Down, French-born diarist
17 57-Across song about a request in a gene lab?
20 Not pro
21 Senescence
22 Prefix with dermal
25 Rocky hill
26 Prepare for printing
27 Prefix with gliding
29 Change over at a factory
31 Pulitzer or Tony, as for 57-Across
33 Star of Scorpio
37 57-Across song about a request in the maritime supply store?
40 Varnish ingredient
41 Dye chemical
43 Pouilly-___ (white wine)
46 Individual
47 Board game from India
51 Shade tree
53 Dover's state: Abbr.
54 Slothful
55 Word said twice before "Don't tell me!"
57 Noted Broadway composer

63 With 68-Across, what Fred MacMurray had in a 1960s sitcom
64 007
65 Famed lab assistant
66 Old catalog maker
67 Swear
68 See 63-Across

DOWN

1 ___-relief
2 Pint at a pub
3 See 16-Across
4 20th-century art movement
5 Synagogue singer
6 Whole
7 A degree
8 Golf bag item
9 Light switch surrounder
10 Battery end
11 Actress Turner and others
12 Lord or vassal
13 It's a plus in accounting
18 C.D. earnings: Abbr.
19 Howler
22 Mileage rating grp.
23 Manhandle
24 Pitcher Hideki ___
26 Honky-___
28 Give ___ for one's money
30 Heads' opposite
32 Small sharks
34 Followers of pis
35 Alleviated
36 Fence crossing
38 "Get it?"
39 53, in old Rome
42 Patriots' org.

44 Some patches
45 African antelopes
47 Fence features
48 ___ drop of a hat
49 Old Oldsmobile
50 Wishful one
52 Central
56 The one here
58 Brian Williams's employer
59 Old French coin
60 Bigheadedness
61 Charged particle
62 ___ Butterworth's

by Stephen Budiansky

ACROSS

1 Lavish entertainment
5 At a distance
9 Russian country house
14 Realtor's unit
15 Exploration org.
16 Actor Hawke
17 Title for Jesus
20 Chi-town team
21 Slimmer's regimen
22 Contents of Bartlett's
23 Peddle
24 Mows
25 Lightest-colored
28 Pre-dye hair shade, often
29 Revolutionary Guevara
32 Champion tennis servers
33 Russia's ___ Mountains
34 "Slow down!"
35 1976 Walter Matthau/Tatum O'Neal movie
38 Private investigators, for short
39 Iranian money
40 Africa's Sierra ___
41 Suffix with book or freak
42 Baseball glove
43 Expired
44 Smooth, as a drive
45 One of the three H's in a summer weather forecast
46 Gas rating number
49 Coarse fiber
50 "Ugh!"
53 1958 best seller by William J. Lederer and Eugene Burdick
56 Concise
57 Shakespeare's stream
58 Major-___ (bigwig)
59 Name on a deed
60 Store
61 One more time

DOWN

1 Chief parts of adipose tissue
2 Sound in a long hallway
3 Big-mouthed carnivorous dinosaur, for short
4 Hosp. brain readout
5 Make sacred
6 No longer bright
7 Aide: Abbr.
8 The old college cheer
9 Second-in-command
10 One of the Three Musketeers
11 Atkins of country music
12 Big-eared hopper
13 "No ifs, ___ or buts"
18 Texas oil city
19 Is, in math
23 Predicate parts
24 Words moving along the bottom of a TV screen
25 Singer Page
26 Suffers after overexercise
27 Bloodsucker
28 Terrific
29 Total confusion
30 Singer Lena or Marilyn
31 Relaxed
33 Come together
34 Tearful
36 Twaddle
37 Sports jacket
42 Christmas display sight
43 Underlying
44 Temporary halt
45 Comedy
46 Director Preminger
47 Prepare to swallow
48 Beach bird
49 Coffee, slangily
50 Universally known figure
51 Arrived
52 "Well, what do you ___?!"
54 Thanksgiving side dish
55 Boise's home: Abbr.

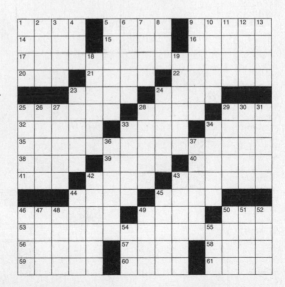

by Janet R. Bender

ACROSS

1 Sign at an A.T.M.
5 Smooth
11 Afternoon social
14 Slender instrument
15 Without delay
16 Columnist Buchwald
17 Actress Moore
18 Ringers
20 Freshwater fish with silvery scales
22 For each
23 Cone producer
25 Punch hard
28 Tiny bit
29 Ringers
33 Actress Hatcher
34 Vessel of 1492
35 Ringers
42 Calais concept
43 Ones with war stories
45 Ringers
51 Tater
52 Butcher's, baker's or candlestick maker's
53 Western tribe member
54 Equips with metal plating
57 Indispensable
59 Ringers
62 Hit the spot
65 Air hero
66 In abundance
67 Some investments, for short
68 Noted Turner
69 Aft ends
70 Certain cobras

DOWN

1 Cape ___
2 Justice Fortas
3 Shade maker for a siesta
4 ___ to the throne
5 Deli meat
6 Kind of clock or number
7 Additionally
8 Voter's finger stainer
9 Scholastic sports grp.
10 Cry of pain
11 Assume responsibility for
12 Raises
13 Confused
19 Late afternoon on a sundial
21 Educated guess: Abbr.
23 Hale

24 Checked a license, informally
26 Trigonometric function
27 Director Kazan
30 Quick drink
31 Old cable TV inits.
32 Jokester
36 Indy 500 locale
37 Summer N.Y. hrs.
38 Hula hoops?
39 A Gabor
40 Habitués
41 Manuscript annotation
44 Copenhagen-to-Prague dir.
45 Evergreen
46 All excited
47 Favorite
48 Rule
49 Showy blooms
50 Encountered

51 Nasser's successor
55 Semis
56 Ella Fitzgerald specialty
58 Largest of seven
60 Barley brew
61 Craggy prominence
63 Utilize
64 Double-180 maneuver

by Gene Newman

ACROSS

1 French cleric
5 Enthusiasm
9 Slightly open
13 "Time ___," 1990s sci-fi TV series
14 1950s candidate Stevenson
16 Art ___
17 56-Across figure
19 Bushy do
20 Birds' homes
21 Stabbed
23 Job application attachments
24 "Bird on ___," 1990 Mel Gibson movie
25 Carrier to Sweden
26 Before: Abbr.
27 Necessary: Abbr.
30 ___ Parks, former "Miss America" host
33 Two under par
34 Man's nickname that's an alphabetic run
35 W.C., in England
36 56-Across figure
38 Metal in rocks
39 Popular card game
40 When some TV news comes on
41 Change for a five
42 Superman's symbol
43 Brings into play
44 Singer Sumac
46 Faux pas
48 Fierce one
52 Vance of "I Love Lucy"
54 Place to buy a yacht
55 Mimicked
56 S. Dakota monument
58 ___ of Man
59 Happening
60 Johnson who said "Ver-r-r-y interesting!"
61 Loads
62 Puts in extra
63 Spick and span

DOWN

1 Battling
2 Indian who may be 1-Down
3 Foundation
4 Tire out
5 Cutups
6 A sphere lacks them
7 Computer keys: Abbr.
8 Neighbor of a Vietnamese
9 Firefighter Red
10 56-Across figure
11 Farm unit
12 Crucifix
15 Place to dip an old pen
18 "___ la Douce," 1963 film
22 Actor David of "Separate Tables"
24 Laser gas
26 Walks outside the delivery room?
28 To be, in France
29 Opposite of an ans.
30 Ocean-colored
31 Millions of years
32 56-Across figure
33 Set foot in
36 Mrs. Bush
37 "My treat!"
41 One who rows, rows, rows the boat
44 Breadmakers' needs
45 Algebra or trig
47 Disney World attractions
48 Headed (for)
49 Taking out the trash, for one
50 Heart line
51 Chirp
52 Colorado resort
53 ___ facto
54 Partner of born
57 Dam project: Abbr.

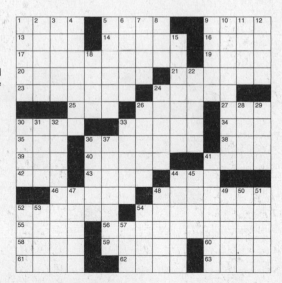

by Sherry O. Blackard

88

ACROSS
1 Retreats
7 Dry, as wine
10 It leaves marks on asphalt
14 Triumphant cry
15 Word often said twice before "again"
16 Numbers game
17 She wed George Washington
20 Niagara Falls' prov.
21 Karel Capek play
22 Church nooks
23 Where Washington relaxed
28 Wrath
29 Pi preceder
34 Friend in the Southwest
37 Forsaken
39 Ready for picking
40 State defense organization headed by Washington
43 Its flight attendants' greeting is "Shalom"
44 Magician's start
45 Word prefixed with poly-
46 Edison's New Jersey lab locale
48 "Welcome" site
49 Where Washington's forces wintered
55 Defense aid
59 Writer Fleming
60 Time Warner merger partner of 2001
61 Colonial force headed by Washington
66 ___ Stanley Gardner
67 Belfry flier
68 ___ corpus
69 Faculty head
70 Not just tear up
71 "Tristram Shandy" author

DOWN
1 Televised sign in football stands
2 Hersey's bell town
3 Love of artistic objects
4 D.C. summer clock setting
5 Fed. biomedical research agcy.
6 Deprive of food
7 Fab Four drummer
8 Directional suffix
9 Dancer Charisse
10 Old record problem
11 Popular sneakers
12 "Picnic" playwright
13 Female deer
18 ___ date
19 Rajah's wife
24 Carp
25 "Star Trek: T.N.G." counselor
26 Bellini opera
27 Prefix with potent
30 "The Count of Monte ___"
31 Film director Martin
32 Mayberry boy
33 Close
34 Swear to
35 Actor O'Shea
36 Investments usually held for yrs. and yrs.
37 Kind of suit found in a courtroom
38 Sculling need
41 Queen in "The Lion King"
42 Page (through)
47 Chapter 57
48 Avian talkers
50 Needing a good brushing, say
51 Ingest
52 Scarcer
53 Beatnik's encouragement
54 "Family Ties" mom
55 Served past
56 Oral tradition
57 "To Live and Die ___"
58 Bingo call
62 Peacock network
63 Musical talent
64 Long.'s opposite
65 Face on a fiver

by Ed Early

ACROSS

1 Livens (up)
5 Snapshot
10 Bedazzles
14 Away from the wind
15 Home run king Hank
16 Retail store
17 Glib responses
19 On the ocean
20 Baffled
21 Canines or bicuspids
23 New Haven collegians
24 Personal bugbear
27 Observer
30 Quattros, e.g.
31 Some sports cars
34 Take into custody
37 Supreme Diana
38 Go bad
39 Indy service break
41 Sport ___ (all-purpose vehicle)
42 Med. school subj.
44 Caviar source
45 Price add-on
46 Subway handhold
48 Make into law
50 Kind of stove
53 Smooch
56 Major company in metallic products
57 Drink often served with a lemon twist
60 Skin woe
62 Portfolio hedges
64 Eliot or Frost
65 One of the nine Muses
66 "Lohengrin" soprano
67 Drags
68 Heroic tales
69 Not shallow

DOWN

1 Mama's partner
2 Fill with joy
3 Flower feature
4 Protect, as freshness
5 Free ticket
6 Hems' partners
7 Source of iron or lead
8 Rich pastry
9 Beginning
10 Not an expert
11 Exhausted
12 Before, in verse
13 Depot: Abbr.
18 "Forget it!"
22 Clean air org.
24 "Blue Hawaii" star
25 Far-reaching view
26 "The Private Lives of Elizabeth and ___" (1939 film)
28 Common newspaper nickname
29 Art Deco designer
31 Understand
32 Jay Silverheels role
33 Go back to square one
35 Surprise greatly
36 Roman robe
40 Bundle
43 Things held by Moses
47 Chest muscle, for short
49 Neatened
51 Easy strides
52 Designer Ashley
54 Item worn around the shoulders
55 Pick up on
57 Teensy bit
58 Navy noncoms, for short
59 "Rush!" order
60 It may be a walk-up: Abbr.
61 Dove's sound
63 Children's game

by Marjorie Berg

90

ACROSS

1 Film mogul Louis B. (whose company mascot was 26-Across)
6 "Funny!"
10 Hard to fluster
14 Mrs. David O. Selznick, daughter of 1-Across
15 Assist in wrongdoing
16 Hodgepodge
17 One lacking courage
19 On the briny
20 ___ Tuesday
21 Take the first step
23 Poland's Walesa
25 Tam sporter
26 Roarer in film intros
29 Sty fare
31 Eucalyptus-loving "bears"
35 Drive-thru dispenser, maybe
36 Gazetteer statistic
38 Sporty Mazda
39 Courage seeker in a 1939 film
43 Top man in the choir?
44 ___ proprietor
45 SSW's opposite
46 Fake
48 Crowe's "A Beautiful Mind" role
50 Suffix with chariot
51 Pack and send
53 Reply to "That so?"
55 Deuterium and tritium, to hydrogen
59 Make unreadable, for security
63 Island near Java
64 One feigning courage
66 Tied in score
67 "___ homo"
68 Put ___ in one's ear
69 An earth sci.
70 Not fake
71 Cake sections

DOWN

1 Fail to catch
2 Keystone's place
3 Reunion number
4 Sign up
5 Superman player George
6 Barn loft contents
7 Basics
8 Puts on the burner
9 Tear into
10 Formal jacket feature
11 What's more
12 In ___ of
13 A drawbridge may span one
18 Render harmless, perhaps, to 26-Across's kin
22 Hardly cramped
24 Round dances
26 Starbucks order
27 Old anesthetic
28 Prophetic signs
30 Argentina's Juan
32 Frankie or Cleo
33 Do penance
34 Less dotty
37 Ike's two-time opponent
40 Exerting little effort
41 Straight: Prefix
42 Former Georgia governor Maddox
47 Sleeping bag closer
49 Suggest subtly
52 Treaty result
54 "Star Wars" genre
55 "___ to differ"
56 Except for
57 Promise product
58 Shelter org.
60 Gape at
61 Whitetail, e.g.
62 Notable times
65 Slithery swimmer

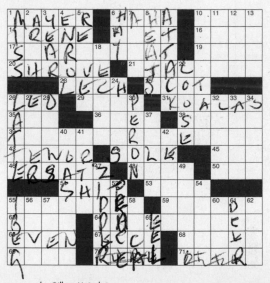

by Gilbert H. Ludwig

ACROSS

1 Look (at), as stars
5 Artist's suffix with land or sea
10 Tortoiselike
14 "___ Around" (#1 Beach Boys hit)
15 Breaking a bad one is good
16 El ___, Tex.
17 ___-a-brac
18 Big kitchen appliance maker
19 Eight, in Spain
20 Wife of King David
22 Prepare to pop the question
23 Nova Scotia clock setting: Abbr.
24 June 14
26 Hamburger meat
30 Peter who is an eight-time Oscar nominee
32 Last full month of summer
34 Departure's opposite: Abbr.
35 Penny
39 Cheater's aid
40 Yellowish shade
42 Asian nurse
43 President before Wilson
44 Australian hopper, for short
45 Igloo dweller
47 "To be or not to be" soliloquist
50 Woman of "Troy"
51 One taking flight
54 That, in Tijuana
56 Scent
57 "Days of Our Lives," for one
63 "The World According to ___"
64 Ne plus ___
65 Slightly
66 Feminine suffix

67 Full . . . and happy about it
68 Mideast's ___ Strip
69 Active one
70 Cursed
71 School before middle school: Abbr.

DOWN

1 Any of the Bee Gees
2 Taj Mahal site
3 Time, in Mannheim
4 Work on glass, say
5 Former Iranian leaders
6 Awoke
7 Basic rhyme scheme
8 "H.M.S. ___"
9 Third letter after delta
10 Light dessert

11 Donned skates, e.g., with "up"
12 Actor Milo
13 Sheeplike
21 Declares
22 ___ Kan (pet food)
25 Peter who played Mr. Moto
26 Agreement
27 Atmosphere
28 End-of-week cry
29 Noisy public speaker
31 California/Nevada lake
33 Singer nicknamed the Velvet Fog
36 Oscar winner Jannings
37 Partner of rank and serial number
38 Ending with tele-
41 Side dish at KFC
46 "Scram!"
48 Old Turkish title

49 Ripper
51 Ran amok
52 Poetry Muse
53 Talent
55 Ditchdigger's tool
58 Director Preminger
59 Newspaper unit
60 And others, in footnotes
61 Completely demolish
62 One who raised Cain
64 Inits. in Navy ship names

by Christina Houlihan Kelly

92

ACROSS

1 Actor Damon
5 Great buy, slangily
10 Go yachting
14 Met solo
15 Inventor Nikola
16 Ides of March utterance
17 Timid creature
18 Big name in chips
19 "Hud" Oscar winner
20 Actor Ben with the gang?
23 ___-mo
25 Cornhusker State: Abbr.
26 Like good soil
27 Chops to bits
29 Best Actress winner for "Million Dollar Baby"
31 Really enjoyed
32 Democratic honcho Howard
33 Roadside sign
36 Marathoner Frank with candy?
40 Layer?
41 Richly adorn
42 Easy mark
43 Nutty as a fruitcake
45 Motor City hoopster
46 Mel Ott, notably
48 Several eras
49 Unlock, poetically
50 Novelist Evan with a small smooch?
54 Man Friday, e.g.
55 Publicist's concern
56 Workbook segment

59 Puts into play
60 "Our Gang" dog
61 Mower maker
62 Document content
63 Dorm annoyance
64 Cashless deal

DOWN

1 "Spy vs. Spy" magazine
2 "You ___ here"
3 Gets soused
4 Pucker-producing
5 Metro entrances
6 Potato sack wt., maybe
7 Renaissance family name
8 K.C. Royal, e.g.
9 Space cadet's place
10 Author/illustrator Maurice
11 First-stringers

12 Europe's "boot"
13 Quiet time
21 Like a stumblebum
22 ___ compos mentis
23 Not just a success
24 Like a ballerina
28 Despicable sort
29 Serta competitor
30 Harry Potter accessory
32 Icicle former
33 Become familiar with
34 Fabulous author
35 "Funny Girl" composer Jule
37 Voyages in vain?
38 Place for a title
39 Used to be
43 Up-to-the-minute
44 White Monopoly bill

45 "I yam what I yam" speaker
46 False front
47 Encyclopedia volume
48 Landscaper's tool
50 ___ monde
51 "You said it!"
52 Defense grp.
53 Roster removals
57 Lyrical Gershwin
58 Blouse, e.g.

by Deb Amlen

ACROSS
1 Baldwin of the silver screen
5 Recur, as arthritis
10 Father of Seth
14 Actress Hatcher
15 Computer item with a tracking ball
16 Aura being picked up
17 Possibly prompting a reply like 25-, 47- or 62-Across
20 Supersede
21 Immature insects
22 Rink surface
23 Rep.'s opponent
24 Singer Sumac
25 "What?!"
31 Companion of Tarzan
32 It's good only for its waste value
33 T-bone or porterhouse
37 Not so much
39 Noted Tombstone family, once
41 Ancient Roman censor
42 Like beer at a bar
44 River's mouth
46 Sign outside a hit show
47 "What?!"
50 Railroad stop: Abbr.
53 End of a proof
54 Chem. thread
55 Meat-packing pioneer
57 Chosen one
62 "What?!"
64 Slugger Sammy
65 Sailor's "Halt!"
66 "The Thin Man" wife
67 European car

68 Nigeria's largest city
69 Son of Seth

DOWN
1 "___ additional cost!"
2 Pope after Benedict IV
3 Folies Bergère designer
4 Kind of acid
5 Atmosphere, as in a restaurant
6 For both sexes
7 Toothpaste holder
8 "It's no ___!"
9 Shotgun shot
10 State unequivocally
11 Split (up)
12 At right angles to a ship

13 Jason's ally and lover, in myth
18 Killer whales
19 Poetic feet
23 Horse with a spotted coat
25 Sign of a saint
26 Unlock
27 Toward sunset
28 Swapped
29 Sheik's bevy
30 And others: Abbr.
34 Facility
35 Gillette brand
36 Wacko
38 Problem with an old sofa
40 Hollywood hopefuls
43 Resentment
45 "Li'l ___" (Al Capp strip)
48 Springlike

49 "Phèdre" playwright
50 Final approval
51 Custer cluster
52 Entertain
56 Kind of history
57 For men only
58 Studebaker's fill-up, maybe
59 Daffy Duck or Porky Pig
60 Continental currency
61 Those: Sp.
63 Eggs

by Robert Malinow

94

ACROSS

1 Frisks, with "down"
5 Muhammad's birthplace
10 Elisabeth of "Leaving Las Vegas"
14 Ranch unit
15 Pong maker
16 Hoopster Malone
17 "All I Wanna Do" singer, 1994
19 Toledo's lake
20 Pekoe server
21 Luggage attachment
23 Threw in
24 French article
26 Like woolen underwear?
27 Salsa scooper-uppers
29 Sun. delivery
30 Yeats or Keats
33 Boys' or girls' room, in London
34 Attack by plane
37 Cleansed (of)
38 First U.S. chief justice
40 Hide-hair link
41 No longer in style
43 Press for payment
44 Palm reader, e.g.
45 Hither's partner
46 Rigid bracelet
48 Bill of fare
50 Needle hole
51 Gut course
55 All riled up
57 Rich's partner
58 Say "Uncle!"
59 "Network" star
62 On the ocean
63 No longer in style
64 Add kick to

65 Flat rate?
66 Actor Davis
67 Chapters of history

DOWN

1 Orzo, e.g.
2 Had a yen
3 Radial pattern
4 Eve's tempter
5 Fountain offering
6 Catchall abbr.
7 Cougar or Lynx
8 Hags
9 Sony competitor
10 Summer pest, informally
11 "The Bridge" poet
12 Dickens's ___ Heep
13 Mournful poem
18 Luke Skywalker's mentor

22 Like the air around Niagara Falls
24 "Looks like trouble!"
25 Lunchtime, for many
28 Congealment
30 Country club figure
31 Mideast export
32 Singer with the 1988 #1 country hit "I'm Gonna Get You"
34 Acted the fink
35 Antagonist
36 Flub
38 Leigh of "Psycho"
39 Month for many Geminis
42 Difficult spot
44 Mariner's measure

46 Guardian Angels toppers
47 Table extension
48 New dad's handout
49 Biscotti flavoring
52 Salvage ship's equipment
53 New Mexico's state flower
54 Cookout leftovers?
56 ___ facto
57 For the asking
60 Profs' helpers
61 Yalie

by Gail Grabowski

ACROSS

1 Brown shade used in old photos
6 Having protected feet
10 Postal delivery
14 Deal maker
15 2:00 or 3:00
16 Skin breakout
17 Head/legs separator
18 Cathedral area
19 Box office take
20 Short-lived success
23 Affirm
26 Congo, formerly
27 Lunch or dinner
28 Hand: Sp.
31 Furthermore
32 Vintage designation
33 Oscar winner for "Scent of a Woman"
35 Short-lived success
40 Octagons, hexagons, etc.
41 The "E" of Q.E.D.
43 Greek cross
46 "___ a man with seven wives"
47 Counterpart of midterms
49 Mary of old films
51 Close of a swimming race
52 Short-lived success
56 10th-grader, for short
57 Skater Lipinski
58 Ballet rail
62 Cleveland's lake
63 Give off
64 Elicit
65 What a detective follows
66 Kind of room
67 Paper size larger than "letter"

DOWN

1 Used a pew
2 Swelled head
3 The "p" of r.p.m.
4 To the degree that
5 Makes amends
6 Former Iranian rulers
7 Mesa dweller
8 Evict
9 Picked from the stack of cards
10 ___ cum laude
11 Maine's ___ National Park
12 Summer office worker
13 Looked lecherously
21 Founded: Abbr.
22 Atmosphere layer
23 Be inquisitive
24 Atoll protector
25 Iridescent gem
28 "Olympia" painter
29 Deeds
30 Disease research org.
33 Prop for Santa
34 Nafta concept
36 Collar site
37 Lunch meat
38 Asia's shrinking ___ Sea
39 "The Lion King" lion
42 Cooking meas.
43 It's on the fringe
44 Toward land
45 Perfect world
47 Blubber
48 Sanford of "The Jeffersons"
50 Marveled aloud
51 Atty.-to-be exams
53 News bit
54 Tattle on
55 Small beam
59 Alternative to a bare floor
60 "His Master's Voice" sloganeer
61 Sushi fish

by Mike Torch

96

ACROSS
1 Hardwood tree
4 Nosed (out)
9 With 69-Across, song from 20-Across
14 Give the umpire grief
15 Mr. Moto player
16 Kid's retort
17 Big inits. in TV comedy
18 1979 musical about a half-mad barber
20 1970 musical about marriage
22 Fury
23 U.S.: Abbr.
24 See 51-Across
29 Container with a screw-top
33 ___ vera
34 Some toy trucks
37 Head of Haiti
38 Broadway composer (of 18-, 20- and 57-Across) born 3/22/1930
43 Rime
44 Oklahoma native
45 "Wishing won't make ___"
46 Encounter, as success
51 With 24-Across, song from 18-Across
55 Height: Prefix
56 Wallach of "The Magnificent Seven"
57 1971 musical about a reunion
60 Song from 57-Across
65 Unforgettable Cole
66 Army inspection?

67 Giant
68 Bell Atlantic merger partner of 2000
69 See 9-Across
70 Refine, as metal
71 One of the Chaplins

DOWN
1 Early '80s political scandal
2 California winemaking county
3 Noted resident of Baker Street
4 "Born Free" lioness
5 Like the answer to this clue
6 Lady Jane ___
7 Before, in verse
8 Jeans material

9 Aspirin maker
10 CPR giver, for short
11 Skater Midori
12 Give the go-ahead
13 The Almighty
19 Noteworthy time
21 Specialist
24 Annoying
25 It's sworn at a swearing-in
26 Peter Fonda title role
27 Reply to the Little Red Hen
28 Consider
30 Utmost
31 Average guys
32 ___ Domini
35 First-rate
36 Old dagger
38 Climb, as a pole

39 Canine from Kansas
40 Bridge hand
41 Ship's front
42 Richard Gere title role
47 ___-Mart
48 Cake toppers
49 Pact
50 Entertained
52 "Die Lorelei" poet
53 Under the weather
54 Light rhythms
57 Party
58 Kind of exam
59 Advanced
60 C.D. holder, maybe
61 Alice's sitcom boss
62 H.S. course
63 "Mazel ___!"
64 Not her

by David J. Kahn

ACROSS

1 Is in a play
5 Layers
11 Tool with teeth
14 Jacket
15 Rang, as bells
16 Swiss canton
17 Famous large deep-blue rock
19 Brooch
20 An hour before midnight
21 Illegally seized
23 Filled with joy
26 Game played on 64 squares
27 Say more
30 Sly maneuver
31 Prophet
32 Make void
34 Money in Mexico
36 Strikebreaker
39 Shows for the first time
41 Yield to desire
43 Similar (to)
44 Cry in court
46 Ordinary
47 Pub projectile
49 Prosperity
51 Maidenform product
52 Hindu social division
54 Admit to wrongdoing
56 Calm down
58 Injuries near beehives
62 Savings for old age, for short
63 Military decoration
66 Get __ of (toss out)
67 Rubs out
68 "Bye"
69 Cheer for a matador

70 Puts trust in, with "on"
71 Site of Napoleon's exile

DOWN

1 Dull hurt
2 Refrigerate
3 Put on reel-to-reel
4 Jobs in the computer field
5 Kind of column
6 Alternative to coffee
7 Male sheep
8 For all to hear
9 Sawbucks
10 Bring forth as evidence
11 Site for eating and entertainment
12 7-Down, astrologically
13 Orchestra section

18 Greek oracle site
22 Kind of monkey
24 __-turvy
25 Hurricane's center
27 Shade of blue
28 Drop, as a doughnut in milk
29 "Just Shoot Me" co-star
31 Daughter's opposite
33 Half of Congress
35 Medium, large and extra-large
37 Ice cream thickening agent
38 Lugosi who played Dracula
40 Hollywood filming locale
42 Minnesota port
45 7-Down's mate
48 Autumn farm worker

50 Estimate the value of
52 Egypt's capital
53 Shower bringer
54 Wild
55 Jigsaw puzzle element
57 Without a doubt
59 Hammer's target
60 Take hold of
61 Portico in Greek architecture
64 Letter before omega
65 __ jeans

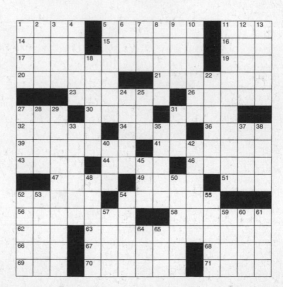

by Elizabeth Babikan

ACROSS

1 Stared stupidly
6 Light bulb units
11 Sweetums
14 Simple counters
15 Potato growers' home
16 Big galoot
17 Convince a G.I.?
19 Cause to fret
20 Peruvian range
21 Not naked
23 Was dependent
26 Bunt result, maybe
27 Like the Wolfman
28 It goes under a top
30 "The Republic" philosopher
31 Work units
32 Secure position
34 Baseball bat wood
35 Random attack
36 Evidence in a paternity suit
39 No pieces of cake
41 Masterstroke
42 Water balloon sound
44 Wind up or down
45 Tropical lizard
46 "As Good As It Gets" film studio
48 Hit on the noggin
49 Gymnast Mary Lou
50 Go-between
52 Frequently, in verse
53 Refuse to work on the weekend?
58 Actor Billy ___ Williams
59 Gives off
60 Hosiery shade
61 Blunder
62 "Belling the Cat" author
63 Casino array

DOWN

1 Burner fuel
2 Justice Fortas
3 Chum
4 Elongated pastries
5 Mickey Mouse operation?
6 Sly trick
7 Tacks on
8 Mai ___
9 Bara of old films
10 Touchy subject
11 Dine on some fish?
12 Gift-giver's urging
13 Abutting
18 Uneven?
22 Unit in a terrorist organization
23 Perlman of "Cheers"
24 Corn units
25 Burn trash?
26 Washed
28 Irritate
29 Violinist's application
32 London forecast
33 Sounds from Santa
35 Set sail
37 Microwave, slangily
38 Like two peas in ___
40 Hops-drying oven
41 Like some air-conditioning
42 Walked briskly
43 Like better
45 Rant and rave
47 Japanese cartoon art
48 Track action
50 Concerning
51 [You don't mean . . . !]
54 Rejoinder to "'Tain't!"
55 Dynamic ___
56 Quick to learn
57 Thumbs-up response

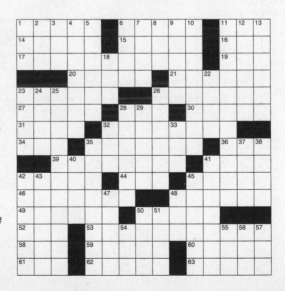

by Victor Fleming and Nelson Hardy

ACROSS

1 Boss
6 Pepsi, for one
10 Not check or charge
14 Event with bucking broncos
15 Banned orchard spray
16 Prefix with suction
17 Woody of "Manhattan"
18 Take a breather
19 Norway's capital
20 "See you later"
21 Check mate?
24 Beyond doubt
25 Some linens
26 Balance beam?
31 "Yow!"
32 Cry heard on a fairway
33 Catch, as a perp
36 Before-test work, informally
37 Simple song
39 Super-duper
40 Brit. word reference
41 Ferris wheel or bumper cars
42 Join
43 Firm offer?
46 Illinois city symbolizing middle America
49 Refusals
50 Vegas spread?
53 Person in a zebra-striped shirt, informally
56 Opposite of gave
57 Whom the cheerleaders cheer
58 Hit musical set in Argentina
60 ___ fixe (obsession)
61 Suffix with major

62 Katey of "Married . . . With Children"
63 Loch ___ monster
64 Film unit
65 Stable enclosure

DOWN

1 One who complains, complains, complains
2 "___ smokes!"
3 Doing nothing
4 Wide shoe designation
5 Cheese dishes
6 Aladdin's transportation
7 Butter substitute
8 Glasgow gal
9 Beautiful skill
10 Deal finalizer
11 Grocery pathway

12 Leave, slangily
13 B-ball
22 Mess up
23 "How do I love ___?"
24 Tread
26 Mispelled, for misspelled, e.g.
27 Irish republic
28 Barely made, with "out"
29 Frequently
30 Kiddie
33 Pinot ___ (wine)
34 Voting no
35 When repeated, Road Runner's sound
37 Fiasco
38 Dictator Amin
39 Relatives of termites
41 Completely botch
42 Futile

43 Car stoppers
44 Tooth layer
45 Boar's mate
46 Yeltsin's successor as leader of Russia
47 Eat away at
48 Woodwinds
51 Red Rose
52 $5.15/hour, e.g.
53 Latvia's capital
54 Footnote abbr.
55 Autumn
59 Dyemaker's container

by Christina Houlihan Kelly

100

ACROSS

1 Throat problem
5 Amorphous movie monster
9 "Quo ___?"
14 Prom night wheels
15 Capital of Italia
16 "No way!"
17 Dermal flare-up
18 Black-bordered news item
19 More up-to-date
20 "Right now!"
23 Gun rights grp.
24 Mandela's org.
25 Rte. recommenders
26 Porker's place
27 Death, to Dylan Thomas
33 Fam. member
34 Morales of "NYPD Blue"
35 Newsman Jim
38 Steams up
40 Where a train pulls in: Abbr.
42 Lamarr of film
43 Hobo's ride, perhaps
46 Ad award
49 Book collector's suffix
50 Part of a love triangle
53 Hole number
55 Friend of Pooh
56 Monument of lexicography, for short
57 Poem of Sappho
58 Hint to the starts of 20-, 27- and 50-Across
64 Innocent ones
66 Mock words of understanding
67 Appear to be
68 Bridge bid, briefly
69 Skirt to twirl in
70 Opposite of "Out!"
71 Rustic
72 Louisiana, e.g., in Orléans
73 "Vissi d'___"

DOWN

1 Pitched too low
2 Rolling in dough
3 Prefix with science
4 Attacks
5 Mile High City team
6 Arcing shots
7 Cut out
8 Philippine peninsula
9 Old, to a car buff
10 Leave speechless
11 Toward the mouth
12 Like krypton
13 Alley cat, perhaps
21 "Bus Stop" playwright
22 Place for some polish
27 "Lou Grant" paper, with "the"
28 One who saves the day
29 His questions are answers
30 Western treaty grp.
31 Deep-six
32 Loser to R.M.N., 1968
36 Author Ferber
37 Meg of "In the Cut"
39 P.T.A. meeting place: Abbr.
41 Inn take
44 Deodorant type
45 Crucifix
47 Resolve, as differences
48 Wasn't in the black
51 So far
52 Black Sea port
53 N'awlins sandwich
54 Hersey's bell town
59 Seal up
60 "The Thin Man" dog
61 Within reach
62 Like a pickpocket's fingers
63 "Peter Pan" pirate
65 Hydrocarbon suffix

by Harvey Estes

ACROSS

1 False god
5 Overly hasty
9 Huge ice chunks
14 Nervously irritable
15 Comic Sandler
16 Mrs. Bush
17 Despot Idi ___
18 String tie
19 Houston baseballer
20 Gentle/not gentle
23 Stops from yo-yoing
24 Conqueror of 1066 England
28 The "I" of T.G.I.F.
29 Old what's-___-name
30 Relative of beer
31 1960s radical Hoffman
35 Interval
36 Assert
37 Former pupil/present pupil
41 Stitch's cartoon pal
42 Closemouthed
43 Twinges
44 Serious drug cases, for short
45 "Man's best friend"
46 Fortune 500 listings: Abbr.
48 Firearm, e.g.
50 Loving touches
55 Furious/not furious
57 Fire starter
60 Inch or teaspoon
61 Measure (out)
62 Having a close resemblance
63 Longtime Yugoslav leader
64 Sign to interpret
65 The present
66 Harry Potter's lightning bolt
67 Rome's fifth emperor

DOWN

1 Grins widely
2 Let in
3 Nimble
4 ___ Carter, who played Wonder Woman
5 Cottontail
6 Loves to pieces
7 Casa parts
8 Group insurance grps.
9 Taste sensation
10 Light in a light show
11 Not at home
12 Say 2 + 2 = 5, say
13 ___ Paulo, Brazil
21 Parisian goodbye
22 Bumbling
25 Expert
26 "I knew it all ___!"
27 Bright salamanders
29 Consumes
31 Luminous
32 One who says 34-Down
33 Model builder's wood
34 Wedding declaration
35 Precious stone
36 Org. for cavity fillers
38 In the middle of
39 Harbor boat
40 Unexpected sports outcome
45 Democratic Party symbol
46 Per ___ (each)
47 Lincoln, e.g., at Gettysburg
49 Arctic jacket
50 Sour sort
51 ___ Says (child's game)
52 "If they could ___ now . . ."
53 Start, as school
54 Shorthand taker
56 Boring routines
57 Was in session
58 Mahmoud Abbas's grp.
59 Pitch in for

by Norma Steinberg

102

ACROSS

1 Insubstantial stuff
6 "Show Boat" novelist Ferber
10 Regarding
14 Cowpoke competition
15 Wiener schnitzel meat
16 Mix together
17 "That is to say . . ."
18 Eliel Saarinen's son
19 Huff and puff
20 Words following an oath, sometimes
23 Writer Roald
24 Take care of
25 Roman god of love
28 Like Easter eggs
31 Govt. code breakers
32 Peace of mind
34 Womanizer
36 Gullible one
39 Avoid technobabble
42 Something some people return from vacation with
43 WWW addresses
44 Paid attention to
45 "Casablanca" pianist
47 Conductor Klemperer
49 Afternoon socials
50 Russian plain
53 Cashmere, e.g.
55 "I didn't understand a thing you said"
60 The good life
61 "Roseanne" star
62 Sees the sights

64 Grandson of Adam
65 Plumbing problem
66 Blue book filler
67 Flat payment
68 Professional charges
69 Catches one's breath

DOWN

1 Work wk. ender, for most
2 Cakewalk
3 Old music halls
4 Pendant gem shape
5 Accord maker
6 Without highs and lows
7 Consider
8 ___ a soul
9 Up in the air
10 Trembling trees
11 Get out of the way
12 Touch of color
13 Garden products brand
21 Words of a worrier
22 Weasel out (on)
25 Unable to move, after "in"
26 City near Phoenix
27 Legal hunting period
29 Dadaism pioneer Max
30 Buck's partner
33 Batting woes
35 Release, as a chain
37 Out of port
38 Highest degrees
40 Worldwide workers' grp.
41 Went wild
46 Most appropriate

48 Pipsqueaks
50 Have the helm
51 Macbeth's title
52 Treble clef lines
54 Aquatic mammal
56 Nearly unique in the world
57 Canal of song
58 Rumple
59 Word after quod
63 Method: Abbr.

by Nancy Salomon

ACROSS

1 Vice President Spiro
6 Many miles away
10 The "T" of S.A.T.
14 Colonial newscaster
15 In ___ straits
16 Prefix with sphere
17 Suffer a serious blow
20 180° from NNW
21 Words repeated in "___ or not ___"
22 Noble's home
23 Withered
24 Bit of butter
25 Old film comic Sparks
26 Boxer Sonny
29 Uncovers
31 Thomas Paine's "The ___ Reason"
32 Dampens
33 "What Child Is ___?"
37 Out, so to speak
40 Sea eagle
41 President's prerogative
42 Boxing venue
43 Noisy fight
45 Fancy, as clothes
46 Number before "Liftoff!"
49 6:00, 7:00, 8:00, etc.: Abbr.
50 Products of Hammond
51 Sore
53 Roof overhang
54 Sault ___ Marie
57 Give up
60 God of love
61 Shower affection (on)

62 ___ and Novak (old news partnership)
63 Mysterious letter
64 Always
65 "Divine Comedy" writer

DOWN

1 ___ of the Apostles
2 Mardi ___
3 New Balance competitor
4 Wide shoe spec
5 Cancellation of a debt
6 Hacienda material
7 & 8 Museum material
9 Practice a part
10 Savoir-faire
11 Revolutionary War hero ___ Allen
12 Strike, in the Bible
13 Quieted, with "down"
18 Shredded
19 Villa d'___
23 Jagger's group, informally, with "the"
24 Medical prefix with logical
26 Put on board
27 Dr. Frankenstein's assistant
28 Mended
29 Singer Midler
30 Mall units
32 Small songbirds
34 Shades
35 Lodges
36 "Don't leave!"

38 Nullify, as a 41-Across
39 Covered, as a floor
44 Masticate
45 Host Letterman, for short
46 Water-loving animal
47 India's first P.M.
48 Company in a 2002 scandal
50 Bill formerly of "Politically Incorrect"
52 Amount of medicine
53 Suffix with major
54 Bird on a lake
55 Campsite sight
56 Additional
58 Oct. follower
59 Lab eggs

by Robert Dillman

104

ACROSS
1 Internet hookup, for many
6 Storybook elephant
11 Piece worn under a blouse
14 Martian or Venusian
15 Utensil with many holes
16 Stadium cheer
17 Arboreal rodent
19 Spanish eye
20 Rich-voiced
21 Mine car carrier
23 Any of the Great Smokies: Abbr.
24 News bit
26 Washer cycle
27 To's partner
28 "___ making myself clear?"
30 Aid in crime
33 Walk leisurely
36 "Later!"
37 Bone-dry
38 17- and 60-Across and 11- and 35-Down
41 PC "brains"
42 Lee's men, for short
43 Bogs down
44 Golfer's bagful
45 Victorian ___
46 Rambler mfr.
47 Telegram
49 Highly energetic
51 Nutritionist's fig.
54 Fixes at the cobbler shop
57 Was philanthropic
59 One of the Gershwins
60 Western raptor
62 Up to, in ads
63 Be of use to
64 Mill output

65 26th of 26
66 Like a pool table, ideally
67 Hardly wordy

DOWN
1 Billiards bounce
2 Red flag
3 Try for, at auction
4 For fear that
5 The National ___ (tabloid)
6 Other half of a hit 45
7 Make public
8 Ernie's Muppet pal
9 Strong dislike
10 Pass again, in a race
11 Grizzly, e.g.
12 Indian prince
13 Sailor's hail

18 "Do ___ others . . ."
22 Full of foul vapors
25 Postal carrier's tote
27 One of the Bobbseys
29 "Serpico" author Peter
31 Writer ___ Stanley Gardner
32 "___ of the D'Urbervilles"
33 Depositor's holding: Abbr.
34 Act gloomy
35 Earth's largest mammal
36 Prompt giver
39 1960s mantra
40 Full of oneself
46 Opposed to, in dialect

48 Kingly
50 Children's author Scott
51 Radioer's "Got it!"
52 Metes (out)
53 Dance partner for Fred
54 Cracker brand
55 Toledo's lake
56 Serb or Croat
58 Stadium receipts
61 Become extinct

by David Bunker

ACROSS

1 "The World According to ___"
5 Peach ___ (dessert)
10 Nobleman
14 Cake decorator
15 Brainstorms
16 Opera highlight
17 Mysterious writing
18 Doc
19 See 24-Across
20 Where actors put costumes on
23 Took care of
24 With 19-Across, where to get on a freeway
28 Buffoons
31 Sounds like a donkey
32 Take steps
35 1950s girl's fashion
39 Make ready, briefly
41 In progress
42 Swing around
43 Witty banquet figure
46 Opposite NNW
47 1964 Olympics city
48 "Time ___ the essence"
50 In the movies
54 "___ my case"
58 Thanksgiving decoration
61 Mongolian desert
64 Czar or king
65 Cozy spot
66 One who might have a prime corner office
67 Obliterate
68 Answer's opposite
69 Scrutinizes
70 Jobs for repair shops
71 Porkpies and panamas

DOWN

1 Strengthens
2 Integra maker, formerly
3 Keep one's subscription going
4 Cousin of "Abracadabra!"
5 Food critic Sheraton
6 Idyllic garden
7 Shelf
8 Scottish child
9 Fancy tie
10 Special features
11 Coach Parseghian
12 Perimeter
13 Once around the track
21 Afternoon TV fare
22 Planets
25 Manicurists' targets
26 Secretary of State Vance
27 Cosmetician Lauder
29 Lather
30 Upholstered piece
32 Is ___ (probably will)
33 Sing softly
34 Trees used in shipbuilding
36 MS-___
37 French novelist Pierre
38 Summers on the Riviera
40 Mediums
44 Matador charger
45 Muddy up
49 Word that can precede the start of 20-, 35-, 43- or 58-Across
51 Flubbed
52 Accustom
53 Pitcher Ryan
55 ___ Gay (W.W. II plane)
56 Not exactly svelte
57 Kiddies
59 Holiday suffix
60 J.F.K. or Dubya
61 "Gosh!"
62 Prefix with acetylene
63 Quilting party

by Alison Donald

106

ACROSS

1 Replaceable shoe part
5 Construction girder
10 $ dispensers
14 Morales of "La Bamba"
15 Paul of "Hollywood Squares"
16 Hatchery sound
17 Two, to four
19 Yes-__ question
20 __-Rooter
21 George Meany's org.
23 Like some risers
26 Holiday dinner insert, perhaps
29 ". . . __ saw Elba"
30 Next in line?
31 Guys' partners
32 Easy-to-prepare, as cheesecake
34 Gambling mecca
36 Troupe member's "closet"
41 "Livin' la Vida __"
42 On the decline
44 Country singer Tucker
48 One taking tel. messages
50 Honoree's spot
51 Medulla's place
53 Hostess Perle
54 Daniel of Nicaragua
55 Sharif of film
57 Amer. counterpart
58 Where 10-Across may be found
64 Changed locks?
65 Nine: Prefix
66 Reason for an R rating
67 Independence achievers of 1991: Abbr.
68 Orchestra group
69 Old Harper's Bazaar illustrator

DOWN

1 Cock and bull
2 Atty.'s title
3 __ de vie
4 1997 Jim Carrey film
5 "__ a song go out . . ."
6 How times tables are learned
7 Brian of ambient music
8 Commotion
9 Rock genre, informally
10 Classic Harlem theater
11 Bygone Toyota model
12 Like a McJob
13 "S.N.L." skits, e.g.
18 Cowboy Rogers
22 Felt topper
23 Velvet finish?
24 Get one's ducks in __
25 Country's McEntire
27 Flyboy's place
28 Jane's role in "Klute"
30 Deli product
33 Frequent duettist with Tony Bennett
35 Food package amt.
37 One-__ (old ball game)
38 Bounceable?
39 Vardalos and Peeples
40 Make a sweater
43 Fed. property manager
44 Some govt. issues
45 Lines up neatly
46 Yak, yak, yak
47 Rates of return
49 Utterly defeated, in slang
52 Rattled weapon?
53 Scratch
56 New corp. hires
59 Suffix with meth- or eth-
60 Vane dir.
61 Fish/fowl connector
62 PC hookup
63 Bray starter

by Sarah Keller

ACROSS

1 Tiny bit of land in the sea
6 Courtroom event
11 Weather London is famous for
14 Thick-skinned critter
15 Vietnam's capital
16 ___ Perón, former Argentine first lady
17 Assault
19 Lobe site
20 Fraction of a joule
21 Danish money
22 Friend in war
23 ___ volente (God willing)
24 Shooting marble
25 Shows approval, as a crowd
28 Citation
32 Big party
35 Batman and Robin, e.g.
36 Scotch whiskey drink
37 Measures (out)
39 Econ. datum
41 Carpenter famous in the 1970s
42 Get situated
44 Critical hosp. areas
46 Nasdaq competitor
47 Affirmed
50 Like Desi Arnaz, by birth
51 Keg opening
52 Greyhound vehicle
55 Kind of speed, in "Star Trek"
57 Number-picking game
59 I

DOWN

1 Annoyed
2 English county
3 Specialized talk
4 Maze goal
5 Began to like
6 Small floor covering
7 Flooding cause
8 Makes a deduction
9 Yahoo! competitor

60 Second letter before iota
61 Rare event in horseracing
64 Show ___
65 Indian title
66 Harassed, as in a fraternity
67 Hog's home
68 Formally change
69 Outbuildings

10 Tell falsehoods
11 Regret
12 Racetrack shape
13 "The Far Side" cartoonist Larson
18 Illegal activity
22 A black one may be worn at a funeral
26 Not just my or your
27 Berserk
28 "Things aren't so bad!"
29 Photocopier need
30 Turndowns
31 "Auld Lang ___"
32 Popular coll. guy
33 Prefix with dynamic
34 1980 Wilder/ Pryor comedy
38 One with a turned-up nose

40 Went on and on and on and . . .
43 Sched. "question mark"
45 The "S" of M.S.U.
48 Surfing the Net, say
49 Long times
52 Hooch
53 Still single
54 Dispatches
55 Spiders' creations
56 Working away
58 Forthright
61 ___-la-la
62 Computer capacity
63 "Go team!"

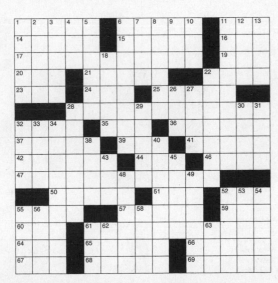

by Tyler Hinman

108

ACROSS
1 Waikiki greeting
6 Speed demon
11 Charlie Chaplin's brother
14 Léhar's "The Merry ___"
15 Dog on "Frasier"
16 Weeding tool
17 Do embroidery
19 River curve
20 Electees
21 Cry repeated in aerobics class
22 ___-ski
24 Bloodhound feature
26 Old TV show that featured "bachelorettes," with "The"
29 Understand
31 Carson's successor
32 Rouse
33 Newborn Newfoundland
35 E.P.A. subj.
37 Giant Mel
38 & 41 Question associated with the last words of 17-, 26-, 55- and 64-Across
43 ID information
44 Stuffed shell
46 Stately tree
47 Dad
49 Catches
51 Duck down
55 Classic toy for budding engineers
58 Fare carrier
59 About
60 Golfer's vehicle
62 Wood finish ingredient
63 Bankbook abbr.
64 It can't light just anywhere

68 Part of NATO: Abbr.
69 Movie star Kevin
70 Play to the back row and then some
71 Myrna of the movies
72 Deep-___ (threw away)
73 Spanish girls

DOWN
1 Shade maker
2 Legal claim holder
3 Black Sea resort
4 Mason's need
5 Cobblers' tools
6 The 21st Amendment, e.g.
7 One taken under another's wing
8 Roman 401
9 German one
10 Put a new price on
11 Popular hotel chain
12 California hikers' mecca
13 A sweet finish
18 Airport schedule abbr.
23 Some movie ratings
25 Cable channel owned by Disney
27 Ancient Peruvian
28 Not a soul
30 Fourth down option
34 Grand or baby grand
36 Grammy winner Lovett
38 Viciously attack
39 In a proficient manner

40 Identifying mark
42 Pass over
43 One-time TV showing
45 Bawdy
48 N.C. State grp.
50 No longer standing
52 007 player
53 Two-horse bet
54 Wealth
56 Work assignments
57 Attempt
61 Some govt. agents
65 Will Smith title role
66 Pickle
67 Overseas friend

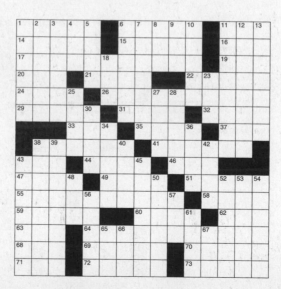

by Gary Steinmehl

ACROSS

1 Shutterbug's setting
6 Playful aquatic mammal
11 S, to a frat guy
14 Scarlett ___ of "Gone With the Wind"
15 Khaki cotton
16 Opposite of vertical: Abbr.
17 Shrinking Arctic mass
19 Singleton
20 Full range, as of colors
21 Hotshot
23 Fibber
24 Run-down joint
25 Lands' End competitor
28 Tends
29 Production from a well
30 Soda bottle unit
32 Salty drops
35 Heavy burden
37 Sub finder
39 Carefully pack (away)
40 A real mouthful?
42 Off-the-cuff
44 "Uncle Tom's Cabin" girl
45 College entrance exams
47 Broccoli piece
49 Naps
51 Baseball's Felipe
52 Washington zoo attractions
53 Ultimate
57 L.B.J.'s successor
58 Competition on an indoor rink
60 Wide shoe spec
61 Gloomy, in verse
62 Painter's stand
63 Archaic verb ending
64 Poker-faced
65 Each has two senators

DOWN

1 Fancy dressers
2 Machinist's workplace
3 Hard-to-believe story
4 Revealer of the future
5 Incomplete
6 Happen
7 The people over there
8 ___ Tacs (breath mints)
9 Allow
10 Most fibrous
11 Very large ham
12 Part of ancient Asia Minor
13 ___ Shorthand course
18 Tehran natives
22 Bill of Microsoft
24 Untamed
25 Stolen goods
26 Queue
27 Texas' official flower
28 Transmits
31 Relatives of frogs
33 Wander about
34 Try to hit, as a housefly
36 Prepared to sing the national anthem
38 One going through papers in a safe, say
41 Sand traps, in golf
43 Ones who "have more fun"
46 Vacation destination
48 Consume more than
49 Shopping jag
50 Directory contents
51 Big maker of office supplies
53 Great flair
54 ___ Major (constellation)
55 Assist in crime
56 Singer Lovett
59 Zodiac lion

by Jim Hyres

110

ACROSS

1 Fix firmly
6 April fools
10 With 69-Across, split
14 Top-notch
15 ___ Bator, Mongolia
16 "Je t'___" (French words of endearment)
17 Adventurer ___ Polo
18 Beatles' meter maid
19 Itsy-bitsy biter
20 Split
23 Cop's badge
25 Regret bitterly
26 Always, in verse
27 Sweetie
28 Perfect plots
31 Engine hums
33 Et ___ (and others)
35 ___ alai
36 Fuel additive
37 Split
43 A little freedom?
44 Darjeeling or oolong
45 Not having a thing out of place
46 Lou Grant portrayer
49 Gift of the Magi
51 Alias preceder
52 Sporty Pontiac
53 Give it a go
55 Penny metal
57 Split
61 Writer Rice
62 Zeus' spouse
63 Soft leather
66 ___-Ball (arcade game)
67 Like Death Valley
68 Eye opener
69 See 10-Across

70 Head honcho
71 Takes a chance

DOWN

1 Tach letters
2 Far-sighted investment, for short
3 Old Dominion
4 Mike holder
5 Play the piccolo
6 Wise guy
7 Set down
8 Crocs' kin
9 Major miscue
10 Pudding starch
11 More benevolent
12 Photocopier, e.g.
13 Dies (out)
21 Work for a jack-of-all-trades
22 Third dimension
23 Persian potentate
24 Pocket problem
29 Musical gift
30 ___-gritty
32 Words before "arms" or "the air"
34 Indolent
36 Frisk
38 Scottish inlet
39 The Zombies' "Tell ___ No"
40 2000, for one
41 Water-skiing locale
42 Headliner
46 Thunderstruck
47 Three sheets to the wind
48 Secondhand
49 "You're a lifesaver!"
50 "What a pity!"
54 Recovery center
56 Newswoman Zahn

58 New driver, usually
59 Tennessee's state flower
60 Wanders aimlessly
64 Rap's Dr. ___
65 Dash widths

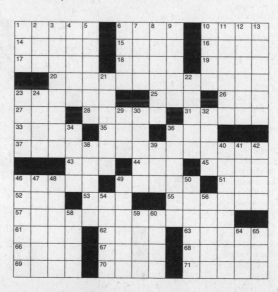

by Nancy Salomon

ACROSS

1 "Tubby" musical instrument
5 What a soldier goes out on
11 Hit on the head
14 On
15 Printed mistakes
16 Suffix with chlor-
17 Dr. Zhivago's love
18 April to October, for baseball
19 Understood
20 Inquire about the leaving time?
23 "___ Rebel" (1962 #1 hit)
24 Way in
25 Comfortable to stay in
28 "The Republic" writer
31 Perfect tennis serve
32 Actress Brennan
35 Ingenuity
39 Endure a comedy routine?
42 Sport with mallets
43 Dinosaur remnant
44 It's dialed before a long-distance number
45 Stew seasoning
47 Earl in Shakespearean England
49 Texas shrine, with "the"
52 The "A" of I.R.A.: Abbr.
54 Substitute for a jittery pilot?
61 "It's c-c-cold!"
62 More diminutive
63 Worsted fabric
64 In the past
65 Draw out
66 Book before Nehemiah
67 Hankering
68 Like rooms on TV's "Trading Spaces"
69 Shallow's opposite

DOWN

1 Fine powder
2 One of the Four Corners states
3 Make yawn
4 Military helicopter named for an Indian tribe
5 Mexican coins
6 Stadium
7 ___ II (razor brand)
8 Hotheaded
9 Siouan tribe
10 Surgeon's tool
11 Intolerant person
12 Scent, in England
13 Small-minded
21 Excited, with "up"
22 Widely recognized
25 Padlock holder
26 Eight: Prefix
27 Breakfast, lunch or dinner
28 Intrinsically
29 Minus
30 Pro's opposite
33 Uncertain
34 Weaving machine
36 Wedding vows
37 Melody
38 X-ray ___ (kids' goggles)
40 "I'm innocent!"
41 Smart ___ (wise guy)
46 Owl, by nature
48 More than tipsy
49 Cornered
50 The "L" of XXL
51 Ohio city
52 Dined at home
53 À la ___ (way to order)
55 Loathsome
56 Lady of Arthurian romance
57 Puerto ___
58 Stuff that seeps
59 Golfer's shout
60 Noisy to-do

by Marc J. Gameroff

ACROSS

1 Fend (off)
5 Puts on
9 Threshold
14 Nerve impulse transmitter
15 Smart-alecky
16 Lefty of 1920s–'30s baseball
17 First trick
20 San Jose-to-Fresno dir.
21 ThinkPad, e.g.
22 Otherwise
23 Capek play
24 Neuter
26 Uninspired reactions
27 Middle part
31 Hard up
33 Second trick
36 Pitts of "Life With Father"
37 Domain of the Hapsburgs, once: Abbr.
38 Like many college dorms
42 Third trick
47 Statistic
49 Eagles on the wing
50 Fall guy
51 Seine feeder
54 They keep "Q" from "U"
55 Samoan port
57 Agassi and Maginot
59 Motherly ministering, for short
62 Trickster's comment, after 17-, 33- or 42-Across
65 Open, as a bottle
66 Suffix with million
67 Twist the arm of
68 Jury composition
69 Place for a bouncing baby
70 Reactions to dirty tricks

DOWN

1 Go in with rolled-up pants?
2 Main line
3 Stood up
4 Crime lab stuff
5 Hat and coat, e.g.
6 Bottomless
7 Mild oaths
8 Razor sharpener
9 Mezzo-soprano Frederica ___ Stade
10 Head start
11 Muddied the waters
12 Cautious
13 Actress Sommer et al.
18 Perpendicular
19 "The smile of beauty" toothpaste
23 Full-bodied
25 "I agree"
27 Cutting tool
28 Top of the lingerie line
29 Criticize, slangily
30 NuGrape competitor
32 Police car with a flashing light, maybe
34 Unhappy response
35 "Sure, why don't we?!"
39 See red?
40 Always, poetically
41 A.M.A. members
43 Status ___
44 Eskimo boat
45 Anticipate
46 Cow catcher
47 Love object of Apollo
48 Each
50 Paid attention, so to speak
52 Move under cover
53 Reagan attorney general ___ Meese
56 Open a bit
58 Pretty pink
59 New kid on the block
60 Nike's swoosh, e.g.
61 Pool sticks
63 Photo ___
64 Gist

113

ACROSS

1 Stogie
6 "Remember the ___!"
11 ___-la-la
14 Place to study, in France
15 Some jazz
16 1975 musical with a Yellow Brick Road, with "The"
17 Mole
19 Place for post-op patients, for short
20 Involves
21 Remover of hides
23 Household power: Abbr.
25 Reagan attorney general Edwin
26 Salad leaf
30 Acquire
33 Terse note from a boss
34 ___ Lee Corp. (Fortune 500 company)
35 End-of-week cry
38 Progresso product
39 Sent, as a letter, by phone line
40 Bring on, as an employee
41 Fairy tale starter
42 Suffered from a cut
43 Prison-related
44 More nervously irritable
46 Sublet
47 Confused
49 Soothsayer
51 More matronly in dress
54 Most adroit
59 ___ Baba
60 Romantic dinner reservation

62 Thick drain-cleaning option
63 Bottled water brand
64 Aired again
65 Takeoff guesstimate: Abbr.
66 Silence markers, in music
67 Track events

DOWN

1 Hand over
2 Computer symbol
3 Joint inflammation
4 ___ Longa, birthplace of Romulus and Remus
5 Substitute for, as a pitcher
6 Humiliate
7 Journey segment

8 Lincoln and others, informally
9 Man in a robe
10 Popular charge card
11 Small plane
12 Reduces to bits
13 Blue shade
18 She, in Cherbourg
22 Nor's partner
24 Persuaders
26 Old U.S. gasoline
27 Gas light
28 Poker variation
29 Blocked
31 Born's partner
32 Itsy bit
34 After-Christmas event
36 Persia, now
37 Hat fabric
39 Secretive org.
43 Play
45 Shoe style

46 Coral formation
47 Saying
48 Sign in a boardinghouse window
50 Perfect places
52 Overhang
53 Sluggers' stats
55 Peach or beech
56 Raison d'___
57 ___ team (police group)
58 Heaps
61 Counterpart of long.

by Robert Dillman

ACROSS

1 Off one's trolley
5 Predatory sort
10 Motorists' citations: Abbr.
14 Plot unit
15 "Not a chance"
16 ___ avis
17 Never
20 Big Apple daily, briefly
21 Source of government revenue
22 Mossy side of a tree
24 Reunion group
25 Fodder storers
28 Actor Davis
31 Cause of a wince
32 Prevents, legally
34 Reporter's question
37 Sometimes
40 "For shame!"
41 Continued ahead
42 Burn soother
43 Excused oneself, with "out"
44 Jazz phrases
45 Wash gently against
48 Cervantes's land
51 Retiree's title
54 Search, as at a sale
58 Always
60 Monied one
61 Chinese "bear"
62 Uncool sort
63 Looks over
64 Some Art Deco pieces
65 Plays for a sap

DOWN

1 Eos' domain
2 Stiff and sore
3 Fingerboard ridge
4 Like a multipurpose tool, perhaps
5 Look of contempt
6 "The Planets" composer Gustav
7 Piercing tool
8 Huck Finn's conveyance
9 Actress Sedgwick
10 High in pitch
11 Internet music-sharing service
12 Lock of hair
13 MS. enclosures
18 Med. care providers
19 Cut out
23 Busy places
25 Catch a glimpse of
26 Fleming and Paisley
27 Beat soundly
29 Go it alone
30 Made, as a web
32 Sufficient, old-style
33 All there
34 Alarmist's cry, in a fable
35 Dance, slangily
36 Small bills
38 Fly ball fielder's shout
39 Primary computer list
43 ___ & Noble
44 Just misses, as a putt
45 River in Hades
46 Home products seller
47 Really annoy
49 Priggish one
50 Saintly glows
52 Pound a keyboard
53 Out there
55 N.Y.C.'s 5th and 7th, e.g.
56 Richard of "Chicago"
57 They may be tight or loose
59 Windsor's prov.

by Mike Torch

ACROSS

1 Chasm
6 Grassy clump
9 Pond organism
13 Provide comfort to
15 Crazy eights spinoff
16 Competed
17 Stuff oneself
18 Enter quickly
20 Response to an insult
21 Angry audience reaction
23 Low point
24 Detail in a builder's plan
26 Infuse with oxygen
27 Store for future use
32 Cleanse totally
33 In a snit
34 Sharp turn
37 Parade spoiler
38 Pasture
39 Continental coin
40 Football distances: Abbr.
41 Spree
42 Home in the Arctic
43 Spend time playfully
45 Have ambitions
48 Wax-coated cheese
49 "One of ___ days, Alice . . ."
50 Sensible
52 Taj Mahal city
56 Devour quickly
58 Pay what's due
60 Planning to vote no
61 Bowling target
62 Not quite a homer
63 Breather

64 "___ the season . . ."
65 Centers of operation

DOWN

1 Nile slitherers
2 Seethe
3 Spiritual exercise
4 Reason to hit the brakes
5 Moo ___ pork
6 Lather
7 Burden
8 Med school grad
9 House that's for the birds
10 Singer Ronstadt
11 Be in on the joke
12 Idolize
14 Potent anesthetic
19 Bread machine cycle
22 Skater's hangout

25 Prefix with schooler
26 Thinking "Gee whiz!"
27 Nimble
28 Campus area
29 Leon ___, who wrote "Mila 18"
30 Feudal lord
31 Spellbound
34 South African native
35 What spinach is rich in
36 Dandy
38 Dandy
39 Extreme self-centeredness
41 Ready for a change
42 S.&L. holding
43 Fish out of water
44 Highly capable
45 Fighting

46 Gleamed
47 Animal hides
50 What V-J Day ended
51 Rustic retreats
53 Swindles
54 Hold sway
55 Pals of Tarzan
57 Decide
59 Sun or moon

by Lynn Lempel

ACROSS

1 Warhead weapon, briefly
5 Like the kiddie rides at a park, relatively speaking
11 ___ Paulo, Brazil
14 "Encore!"
15 Not dismissive of, as suggestions
16 Smidge
17 Beach community near LAX
19 Khan who wed Rita Hayworth
20 "It'd be my pleasure"
21 "Norma ___"
22 Bikini parts
23 Like a bump on a log
24 Outermost strata
26 Lengthy lurkers of the deep
27 Like Bo Peep's sheep
28 Beetle Bailey superior
29 Foxy
30 Air force?
31 2004 Liam Neeson film
32 & 33 Anagrams and puns (or parts hidden in 17-, 24-, 44- and 51-Across)
34 "Never on Sunday" star ___ Mercouri
37 Hammer part
38 Dipstick wipe, often
41 Sans friends
42 Philosopher Descartes
43 Psychologist Jung
44 Soldier's reassignment papers
46 Backyard party spot
47 Who-knows-how-long
48 Tempe sch.
49 Main arteries
50 Surfacing stuff
51 Duel (with)
53 Pittsburgh-to-Boston dir.
54 Multicar accident
55 Highway division
56 Takeoff stat: Abbr.
57 Guitarist Segovia
58 Went like the wind

DOWN

1 Hints at
2 Cavalry V.I.P.
3 With courage
4 Ari of "Kate & Allie"
5 Heading on a list of errands
6 King Kong, e.g.
7 "Place" name on TV
8 Wholly absorbed
9 Girder material
10 Cracker Jack bonus
11 People around a 54-Across, typically
12 Egg carton spec
13 Amazing adventure
18 QB's pass, whether completed or not: Abbr.
22 ___ means possible
24 Ratted
25 Iraqi or Thai
27 "Tomb raider" Croft
30 One who's done for
31 Swiss artist Paul
32 Skid row sights
33 Confident solvers' supply
34 Animal on a Florida license plate
35 Tastefully beautiful
36 Revised downward
37 Reader
38 Seedy stopover
39 She helped Theseus escape the labyrinth
40 Smoothed (over)
42 Auctioned again
43 Holiday music
45 "Splish Splash" singer, 1958
46 Impact sound
49 Nile snakes
51 Tax prep. expert
52 "So ___ me!"

by Merl Reagle

ACROSS

1 Blackguard
4 Coin with Monticello on its back
10 Mlle. from Acapulco
14 Sport ___ (all-purpose vehicle)
15 Tennis champ Goolagong
16 His and ___
17 Automated device in a bowling alley
19 Give off
20 Epic that ends with Hector's funeral
21 Grand Prix, e.g.
23 Nail on a paw
24 Garden item cut up for a salad
26 Grope
28 Historical time
29 Berlin maidens
34 Naked ___ jaybird
37 Legislative act that imposes punishment without a trial
41 Little troublemaker
42 Example of excellence
43 Cry loudly
46 Part of a tied tie
47 Cotton menace
52 Expensively elegant
56 What a lumberjack holds
57 River of oblivion
58 Tilt
59 1988 Kevin Costner movie
62 Pioneering computer game
63 Important parts of dairy cows
64 "Green Acres" star Gabor
65 Nays' opposites
66 "Brace yourself!"
67 ___ and Stimpy (cartoon duo)

DOWN

1 Three-dimensional
2 To any degree
3 Shepherdess in Virgil's "Eclogues"
4 Dweeb
5 "___ Got the World on a String"
6 Army bed
7 Small knob
8 Become a member
9 Delaware tribe
10 Himalayan mountain guide
11 Chart again
12 Instant
13 Fall bloom
18 Within the rules
22 German "the"
24 Steak or ground round
25 Inventor Howe
27 Jeff Lynne's rock grp.
29 J. Edgar Hoover's org.
30 Place for a basketball net
31 Mont Blanc, e.g.
32 To the ___ degree
33 Popular vodka, informally
34 Ending with Gator or orange
35 Instant
36 "Where ___ you?"
38 Base truant
39 Wall Street event: Abbr.
40 RCA dog
43 Biases
44 Hold the rights to
45 Nighttime biter
47 Touched in the head
48 Common daisy
49 ___ apso (dog)
50 Get away from
51 African terrain
53 "None of the above"
54 Use a razor
55 One with big biceps
57 Insatiable desire
60 "___ Misérables"
61 Rap's Dr. ___

by Raymond Hamel

118

ACROSS

1 Wet snowball sound
6 Radio choice
10 Hair goops
14 ___-Roman wrestling
15 1971 Cy Young Award winner ___ Blue
16 Not written
17 Stuffed animals
19 Festive
20 Business V.I.P.
21 Jeer
23 Like meat thrown to a lion
26 Stuffed headrests
30 Pinza of "South Pacific"
32 Went yachting
33 Stuffed appetizers
35 Contents of a big bowl
40 "Am not!" response
41 Most of Libya
42 Cuban bills
43 Stuffed mailers
46 College graduate's goal
48 Furnace's output
49 Stuffed polling receptacles
54 Sun spot?
55 Momentarily
56 Teacher's grp.
58 Lemon-lime malt brand
59 Stuffed diners
66 Coup d'___
67 With no help
68 Dewey, to Truman
69 Cold war news service
70 Either half of Gemini
71 Community workout spots, for short

DOWN

1 Police dept. rank
2 Relative of ante-
3 Headed
4 Kind of converter
5 Trifled (with)
6 Greeting on the Appian Way
7 "Mamma ___!"
8 T.V.A. promoter
9 Number 5 iron
10 "Dead Souls" novelist Nikolai
11 Poet's Muse
12 Early Steven Bochco series
13 Blind parts
18 Miscue
22 Buddy from way back
23 Plot again
24 Shade of blue
25 Smartens (up)
27 Try to win
28 '60s war zone, briefly
29 Scoreboard fig.
31 "___ be in England"
34 Pistol, slangily
36 "Now we're in for it!"
37 Puppy pickup places
38 Haunted house sound
39 Like many a retreat
41 Calm
43 Tarzan creator's monogram
44 Prefix with natal
45 Irk
47 Even less than wholesale
49 "Carmen" composer
50 Author Loos
51 Holy Tibetans
52 Exams before some postgrad. studies
53 Serta alternative
57 Positron's place
60 Solemn pledge
61 Yalie
62 1980s White House nickname
63 Top left PC key
64 Stephen of "Still Crazy"
65 Soon-to-be-alumni: Abbr.

by Lee Glickstein and Nancy Salomon

ACROSS

1 Tams
5 Wood that repels moths
10 "Ali ___ and the 40 Thieves"
14 Natural burn medication
15 Speechify
16 Dutch cheese
17 Rod at a pig roast
18 United Nations' goal
20 Sweetie pie
21 Termite, e.g.
22 "Wait a sec!"
23 Romanov ruler
25 Study of plants: Abbr.
26 Terminus
27 Bubbly drink mixer
32 Black-and-white cookie
33 Roald who wrote "Charlie and the Chocolate Factory"
34 Katmandu's land
38 Thpeakth like thith
40 Vietnamese holiday
41 Like old bread
42 Come after
43 Part of the eye
45 Length × width, for a rectangle
46 Musician's asset
49 Boom box abbr.
52 Bashful
53 With proficiency
54 Slowly, in music
56 Giants great Willie
58 Chem class
61 Something caught near the end of a race?

63 Word that can follow the end of 18-, 27-, 46- or 61-Across
64 "Off for now, love"
65 Soother
66 Change for a five
67 Narrow opening
68 Ostentatious
69 Words

DOWN

1 An A.T.M. dispenses it
2 Brand for Fido
3 Futile
4 Harden
5 Cringed
6 Deity with a bow and arrow
7 Feathered missile
8 Capital of Ga.
9 Making the mouth burn
10 "___ here long?"
11 Maxim
12 Breakfast strip
13 Revise
19 Communion plates
21 La ___, Bolivia
24 Plug, as a hole
25 Purple Monopoly avenue
27 Shoe bottom
28 Land o' blarney
29 Confirm with a vote
30 Question in a geography quiz
31 Sell in stores
35 Political platform
36 Knighted Guinness
37 Wife of Jacob
39 Meets, greets and seats
44 Keep out of the rain
47 Colossus of ___ (one of the Seven Wonders)
48 "Sesame Street" network
49 Sail holders
50 Perfect
51 Desert plants
55 Animal with a beard
56 ___ soup (sushi starter)
57 From square one
59 Top spot
60 Top spot
62 Baby's bawl
63 Place to put bets

by Earl W. Reed

120

ACROSS

1 The Righteous Brothers and the Everly Brothers
5 Wall St. letters
9 Actors Robert and Alan
14 Other, in Oaxaca
15 "The Clan of the Cave Bear" author Jean
16 Athletic events
17 ___ riot (very funny skit)
18 Bruins' sch.
19 Picture with a posse
20 After 29-Down, a movie starring Diane Lane
23 Stir-fry vegetable
24 Athletic sites
28 Cry said while pointing
29 Samovar
31 Singer who definitely has her own dressing room
32 Chicago airport
35 South American range
37 ___-Mex cuisine
38 After 29-Down, a James Grippando thriller
41 Prefix with sac or duct
42 Some Art Deco works
43 Life line
44 Cry for attention
46 Swiss river
47 Call letters?
48 Storyteller Hemingway
50 Thinks
54 After 29-Down, a Drifters hit
57 Like whitecaps

60 Shot, for short
61 Song that may include some high notes
62 Swashbuckler Flynn
63 Actress Osterwald
64 Brand of smokes
65 Teary-eyed
66 Keep ___ (persevere)
67 Roughly computed: Abbr.

DOWN

1 Boneheads
2 Salt Lake City native
3 Monteverdi opera
4 Computer programs
5 Deep disgust
6 State flower of New Mexico
7 Ward of "Once and Again"
8 Verve
9 Love in Lyon
10 Wasn't quite a ringer
11 Police rank: Abbr.
12 Had a bite
13 Lith., once
21 "Psst! In the balcony!"
22 More clear-headed
25 Warmer and sunnier
26 Sailor's "halt!"
27 Latin dance
29 See 20-, 38- and 54-Across
30 Suggestions on food labels: Abbr.
32 Carol starter
33 What helicopters do

34 Par ___ (by air)
35 Popular shaving lotion
36 Did figure eights
39 Pontificate
40 Asleep
45 Floor cleaner's implement
47 Skillful
49 In a bashful manner
50 Metrical feet
51 Tropical roots
52 Writer George or T. S.
53 Bard of old
55 ___ Wawa, role for Gilda Radner
56 Leave out
57 Not very many
58 Assayer's stuff
59 "___ we there yet?"

by Sarah Keller

ACROSS

1 Younger brothers, stereotypically
6 Char
10 Exploding star
14 Betray à la a snitch
15 Miss from Marseille: Abbr.
16 Greek war god
17 Classic Charles Darwin work
20 Game at the corner store
21 Globe
22 Card that wins lots of tricks
24 Website address starter
27 Sharpens
28 Sheraton or Ritz-Carlton
31 Terre ___, Ind.
33 N.F.L. scores
34 Sketcher's eraser
36 Stomach soother, for short
38 What the love of money is, they say
42 Pumps and clogs
43 Go looking for, as business
45 Driver's lic. and company badge
48 Decree
50 Not in short supply
51 Indian stringed instrument
53 Dark film genre, for short
55 Home for Ger. and the U.K.
56 Scents
58 More pleasant
61 The Big Bang, to a physicist
66 Yale students
67 Slender woodwind
68 Broadcasting
69 Soapmaking substances
70 Mercedes competitors
71 Seasons, in a way

DOWN

1 Old hand
2 "Lent" body part
3 Short dagger
4 Like takeout orders
5 Pique
6 Like satin to the touch
7 North Pole worker
8 Gore and Sharpton
9 Salespeople, in brief
10 Cheese-covered chip
11 Cathay and environs, with "the"
12 Swerved
13 Impose, as a tax
18 Utmost
19 Short-lived things
22 "So that's it!"
23 Not wrong: Abbr.
25 Tangy hot sauce
26 Knit and ___
29 They're sometimes inflated
30 Certain Protestant
32 Snitched
35 Atmosphere
37 Egg cell
39 Ireland's Sinn ___
40 Magnificent
41 Lollapalooza
44 The "p" in r.p.m.
45 Santa ___, one of the Solomon Islands
46 With ominousness
47 "Smoke" to chew on
49 Traces of color
52 Wrongly
54 Brazilian vacation spot, informally
57 One whose nose is in the air
59 Corp. money managers
60 Sicilian volcano
62 Hewlett-Packard rival: Abbr.
63 At once
64 Sch. near Harvard
65 Hosp. areas

by Alison Donald

ACROSS

1 Set-to
6 Carpet type
10 Meat on a kabob, maybe
14 Cute "bear"
15 Contented sound
16 Decorative pitcher
17 Bear and Berra
18 One opposed
19 Big do
20 One liable to get hurt
23 Ally of America
27 It may need massaging
28 Sodium hydroxide
29 Provision for late-arriving spectators
33 Prayer start
34 Potato bud
35 Star in the constellation Cygnus
39 Declare
40 Like hilly beaches
43 Be the master of
44 French mothers
46 The last King Richard of England
47 Abstraction
48 Insect that's well-camouflaged on a tree
52 Grow old
55 China's Chiang ___-shek
56 Atlas features
57 Co-nominee
61 Keen on
62 Paint unskillfully
63 Originator of the phrase "Familiarity breeds contempt"
68 Barely gets, with "out"
69 Other than
70 Maker of Seven Seas salad dressing
71 Ancient harp
72 Losing proposition?
73 Busybody

DOWN

1 Poseidon : sea :: Uranus : ___
2 Avian sound
3 Cleaning cloth, often
4 MacGraw of "The Getaway"
5 Said "no thanks"
6 Set-to
7 Event for hounds
8 More pretentious
9 "Old ___" (1989 Jane Fonda film)
10 Show the way
11 Just terrible
12 Something asked of the 33-Across
13 Out of money
21 Fibber's words
22 "Well done!"
23 Belief of 4½ million Americans
24 Griddle locale
25 Harder to find
26 Fergie's ex
30 Big Apple educ. institution
31 They may be rubbed out
32 Is worthy of
36 Skin flick
37 Vote in
38 Woodpeckers' peckers
41 German article
42 Finger or toe
45 "The Square Egg" writer
49 Got, as a job
50 Capital of Rwanda
51 Underhanded
52 Sharon of 23-Across
53 Gooey
54 Keyboard key
58 Sniffer
59 Inspiration source
60 Help in a heist
64 Before, before
65 ___ Andreas fault
66 Frequently
67 Mom-and-pop org.?

by Nancy Kavanaugh

123

ACROSS

1 Smile
5 Body of water in Italy
9 Alternative to U.P.S.
14 City for a quickie marriage or divorce
15 Push up against
16 Fred's dancing partner
17 Aide: Abbr.
18 Filet of __
19 Stirs up
20 Choice at a supermarket checkout
23 Ram's mate
24 Sculptures and oils
25 52, in old Rome
26 Choice offered at an electronic payment machine
33 Man's name that's an alphabetic string
34 Actress Gardner
35 Group of 100 in Washington
36 Singer Sedaka
37 Squeeze (out)
39 Cap and gown wearer
40 Single-celled creature
43 Finish
45 Pipe bend
46 Choice at an airplane ticket counter
49 Neither's partner
50 __ tai (drink)
51 Singer Sumac
54 Choice at a coffee bar
59 Runs across the field

60 Hatcher of "Desperate Housewives"
61 Actress Anderson
62 Dress style
63 Sporting blade
64 __ Rabbit
65 Religious offshoots
66 Grass clumps
67 The "a" in a.m.

DOWN

1 Vineyard fruit
2 Cut again
3 State auto requirement
4 Middle C, e.g.
5 Longtime Dodger manager Tommy
6 Cut short, as an attempt
7 Big swallow
8 Verdi's Moor

9 Gary Larson comic, with "The"
10 Rewrite
11 Meat slicer locale
12 It's AC or DC
13 Crosses (out)
21 "Norma __"
22 Shows, as programs
27 Governed
28 Giver's opposite
29 TV actress Georgia
30 Malt liquor base
31 Slanted, as type: Abbr.
32 Excellent adventurer with Bill
33 18-wheeler
36 No, slangily
38 Smitten
41 Job rewards
42 Illegally off base

44 Journals
47 Speechifies
48 Half-brother of Tom Sawyer
52 "A Bar at the Folies-Bergère" painter
53 In flames
54 Actor's part
55 Movie best seen on a wide screen
56 Lady's man
57 Used auto, perhaps
58 Isle of exile for Napoleon
59 __ Cruces, N.M.

by Kurt Mengel and Jan-Michele Gianette

124

ACROSS
1 Wagering sites, for short
5 Rosary component
9 Big name in kitchen foil
14 When shadows are short
15 "__ want for Christmas . . ."
16 Elementary school door sign
17 Breakfast order
20 Lend __ (listen)
21 Lug
22 Last of 26
23 "Wild Kingdom" host Marlin
26 What apartment dwellers have to pay
28 Actress Verdugo
30 Summer, in Somme
31 Lucky charms
38 Astronaut Grissom
39 Rock's __ Fighters
40 Kind of instinct
41 U.S. senator's salary, e.g.
48 Crazy eights cousin
49 Jazz pianist Blake
50 House wrecker
54 Place for a Ping-Pong table
58 Inventor Whitney
59 Absorbs, with "up"
61 Redhead's helper
62 Bygone music collection
66 1008 on a monument
67 Jai __
68 NBC's peacock, e.g.

69 Passover feast
70 Stampeders
71 __ Smith, who won the 1972 Wimbledon

DOWN
1 Like draft beer
2 Oscar-winning screenwriter Robert
3 One voicing displeasure
4 Air Jordan, for one
5 Groceries holder
6 Chicago transports
7 Tons
8 Duffer's gouge
9 Go along with
10 Tell a "story"
11 Mania

12 Showbiz twin Mary-Kate or Ashley
13 So far
18 Give the third degree
19 Lucy and Ricky's landlady
24 Once known as
25 Big mess
27 Person of the cloth, for short
29 Prior to, old-style
31 N.F.L. 3-pointers
32 French affirmative
33 Onetime steel company name
34 __ d'Alene, Idaho
35 It may be stroked
36 Bacardi, e.g.
37 Sault __ Marie
42 Jocularity
43 Agitated

44 Classic Beckett play, informally
45 "May __ of service?"
46 Not, in Nuremberg
47 Kix and Trix
50 Abounds
51 Popeye's love
52 Unbending
53 Where Dr. Phil got famous
55 High, in a way
56 Russia's Lake __
57 Building subcontractor
60 Sign that attracts crowds
63 Step on it
64 Cougar or Jaguar
65 Tease

by Jim Hyres

ACROSS

1 President before Jefferson
6 Couch
10 "Picnic" Pulitzer winner William
14 Performing poorly in
15 Knocks for a loop
16 Gas in advertising lights
17 With 59-Across, lyric from "America, the Beautiful"
20 Bro's counterpart
21 U.N. working-conditions agcy.
22 Molecule part
23 Guinness suffix
24 Dict. info
26 For adults, as films
30 Lyric from "The Star-Spangled Banner"
33 Numbskull
34 Perlman of "Cheers"
35 Society newcomer
36 These break the silence of the lambs
39 Derisive laugh
40 Huff and puff
41 Prints, pastels and such
42 Hollywood's Ken or Lena
44 Nasdaq debut: Abbr.
46 Lyric from "America"
51 Lunatic
52 Japanese wrestling
53 Smallish batteries
55 Thick slice
57 Band booking

58 Air conditioner meas.
59 See 17-Across
64 "Garfield" dog
65 Talk wildly
66 Etc. and ibid., e.g.
67 Magician's stick
68 Jazz singer James
69 Unlike a rolling stone?

DOWN

1 Humiliate
2 Breakfast roll
3 Extends
4 Apple computer, for short
5 Large steps
6 Took to the airport, say
7 Confess, with "up"

8 Greek salad cheese
9 Wood source for a baseball bat
10 Director Bergman
11 Newcomer, briefly
12 Moo ___ gai pan
13 Finish up
18 Bread spreads
19 ___ Linda, Calif.
25 Leaves in the lurch
27 "Look what I did!"
28 Fifty-fifty
29 Borrower's burden
31 Apron wearers, traditionally
32 L.B.J.'s veep
36 Soothing ointment
37 Neck of the woods
38 Env. notation
39 Get a move on, quaintly

40 Luau paste
42 Toothbrush brand
43 Spy novelist John
44 Shooting marble
45 Write computer instructions
47 Dropped a line in the water
48 Should, informally
49 Bigwigs
50 Swamp swimmers
54 Like dishwater
56 Dinghy or dory
59 "I'm impressed!"
60 Rhoda's TV mom
61 10th-anniversary metal
62 Blasting stuff
63 "The Sopranos" network

by Nancy Salomon

126

ACROSS

1 Tough trips
6 Poster holder
10 Shiites, e.g.
14 Two under, on the links
15 Double-reeded woodwind
16 Pertaining to
17 Tee off
18 Elbow/hand connector
19 Marked, as a box on a test
20 Noted actor's writing implements?
23 "Nope"
25 Actress Hatcher
26 Candidate's concern
27 Instruction to a woman in labor
30 Get-up-and-go
32 Danger signal
33 Yo-Yo Ma's instrument
34 Rodeo wear, often
36 Noted actor's sons?
41 Farmer's spring purchase
42 Orderly grouping
44 Dear old ___
47 Headlight setting
48 Public face
50 "Wheel of Fortune" purchases
52 Huge-screen film format
54 Church perch
55 Noted actor's underarms?
59 Shopper stopper
60 Fiddle sticks
61 California/ Nevada lake

64 Keep ___ (persist)
65 A couple of chips in the pot, maybe
66 Tempest
67 Perfect Olympic scores
68 Makes calls
69 "Breaking Away" director Peter

DOWN

1 Lipton product
2 Made haste
3 Shade of white
4 Swiss artist Paul
5 Word repeated after "Que" in song
6 Rug with nothing swept under it?
7 More competent
8 Plotted
9 9/11 commission chairman Thomas
10 Rush-hour hr.
11 Win over
12 Shrink in fear
13 Made tight, as muscles
21 Highest degree
22 Analogous
23 "The West Wing" network
24 Plane measure
28 Resigned remark
29 Cut down on the flab
31 Electees
34 Dentist's deg.
35 Neighbor of Earth
37 Floral necklace
38 Movie ticket mandate
39 Finesse stroke in tennis
40 With it, mentally

43 Not fly absolutely straight
44 Blots lightly
45 Supply with oxygen
46 Join a teleconference
48 Written permissions
49 Abbr. before a date on a pkg.
51 "Golden Boy" playwright
53 Workweek letters
56 Construction beam
57 Wee
58 "See ya!"
62 Miner's find
63 German spa

by Beth Hinshaw

ACROSS

1 "Mamma Mia" group
5 Play chauffeur
10 Money to help one through a tight spot
14 Either of two directing brothers
15 All gone, as dinner
16 Mayberry boy
17 Daydreamer's state
20 Directional suffix
21 A choir may stand on it
22 Good thing
23 Sailor, colloquially
24 Digit in binary code
25 Joseph Conrad novella
34 Edward who wrote the play "The Goat, or Who Is Sylvia"
35 Pastor's flock
36 Rebellious Turner
37 Vintage autos
38 Kind of club that's a hint to this puzzle's theme
39 Prefix with lock or knock
40 ___-cone
41 Colonial settlement
42 Bobby Orr, notably
43 Vocational school instruction
46 Superannuated
47 Ring outcome, briefly
48 ___ pants (multipocketed wear)
51 Room plus, in a hotel
54 "Don't ___"
57 Common employment benefit
60 Cleveland's lake
61 Enlarge a house
62 Men-only
63 "The World of Suzie ___"
64 Sierra ___, Africa
65 Certain vanity plate for husband-and-wife cars

DOWN

1 Suffer from a charley horse
2 Transvaal trekker
3 Vanilla ___
4 "What else?"
5 "Meet the Fockers" co-star, 2004
6 Hamelin's problem
7 "___ Jury" (Spillane novel)
8 Zig or zag
9 S.A.S.E., e.g.
10 Relax, as rules
11 Berkeley Breathed comic strip
12 Lieutenant
13 Fit snugly
18 Really hot under the collar
19 Like Lincoln, in physique
23 Uno + dos
24 Straight: Prefix
25 Hard on the ears
26 "Maria ___" (Dorsey tune)
27 ___ to mankind
28 Taken wing
29 Intimidate
30 Station with a show
31 The blahs
32 Participated temporarily, as with a band
33 Police con
38 Victuals
39 Florence's river
41 Letter-shaped opening for a bolt
42 Harley rider
44 Links bend
45 Bring into harmony
48 Stick of gum, e.g.
49 Prefix with -postale
50 Common Seattle forecast
51 Slaw or fries, e.g.
52 Reverse, on a PC
53 "The shoe ___ the other foot"
54 A couple of chips, maybe
55 Injury reminder
56 Purchases for a shindig
58 ___ 9000, sci-fi computer
59 Bit of air pollution

by Adam G. Perl

128

ACROSS

1 Peeling knives
7 "See ya"
10 Katie Couric's network
13 Kansas city where Dwight Eisenhower grew up
15 Symbol of sturdiness
17 High hit behind the catcher, say
18 Do surgery (on)
19 End of a school Web address
20 Salves
22 "My life ___ open book"
23 Ward off
26 Safety item for a tightrope walker
27 Pep rally shout
28 Refused
30 Tallied up
33 Neurologist or orthopedist
36 Graceful swimmer
38 Nuptial agreement
39 Spotty
41 Tidy savings
43 Miss. neighbor
44 ___ of Man
46 Paths from here to there
47 Stretchy fabric
49 Self-assurance
51 Family
52 Vegetable that rolls
53 Looks to be
57 Treble's counterpart
59 Thorny parts of roses
61 III + IV
62 Miss terribly

64 Theory of the universe, or a hint to the starts of 17-Across and 7-, 10-, 35- and 40-Down
67 Scene at a natural history museum
68 Observed secretly
69 Summer hrs. in D.C.
70 One doing leg. work
71 Derisive looks

DOWN

1 Post or Trib
2 Residence
3 Shred
4 Aide to Santa
5 Old auto inits.
6 Rebuff
7 Prosperous place
8 Kennel cries
9 ___ out (barely make)
10 Extreme effort at weight loss
11 Alpha, ___, gamma . . .
12 Glimpsed
14 Twisty-horned antelope
16 Musical chord
21 Eye part
24 "Cómo ___ usted?"
25 Vientiane native
27 Abductors' demands
29 Eye part
31 Periphery
32 Lady and the Tramp, e.g.
33 Start a card game
34 Air France destination
35 Skilled marksman

37 Aviation-related prefix
40 Baloney
42 Inside of a paper towel roll
45 Sporting sword
48 One heeding the alarm clock
50 Symbols of meekness
54 Dodge
55 Petty
56 + and –
57 Ordered
58 Carbolic ___
59 A few
60 Nurses a drink
63 Lead-in to fetched or sighted
65 Card game with knocking
66 Spelling competition

by Lynn Lempel

ACROSS

1 Desktop folder, e.g.
5 John Candy's old comedy show
9 William of ___, known for his "razor"
14 Bay of Pigs locale
15 Rock's Mötley ___
16 He didn't give a damn
17 Fedora feature
18 Boot from office
19 Angora and merino
20 What you really saw?
23 Sonora snack
24 Pass by
28 What you really saw?
32 First secretary of homeland security
33 ___ Lingus
34 Quito's land: Abbr.
35 Co. that owns Parlophone records
36 Z's
40 Tolkien humanoid
41 Many want-ad offerings: Abbr.
43 Play for a sap
44 "I ___ amused!"
46 What you really saw?
50 "Super!"
51 N.R.A. part: Abbr.
52 What you thought you saw?
58 Tiny hairs
61 "Scarface" star, 1932
62 Economy-___

63 Don't exist
64 Sidewalk stand drinks
65 Raison d'___
66 Sheriff's symbol
67 Abominable Snowman
68 Circus barker

DOWN

1 Minuteman, e.g.: Abbr.
2 Make perfect again
3 End piece?
4 "Hello" sticker
5 Burn with an iron
6 Defoe castaway
7 Keister
8 Challenge to Congress
9 Big Brother's creator
10 Bach work
11 Corp. V.I.P.
12 Turner Field locale: Abbr.
13 See 25-Down
21 Hall's singing partner
22 Pooped
25 With 13-Down, Pa. range
26 Grow sick of
27 Make into law
28 Part of a nun's habit
29 Blue-pencil wielder
30 Judge of sex and violence in films
31 Swarm member
32 Flinch, say
37 Peeved and showing it
38 Grp. helping those on shore leave

39 ___ hole in (corrodes)
42 Web recreation
45 Grade lowerers
47 Get wider
48 Refrigerator adornment
49 St. Francis's home
53 "If ___ be so bold . . ."
54 Pantyhose shade
55 Summon to court
56 Poet Pound
57 Fiddler's tune
58 It may have a medallion
59 Roth ___
60 Had charge of

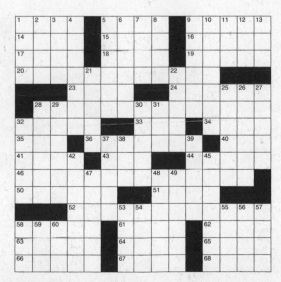

by Malia Jackson and Noah Snyder

130

ACROSS

1 Bay State sch.
6 Juicy fruits
11 Target of many a boxing blow
14 Sophomore's grade
15 Old Testament prophet
16 "It's no ___!"
17 Good sign on a highway
19 Reverse of NNW
20 Dollar or Budget competitor
21 Like the season before Easter
23 Floated gently in the air
26 7 on a grandfather clock
28 Prefix with potent
29 Use a rasp on
30 Comment on, as in a margin
32 Expected
33 Org. for the humane treatment of pets
35 Bobby of the N.H.L.
36 Alcoholics Anonymous has 12 of them
39 Once around a track
40 Catnip and fennel
43 Safe box opener
44 White ___ (termites)
46 Cousin of a Keogh, briefly
47 Arizona's Petrified Forest dates from this period
50 Optimistic
53 Sups
54 "___ luck?"
55 Heavy hammer
56 Bear witness
58 Consequently
59 Fr. holy woman
60 Good sign on a candy box
66 Dark time, in poetry
67 Vice President Burr
68 Weights abroad, informally
69 Scores in the end zone, for short
70 Velocity
71 Appears

DOWN

1 Western tribe
2 "___ in Black," Will Smith film
3 &
4 Layers
5 Acted rudely while in a line, maybe
6 Academics' degrees
7 High's opposite
8 Grp. that entertains the troops
9 Magician in Arthurian legend
10 Hot Japanese drink
11 Good sign on a car trunk
12 Concurrence
13 Ineffectual one, slangily
18 Helpers
22 ___ Dame
23 Bankrolls
24 Be next to
25 Good sign on a lawn
26 Good sign at a motel
27 Not well-put
31 "That feels gooood!"
34 "Above the fruited ___"
37 Kind of porridge
38 The "S" in CBS: Abbr.
41 Boast
42 Fill the stomach of
45 Dish often served with 10-Down
47 Group of cups and saucers
48 Squealed (on)
49 Despotic ruler
51 Sets (down)
52 Nickname for Elizabeth
57 Places to be pampered
58 Manage, as a bar
61 Anger
62 Actress Caldwell
63 ___ de France
64 Suffix with official
65 Twisty curve

by Robert Dillman

ACROSS

1 Some charity fund-raisers
6 Outspoken
11 Org. with a code
14 Singer Davis with the 1998 hit "32 Flavors"
15 Airplane seat choice
16 Old ___, London theater
17 Joie de vivre
19 Lab eggs
20 Accomplish
21 Star-related
23 Prank player
26 "South Park" kid
27 Preceder of Bell or shell
31 Speed-happy driver
33 Book in which the first Passover occurred
35 Castle protector
36 Middle-earth meanie
39 Teacher's charge
40 Paris's ___ Invalides
41 Colder and windier
43 "___ a Tramp" ("Lady and the Tramp" tune)
44 Singer Pinza
46 Popular setting for a wedding
47 Fantastically wonderful
50 Snare
51 Daughter of Czar Nicholas I or II
53 Arctic bird
55 Newswoman Katie
57 Diner sign filler
62 ___-la-la
63 Speaking manner
66 Go wrong
67 Proficient
68 O.K.

69 Newsman Koppel
70 Fix, as laces
71 This puzzle's theme

DOWN

1 ___ Strip (much-fought-over area)
2 British P.M. ___ Douglas-Home
3 Whip
4 Prefix with matter
5 Like wearing a seat belt, e.g.
6 Lombardy province or its capital
7 De-squeak
8 CBS forensic drama
9 "Our Gang" kid
10 Famous Virginia family
11 Lofty place for an academic
12 Pepsi vis-à-vis Coke
13 Symbol of justice

18 Racetracks
22 Bout decision
24 Didn't stay on
25 Kerfuffles
27 Part of M.I.T.: Abbr.
28 Highway toll unit
29 Its academy is in New London, Conn.
30 Some E.R. cases
32 ___ vez (again, in Spanish)
34 Preowned
37 Singer McEntire
38 Wheat, barley or beans
40 In ___ of
42 First drug approved to treat AIDS
45 90210, for Beverly Hills
46 Feeling of loss
48 Person obeying a coxswain

49 Significant
51 Four duos
52 Peter of "M"
54 Super stars
56 ___-Tass news agency
58 Court plea, informally
59 Tributary of the Colorado
60 Rent-___ (security person for hire)
61 Wraps (up)
64 Snare
65 Prefix with dermis

by Stella Daily and Bruce Venzke

132

ACROSS
1 Lascivious
5 Dopey or Doc
10 Say jokingly
14 Zone
15 More unusual
16 Great Salt Lake's state
17 Triumph, but just barely
19 Hawaiian island
20 Badminton court divider
21 Actor Ed of "Daniel Boone"
22 Declining in power
24 False fronts
27 God, to Muslims
28 Smug smiles
30 TV, slangily, with "the"
32 Legal wrong
33 Find a new purpose for
35 Org. with admirals
38 Fall off a beam, e.g.
42 Baseballer Mel
43 Ice cream holders
44 Fusses
45 Politico Gingrich
46 Marks that look like inverted v's
48 Pago Pago's locale
51 Less drunk
54 Graduates
56 Opposite of an intro, musically
57 Parisian yes
60 MasterCard rival
61 Momentarily forget (or get lucky in Scrabble?)
64 Barely earned, with "out"
65 Ship from the Mideast
66 Suffix meaning "little"

67 M&M's that were removed from 1976 to 1987 out of a health concern for a coloring dye
68 A ton
69 Command to a steed

DOWN
1 Home turf?
2 Shallowest Great Lake
3 Led off
4 Amount of hair cream
5 All soap operas, basically
6 Declined in power
7 Got up
8 Thing, in legal briefs
9 Unoccupied, as a theater seat

10 Popular newspaper puzzle subtitled "That Scrambled Word Game"
11 Online commerce
12 Finnish bath
13 Chicken piece
18 Talk idly
23 Biblical tower site
25 Comic Johnson
26 Cigar ends
28 Capital of Manche, France
29 No longer worth debating
31 "The Star-Spangled Banner" land
33 Leases
34 WNW's opposite
35 Sworn to tell the truth
36 Glaswegian, e.g.
37 Loch ___ monster
39 Atlantic or Pacific
40 At this moment

41 Swiss river
45 Wanderers
46 Trees whose wood is used for chests
47 United ___ Emirates
48 Lifeguard, at times
49 Similar
50 Meditated (on)
52 City between Gainesville and Orlando
53 Took a curtain call
55 Fox hit "American ___"
58 "Render therefore ___ Caesar . . ."
59 Scandinavian furniture giant
62 ___ de Janeiro
63 Actor Ayres

by Andrea Carla Michaels

ACROSS

1 Ooze
5 Neighbor of Kan.
9 Go after
14 Island dance
15 Do perfectly
16 Go online
17 Final notice?
18 Coastal flier
19 Take away little by little
20 Diana Ross musical, with "The"
21 They require signals
23 Neptune's domain
24 __ carte
25 Number of operas composed by Beethoven
26 Play the slots, e.g.
28 Ohio university whose team is the Golden Flashes
34 Fancy flapjacks
37 Comstock __
38 Touch with a hanky, say
39 Pro __ (proportionately)
40 Slacks material
42 Facts and figures
43 Baseball bat wood
44 P P P, in Greek
45 Liechtenstein's language
47 Fibs
50 Stephen of "The Crying Game"
51 Beehive State native
52 Timeline division
54 Carpet fuzz
57 Publication that is the key to this puzzle's theme

62 Conk out
63 Tunesmith's org.
64 "That's a shame"
65 Exec's note
66 Peach pit
67 Treat with grandmotherly love, with "on"
68 Kitchen dial site
69 Sharpened
70 Proofer's mark
71 Takes as one's spouse

DOWN

1 Exhibits
2 Blake of jazz
3 1998 role for Cate Blanchett
4 Butter slice
5 N.B.A.'s Shaquille
6 Egyptian temple site
7 Airport delay?

8 Guinness of stage and screen
9 Make spotless
10 Big buzzer
11 Bug-eyed
12 Slaw, e.g.
13 Hydrocarbon suffixes
21 After the buzzer
22 "Oh, goody!"
27 Air quality grp.
29 Beethoven dedicatee
30 "Smoking or __?"
31 Genesis duo
32 "Ciao!"
33 Israel's Abba
34 Sticking point?
35 Too hasty
36 Haul, slangily
41 __ polloi
42 Rap's Dr. __
44 Entered again

46 Part of Q.E.D.
48 New Orleans school
49 Hundred on the Hill
53 Bowling alley button
55 Pointed
56 Doers of drudgery
57 Track meet event
58 Regarding
59 Revered one
60 Little shavers
61 Jillions
65 Use a Lawn-Boy, e.g.

by Adam G. Perl

134

ACROSS

1 Baby's first word, in Italy
6 Commercials
9 Touches
14 Skip ___ (lose tempo)
15 Tennis do-over
16 Katmandu's land
17 ___ firma
18 Mai ___ (tropical drink)
19 "Yum!"
20 "Future Shock" author
23 Prefix with -lithic
24 Wetland
25 Antique restorer's efforts, for short
28 Late hunter of Nazi war criminals
34 Comedian Philips
35 Aria singer
36 Brewing coffee produces one
37 Designer Christian
39 Semesters
42 Muslim holy man
43 Shake hands (on)
45 Former senator Trent
47 ___ dye (chemical coloring)
48 "Sister Carrie" author
52 Airport schedule abbr.
53 The 1919 Treaty of Versailles concluded it: Abbr.
54 Directional suffix
55 Singing group suggested by the starts of 20-, 28- and 48-Across
61 Dragon Ball Z game company
64 ___ Solo of "Star Wars"

65 Actress Papas or Ryan
66 Thesaurus author
67 Superlative suffix
68 Girlish laugh
69 Bullwinkle, for one
70 Letter between pi and sigma
71 Actress Falco and namesakes

DOWN

1 ___ Hari
2 Brother of Cain and Seth
3 "___ Griffin's Crosswords"
4 Dolphins QB Dan
5 Finished
6 Choir voice
7 Like most users of sign language
8 Cadavers, slangily
9 Insect or radio part
10 Yogi, for one
11 FedEx competitor
12 Tit for ___
13 Crafty
21 Namely
22 Former auto executive Iacocca
25 Clarence of the Supreme Court
26 Kind of class for expectant mothers
27 Noisy shouting
28 Anesthetize, say
29 "Put me down as a maybe"
30 Tied down, as a boat
31 "___ changed my mind"
32 Country rocker Steve
33 Prefix with lateral
38 Old Olds car
40 "The ___ Squad" of '60s-'70s TV
41 Throat problem

44 First American to walk in space
46 Orkin target
49 Be in the red
50 Wealthier
51 Accustomed
55 ___ chic
56 Corned beef concoction
57 Absorbed by
58 Soda pop brand
59 Thigh/shin connector
60 Understands
61 Slot machine part
62 Excessively
63 In the past

by Michael Blake

ACROSS

1 Prominent feature of Dracula
6 Reunion group
11 Showman Ziegfeld
14 "Let's Make ___"
15 Search engine name
16 Designer Claiborne
17 It may end up in the gutter
19 In the style of
20 ___ acid (protein component)
21 Schindler of "Schindler's List"
23 Spy's device
26 Sweater style
29 Runs out
32 Slave girl of opera
33 Exploding stars
34 Fuel economy org.
35 City in Italia
39 What 17-, 26-, 50- and 60-Across have in common
43 Pageant accessory
44 Tony Soprano and cohorts, with "the"
45 Cheese hunk
46 One on a pedestal
48 Old timer?
50 Classic breakfast fare
54 Suffix with butyl
55 Reporting to
56 How-to presentations
59 ___ glance
60 Item on a set
66 Fix illegally
67 Disney mermaid

68 Sees red
69 Informal top
70 Center of power
71 Some retired racehorses

DOWN

1 Wonderful, slangily
2 Fuss
3 Partner of improved
4 Big bash
5 ___ to none (long odds)
6 Stellar swan
7 Part of a repair estimate
8 "Got it!"
9 Showman Hurok
10 Went at it alone
11 Cereal morsel
12 Purple hue
13 Country/rock's ___ Mountain Daredevils
18 Nick at ___
22 Tangled, as hair
23 Big tops
24 Lei Day greeting
25 Blacktops, say
27 Surveillance evidence
28 Fact fudger
30 Common union demand
31 Part of a min.
34 Flow back
36 Nostalgic tune
37 Mullally of "Will & Grace"
38 Fred Astaire's sister
40 Bow-toting god
41 Certain plea, for short
42 Of one's ___

47 Skin-related
48 Makes hard
49 "Semper Fi" org.
50 Milk purchase
51 Loosen, in a way
52 Bit of wisdom
53 Parting word
57 Klutzy sorts
58 Dirty reading
61 "___ y plata"
62 Trader ___ (old restaurateur)
63 Rhea relative
64 Like Republican states on an electoral map
65 Braying beast

by C. W. Stewart and J. K. Hummel

136

ACROSS

1 "___ upon a time . . ."
5 Like a score of 10 out of 10
10 Speedy
14 "Star Wars" princess
15 Dated yet trendy
16 Knowing of
17 "See you again!"
20 Longtime CBS and NBC newsman Roger
21 Touchdown destination
22 Blacktops
25 Tricky curves
27 Bud's partner in comedy
28 Had dinner
29 ___ B'rith
30 Coarse file
31 "Veni, vidi, vici" speaker
34 The "R" of NPR
37 "See you again!"
41 Henry Blake's rank on "M*A*S*H": Abbr.
42 Many IM recipients
44 Letterhead design
47 "___ Green" (Kermit the Frog song)
49 Snooze
50 In the style of
51 Mah-jongg pieces
53 Domineering
55 The dole
57 Chief Norse deity
59 "See you again!"
64 Suffix with sock
65 Ship-related
66 Lawman Wyatt
67 Former Cub ___ Sandberg
68 Entrap
69 Where "you can do whatever you feel," in a hit 1978 song

DOWN

1 Outdated
2 Recent: Prefix
3 The Reds, on scoreboards
4 Words on a Wonderland cake
5 Steamed
6 Muffle, as a sound
7 U.F.O. fliers
8 Kind of well
9 Michaels of "Saturday Night Live"
10 "Happy Days" cool cat, with "the"
11 Country north of Namibia
12 Dictation takers
13 Shredded
18 Greyhound vehicle
19 TV spots
22 Grp. funding 19-Down in campaigns
23 Just slightly
24 Swerve
26 "Nobody doesn't like" her, in a slogan
29 ___-a-brac
30 Stir up
32 Lindbergh's classic flight, e.g.
33 Fitting
35 Actress Cannon
36 "How was ___ know?"
38 Duke or earl
39 Restroom door word
40 Chapters in history
43 Austin Powers, e.g.
44 Perry Mason, e.g.
45 Clinton cabinet member Hazel
46 Gasoline unit
48 Weather map line
51 Tic-___-toe
52 Cattle branding tools
53 Lighter and pen maker
54 Perfectly pitched
56 A polar bear might be found on one
58 Valley
60 Actress Mendes
61 '60s conflict site
62 Tolkien creature
63 F.D.R. initiative

by Dave and Tracy Mackey

ACROSS

1 Ashen
5 Decorative molding
9 Yellow shade
14 Gen. Robt. ___
15 "Look both ways before crossing," e.g.
16 Lax
17 In front of a hydrant, say
20 Notice for late ticket-buyers, maybe
21 "Waking ___ Devine" (1998 film)
22 Ignited
23 "Uh-oh"
27 Cool, to a cat
30 They might be near I.C.U.'s
31 Hair removal product
32 Tic-tac-toe loser
33 Atlanta university
36 Fran of "The Nanny"
38 School lady
39 Things hidden in 17-, 23-, 49- and 57-Across
41 Pawn
42 Loch Ness monster, e.g.
44 Dictatorial
45 Umberto who wrote "The Name of the Rose"
46 1998 song by the Goo Goo Dolls that was #1 for 18 weeks
47 Part of m.p.g.
48 Aurora's Greek counterpart
49 Publicists
54 Nafta signatory
55 Opposite of post-
56 Only Super Bowl won by the New York Jets
57 Business sessions that drag
63 Seed-to-be
64 Israel's Abba
65 French seas
66 Mythological reveler
67 Hair line
68 Zebras, to lions

DOWN

1 "Taste that beats the others cold" sloganeer, once
2 Morning waker-upper
3 "Vive ___!"
4 "Horrors!"
5 Directives
6 Father ___ Sarducci, longtime "S.N.L." character
7 Pipe joint
8 Epitome of slipperiness
9 Home of the Casbah
10 Castle defense
11 Ex-hoopster Manute ___
12 Course for a recent émigré: Abbr.
13 King in un palacio
18 Contestant's mail-in
19 The Oscars of magazine publishing
24 ___ Jean (Marilyn Monroe, affectionately)
25 Disrobe
26 Zinger
27 Ding Dongs competitor
28 Board members, for short
29 Looney Tunes pig
33 Maker of introductions
34 ___ Polo
35 Snacks dipped in milk
37 Dusting or taking out the garbage
39 "Yippee!"
40 Lake ___, outlet of the Maumee River
43 Racetrack tout
44 Father
47 Father, e.g.
50 Stab
51 Forty-___
52 Un gato grande
53 Girlish boy
54 Hard on the eyes
57 ___ Lobos
58 TV's Longoria
59 Kook
60 Opposite of "naw"
61 Wall St. hire
62 Little troublemaker

by Peter A. Collins

138

ACROSS

1 Black-bordered news item
5 Anne of "Wag the Dog"
10 Dull-colored
14 Internet connection at a restaurant or airport
15 Fanfare
16 Seized vehicle
17 Snoop
19 Height: Prefix
20 Steak that a dog might end up with
21 "Huckleberry Finn" author
22 Wet mascara worry
25 Felix and Oscar, with "the"
28 Bathroom powder
30 Wyatt of the Wild West
31 Magazine V.I.P.'s
32 1980s video game with a maze
35 Down, usually, on a light switch
38 Carouse
42 Golf peg
43 Boxed stringed instrument
44 "___ solemnly swear . . ."
45 Ax or awl
47 Judicial assertion
49 Symbol of purity
54 Figure of speech
55 Wall art
56 Mutual of ___
58 "Gotcha," to a beatnik
59 Want ad heading . . . or a hint to the starts of 17-, 25-, 38- and 49-Across
64 Queue
65 More than steamed
66 March Madness org.
67 Brain readings, for short
68 Parceled (out)
69 Safecracker

DOWN

1 To have and to hold
2 Life story, for short
3 Conditions
4 Men's fashion accessory
5 Submarine sandwich
6 Commercial prefix with Lodge
7 Informed, with "in"
8 ___ Solo of "Star Wars"
9 Flight board info: Abbr.
10 Use, as past experience
11 CliffsNotes version
12 "___ Love," 1957 #1 hit by 13-Down
13 Singer Pat
18 Brusque
21 The Blue Jays, on a scoreboard
22 Rung
23 Furious with
24 Pitcher of milk?
26 John Donne's "___ Be Not Proud"
27 Went by dugout
29 Passover bread
33 Spicy dish that may have a fire-alarm rating
34 Encountered
36 ___-Lay (snack company)
37 At the end of one's patience
39 Take-home pay
40 Squirm
41 Capitol's top
46 Bird that hoots
48 Crevice
49 Photographer's request
50 Peep show flick
51 Circular gasket
52 Go ___ for (support in time of need)
53 Overact
57 Copied
59 Huck's raftmate
60 Metal from a mine
61 Sno-cone filler
62 Re-re-re-remind
63 Respond to a really bad joke, maybe

by Ken Bessette

ACROSS

1 Olympics prize
6 "Zounds!"
10 "In your dreams!"
14 Vega of "Spy Kids" movies
15 Marilyn Monroe facial mark
16 It may be tempted
17 Reminisce about a nice facial outline?
20 "I'll take that as ___"
21 Cartoon villain Badenov
22 Gangsters' gals
23 Ambassador's forte
25 Nada
26 Sidney Poitier title role
27 Reminisce about spring cleaning?
33 "Daggers" look
35 Rap sheet letters
36 Trifling amount
37 Common breakfast fare
40 Tense subject?
43 Brit. record label
44 Catchword of 6-Down
46 Wise up
47 Reminisce about working in a restaurant?
52 Pool tool
53 Messenger ___
54 Starch-yielding palm
57 Santa ___, California city, county or river
60 Not spoken
62 Buddhist sect
63 Reminisce about a pig-out?
66 Census data
67 Jungle menaces
68 Minister's home
69 Physiques, informally
70 Cathedral area
71 Like dessert wines

DOWN

1 Corday's victim
2 Actress Verdugo
3 Like a blue state
4 Give the boot
5 Mild-mannered type
6 Television chef Lagasse
7 Big bully
8 "The Sound of Music" setting
9 "___ Rosenkavalier"
10 Be able to meet the expense of
11 Go yachting
12 "___ be a cold day in hell . . ."
13 Honoraria
18 U2 frontman
19 Skip
24 Time in a seat
26 Mark permanently
28 Middling grade
29 Heart chart, for short
30 People rival
31 Wing it?
32 Roll of the dice, maybe
33 Attendee
34 Poor, as an excuse
38 Having the resources
39 Postgraduate study
41 Boxer Laila
42 Department store department
45 Salsa percussion
48 Unlike this answer
49 Waikiki wingding
50 As a precaution
51 Follow, as a suspect
55 Honkers
56 Get-go
57 Kvetching sort
58 Toy block brand
59 Got 100 on
60 'Vette roof option
61 Parts of a drum kit
64 Home for Bulls, but not Bears: Abbr.
65 Like a new recruit

by Deb Amlen

ACROSS

1 Bounce to the surface
6 Botch
10 Sports equipment
14 Belittle
15 Least bit
16 Present opener?
17 Free health and dental care, and then some
20 List of test answers
21 Aviates
22 Limerick or sonnet
23 Luke's twin sister in "Star Wars"
24 Price __ pound
25 Math symbol for extraction of a root
30 Pilot's stat.
33 Warnings
34 Entree in a bowl with beef or lamb, say
36 Pelvic bones
37 Boat propeller
38 Clark's crush on "Smallville"
39 "Hey, come back a bit"
42 Enter en masse
44 Where pigs wallow
45 In limbo
47 Wood-shaping tool
48 Nays' opposites
49 Flair
52 Peppermint __ of "Peanuts"
54 Sombrero, e.g.
57 Eyeglass option for different distances
60 Early state in the presidential campaign
61 Reclined
62 Major artery
63 The Big Board: Abbr.
64 Doe's mate
65 Winona of "Girl, Interrupted"

DOWN

1 Pitcher's faux pitch
2 New York theater award
3 One often needing a change
4 Take advantage of
5 "Couldn't be better!"
6 Pertaining to a son or daughter
7 Ear or leaf part
8 Four Corners-area Indians
9 Prohibition
10 Errand runner
11 Dubai dignitary
12 Six-legged scurriers
13 Move skyward
18 Fake identity
19 Occurrence
23 Bygone Italian coins
24 Tour grp.?
25 Monsoon occurrences
26 Apportion
27 God or goddess
28 Brainy
29 Suffix with bombard
30 Trailblazing video game maker
31 His tomb is in Red Square
32 Banjo sound
35 Hits hard
37 Lummox
40 Like 16 vis-à-vis 15, agewise
41 Turk's topper
42 Home viewing for a price
43 Subscription period, often
46 Loathing
47 Aquatic plant life
49 Pirouette
50 "Iliad" setting
51 Cries after being burned
52 H.S. junior's exam
53 Where most of Russia is
54 Group of buffalo
55 Prefix with chamber
56 Ruler before 31-Down
58 Ernie of the 24-Down
59 Silver screen star Myrna

by Lynn Lempel

141

ACROSS

1 Puppies' plaints
5 Cobb of "12 Angry Men"
9 Icy look
14 Oratorio highlight
15 Di or da preceder in a Beatles song
16 Moves like sludge
17 "What __ Did" (classic children's book with a punny title)
18 __ Spee (old German warship)
19 Catcher's position
20 Enjoying an outing, of sorts
23 "Gets the red out" sloganeer
24 Italian auto, for short
25 Scientology founder __ Hubbard
28 For no profit
32 Sister of Marge Simpson
36 Forsaken
38 Get __ the habit
39 Enjoying an outing, of sorts
42 Homecoming figure, for short
43 Yin's counterpart
44 Checking out
45 Michelin offering
47 Flagston family pet
49 Gin flavoring
51 Edit
56 Enjoying an outing, of sorts
61 Like wild tigers
62 Drought relief
63 Hi Flagston's wife, in the comics

64 Garden plant support
65 One hired by a corp. board
66 McCann of country music
67 Cheated, slangily
68 One of "The Addams Family," informally
69 Comrade in arms

DOWN

1 Comic Smirnoff
2 Tehran denizen
3 Actress ZaSu
4 Greet cordially
5 Paul Bunyan, e.g.
6 River of Spain
7 Mideast airline
8 Port of Israel
9 Treat leniently, with "on"

10 Talkativeness
11 France's Côte d'__
12 Actor Stephen and kin
13 Renaissance family name
21 China's Zhou __
22 Trolley sound
26 Gymnast Korbut
27 Ad infinitum
29 "The __ Love" (R.E.M. hit)
30 British W.W. II–era gun
31 Chinatown gang
32 Exchange jabs
33 Former Connecticut governor Grasso
34 Speak well of
35 "I can't blame anyone else"
37 Latvia's capital

40 Fishing line material
41 Georg who wrote "The Philosophy of Right"
46 Trued up
48 Twist badly
50 Everglades wader
52 Home overlooking the sea, maybe
53 How some tuna is packed
54 Dexterity
55 Lamb or Bacon piece
56 __ browns (diner fare)
57 Analogy part
58 Havana aunts
59 Kind of stand
60 Doesn't dally

by Victor Fleming

142

ACROSS

1 Boston orchestra
5 Seaboard
10 30 minutes, in the N.F.L.
14 Once more
15 God of the Koran
16 Mixed bag
17 X-rated dance
19 Miniature plateau
20 Top secret?
21 "Thar ___ blows!"
22 Something to cram for
23 Banjo picker Scruggs
25 Org. that publishes American Hunter
27 Some Caribbean music
30 Beach find
36 Referred to
39 ___ Speedwagon (1970s–'80s band)
40 Rotgut
41 "___ of Two Cities"
42 Fabergé collectible
43 Acquire, as a debt
44 ___ badge, boy scout's award
45 Dover's state: Abbr.
46 ___ jacket, 1960s fashion
47 Initial power source
50 One of a D.C. 100
51 401(k) alternative, for short
52 Oodles
55 Object of the actions suggested by the starts of 17-, 30-, 47- and 66-Across
58 "You've ___ Mail"
61 Lose all one's money in gambling
65 Thomas Edison's middle name
66 Pinto

68 Plane assignment
69 Ryan of "The Beverly Hillbillies"
70 Julia Roberts's role in "Ocean's Eleven"
71 Golfer's target
72 Krupp Works city
73 Alphabetize, e.g.

DOWN

1 It might be checkered
2 Not fooled by
3 Llama country
4 Slide, as a credit card through a reader
5 Supplies, as food for a party
6 Cheer for El Cordobés
7 "Ah, me!"
8 Part of a girl scout's uniform
9 Finis
10 1990 Macaulay Culkin film
11 The "A" in A-Rod
12 Kudrow of "Friends"
13 Cappuccino head
18 ___ brain (nitwit)
24 "Streets of ___" (classic cowboy song)
26 Bird that comes "bob, bob, bobbin'"
27 Little rascal
28 Ben Franklin, famously, in an electrical storm
29 Arcade game maker
31 Israeli desert
32 Sharp turn on a golf course
33 Sources of Scottish streams
34 Sky-blue
35 Twice-seen TV show
37 Competitor of "The 5th Wheel," in reality TV
38 Scare off
48 Chatterbox
49 Spoiled
53 Scrooge's cry
54 Dalmatian markings
55 Launder
56 Margarine
57 White House office shape
59 Crew's control?
60 Deadlocks
62 Cookie with a creme center
63 Stalingrad's land, for short
64 The "T" of S.A.T.
67 U-turn from SSW

by Randall J. Hartman

ACROSS

1 Its eye may be part of a witch's brew
5 Daddy-o
9 Sleep soundly?
14 Popular cornstarch brand
15 "___ my word!"
16 Prenatal sites
17 Low-fat, as beef
18 Not on time
19 Business on the Internet
20 Polishing machines at an Ithaca campus?
23 CPR giver
24 Opposite of throw away
25 Geometry symbols
28 Recipient of "G'day"
31 Puts into effect
35 Trustee group at an Atlanta campus?
38 Peel
39 Musical closings
40 Old Michael Jackson 'do
41 Zellweger of "Chicago"
42 In a bit
43 Thoroughfare at a New Orleans campus?
45 Broadway Joe
47 Flip out
48 U.F.O. crew
49 Fishing float
51 Swiffer, e.g.
53 Rental arrangement at a Milwaukee campus?
60 Letters that must be bought on "Wheel of Fortune"
61 Versifier
62 Kind of hygiene
63 Analyze in English class
64 Mental flash
65 Lice-to-be
66 Cross over?
67 Dance's partner
68 Let (up)

DOWN

1 Face powder ingredient
2 Lunchbox goody
3 Food thickener
4 John who wrote "Love built on beauty, soon as beauty, dies"
5 Can opener
6 October gem
7 What Texas hold'em tables hold
8 Take furtively
9 Volvo's home
10 Stationer's supply
11 Sharif of "Funny Girl"
12 Baseball stat
13 Night school subj.
21 Outstanding Comedy Series awards
22 Addiction
25 Pie nut
26 "___ roll!"
27 Sin city
29 Vegetarian's protein source
30 ___ Court (London tube station)
32 Paddled vessel
33 One of two choices on Halloween
34 Tournament favorites
36 Discovered by accident
37 A horse of a different color?
41 Towed items, sometimes
43 No ___ traffic
44 Conventioneer's wear
46 Close-fitting hats
50 French military hats
52 Nokia offering
53 Repast
54 Suffix with billion
55 Fuss
56 Adolescent
57 Melody for Dame Nellie Melba
58 Piper's followers
59 Ultimatum's ultimate word
60 N.Y.P.D. alert

by Sarah Keller

144

ACROSS
1. ___ Antoinette
6. Tallies
10. Series of scenes
13. Actress Blake or Plummer
15. Not having a stitch on
16. Letter before sigma
17. Lump in the throat
18. "Calm down!"
20. Neighbor of Scot.
21. Dabbling duck
23. Years and years and years
24. "Move!"
29. One-named Art Deco master
30. Stephen of "The Crying Game"
31. Bear in constellation names
34. Cap or helmet
39. "Pay attention!"
43. Cared for a home while the owner was away
44. Pink wine
45. Hang back
46. Sail support
49. "Lookie there!"
56. Like many a wiseacre's comment: Abbr.
57. Part of F.Y.I.
58. Lots of laughs
60. "Oh, be serious!"
64. Car model with a musical name
66. Metalliferous rock
67. Done with
68. Passes, as a law
69. Auction motion
70. Farewells
71. "Savvy?"

DOWN
1. Crew member
2. Honor ___ thieves
3. Poconos or Tetons
4. Write-___ (some votes)
5. Manuscript receiver
6. White, in Mexico
7. Owing
8. Banned insecticide
9. Caribbean, e.g.
10. "This way" sign
11. Dishes for fancy meals
12. ___-turvy
14. Native seal hunter
19. "Golly!"
22. Breakfasted, e.g.
25. Parts of an udder
26. Stew
27. Go like mad
28. "If I ___ hammer . . ."
31. "Yuck!"
32. Rock's ___ Speedwagon
33. Sutcliffe of the early Beatles
34. F.D.R. successor
35. Middle measurement
36. It may be puffed up
37. Sighs of contentment
38. Letter carrier's assignment: Abbr.
40. Hades
41. Golfer ___ Aoki
42. Heroic legend
46. Call to a calf
47. Blow ___ (become enraged)
48. Brawny
49. Not be able to swallow
50. When to celebrate el año nuevo
51. Schlepped
52. "Gimme ___!" (frequent Alabama cheerleader's cry)
53. Color specialists
54. "It's ___" ("There's no doubt")
55. ___-frutti
59. Cartoonist Thomas
61. High tennis shot
62. Some Christmas greenery
63. Doctor's quote
65. Scottish refusal

by C. W. Stewart

ACROSS

1 It's full of holes and traps
5 Gastric juices, e.g.
10 Remnant of a tattoo removal, maybe
14 Zone
15 Herb popular in Indian food
16 Staff note
17 Glam rocker's accessory
19 Jessica of "Fantastic Four" films
20 The "F" in the equation "F = ma"
21 Pat on the back, as a baby
22 Sleigh
23 Get up
25 Loathes
27 Usurer's victim
30 Throat condition
31 Parisian streets
32 Tiptop
35 Drained of color
38 "What ___ the odds?"
39 Dumps (on)
41 Guitarist's guitar
42 Succeed in life
44 It fills barrels
45 Freshly
46 Make believe
48 Espy
50 Like trees on a prairie
52 Hooch
54 "Mr. ___ risin' " (classic Doors lyric)
55 One always on the lookout for a deal
57 Hotel room posting
61 Wife of Osiris

62 Director's cry . . . or a statement about 17-Across and 11- and 29-Down
64 Longtime Yugoslav chief
65 Flood preventer
66 Surrounding glow
67 List ender
68 Play to the back of the audience
69 Longings

DOWN

1 Sailor's hook
2 Nabisco cookie
3 King who was the father of Cordelia
4 Moneybags types
5 Starting pitcher
6 Places to park
7 Saturate

8 New Look designer
9 Answer in anger
10 Overhead shots
11 Transparent packaging material
12 Color meaning "caution" on 13-Down
13 See 12-Down
18 Guitar ___ (hit video game series)
24 Oil-rich land
26 They're uplifting
27 Bummer
28 Money since 2002
29 Taco alternative
30 Coal bed
33 Extended family
34 Stereotypical tattoo

36 Company V.I.P.
37 Former speaker Gingrich
39 "Exodus" author
40 Long-gone bird
43 Kind of can
45 Eroded
47 Like caresses
49 Writer Pound
50 Beat, biblically
51 Take as a given
52 "Wonderful!"
53 Wedding band, maybe
56 Polite way to interrupt someone
58 Loyal
59 Pull in
60 Watering holes
63 "Get it?"

by Kevin Donovan

146

ACROSS

1 Stars and Stripes, e.g.
5 Places where lines meet
9 French greeting
14 ___ of Sandwich
15 Cause of a game cancellation
16 Unaccompanied
17 "Here he is now!"
20 Black card
21 Talks one's head off
22 French summer
23 Twinings selections
26 Sign before Virgo
27 Big Apple ave.
28 Be undecided
33 ___ Wednesday
34 Suds maker
35 Mounted, as a horse
38 Talking maybe a little too fast
40 Snapshot
43 Sgt. Snorkel's dog
44 Fable writer
46 No. on which a magazine's ad rates are based
48 Freudian one
49 Persist to completion
53 Prefix with center
55 Column's counterpart
56 Interstate entrance or exit
57 Fish after which a cape is named
58 Logic diagram
60 Long Island airfield town
64 Command center? . . . or where you might hear the starts of 17-, 28- and 49-Across
68 Nephew of Donald Duck

69 For whom the bell tolls, in a John Donne meditation
70 Numerical prefix with -ber
71 Bygone Montreal ball club
72 Quiet exercise
73 Remove from the freezer

DOWN

1 Admit (to), with "up"
2 Reindeer herder
3 Geometry calculation
4 "My pleasure"
5 Black power hairdo, for short
6 Dunderpate
7 The "C" in N.Y.C.
8 Divided 50-50
9 Dirge
10 Schooner fill

11 Billet-doux
12 Join
13 Old message system
18 Wails
19 Dueling sword
24 Perched on
25 Deposed Iranian
28 "Roots," for one
29 ___ of Wight
30 Message on a shipping crate
31 Geologic time unit
32 Pigeon's sound
36 Big elevator manufacturer
37 ___ too soon
39 Droid
41 Wedding cake feature
42 Killer whale
45 Republican, Democratic, Green, etc.

47 "Luann" or "Blondie"
50 Knight time?
51 A score
52 End result
53 French place of learning
54 Mail receiver, in brief
59 Repeat
61 ___ Ness monster
62 Itsy-bitsy bit
63 Winter truck attachment
65 God, in Italy
66 Brain scan, for short
67 Bounding main

by Ken Bessette

ACROSS

1 Where to tie the knot
6 "Bearded" bloom
10 Captain Hook's henchman
14 Exotic jelly flavor
15 "___ a deal!"
16 Boston suburb
17 Is pessimistic
20 Waterborne youth group member
21 "I agree completely"
22 Follows orders
24 Ballpark worker
25 Stuffed mouse, maybe
29 Diving bird
31 Intergalactic traveler
32 ___ shui
34 Hellenic H's
38 Is optimistic
41 Eliot of the Untouchables
42 Taj Mahal site
43 Hobby knife brand
44 Bearded grazer
45 Springing bounce in tall grasses, as by an animal, to view the surroundings
46 Garbage
50 A dwarf planet, now
53 Makes use of
55 Binging
60 Is apathetic
62 March plaything
63 "Hurry!"
64 Frolics
65 Sapphic verses
66 Attack, as with eggs
67 Attack with rocks

DOWN

1 Dark ___
2 Elegance
3 Bite-size appetizer
4 Forum greetings
5 Masked scavengers
6 One Time?
7 Like a bad dirt road
8 "___ bin ein Berliner"
9 Tom Jones's "___ a Lady"
10 Job openings
11 Gift of the Magi
12 Come after
13 Key in
18 Shakespeare's Sir ___ Belch
19 Captain Queeg's creator
23 Year-end temp
25 "Love and Marriage" lyricist Sammy
26 Natural emollient
27 A lot of a car valet's income
28 Buttonless shirts, informally
30 "Disgusting!"
32 Get all steamy
33 Flub
34 24/7 auction site
35 PC whiz
36 Regarding
37 Halt
39 "Go, team!" screamer
40 Whistle-blowers
44 Neuter, as a horse
45 Walk of Fame embedment
46 Screwy
47 Steer clear of
48 Cook in a wok, maybe
49 Scrabble pieces
51 Opposite of express
52 Not suitable
54 Start of a play to the quarterback
56 Storyline
57 San ___, Italy
58 Nascar airer
59 In ___ (actually)
61 China's Lao-___

by Eugene W. Sard

148

ACROSS

1 "I saw ___ sawing wood . . ." (old tongue twister)
5 Lawn base
8 Finally
14 Outlaws
15 "I won! I won!," e.g.
16 Amp toter
17 What President Washington said upon winning the lottery?
19 Professor's goal
20 "I've got a mule, her name is ___"
21 Once around the sun
22 Hidden valley
23 What flagmaker Ross said . . . ?
28 Colonial Franklin, familiarly
29 Cheer to a matador
30 Just watched
33 What Miss Molly said . . . ?
39 End in ___ (draw)
40 In a huff
41 Captain who said "Eat your pudding, Mr. Land"
42 What Galileo said . . . ?
44 "I can't ___ satisfaction" (Rolling Stones lyric)
45 "___ shocked . . . SHOCKED!"
46 Collide
47 What the Big Bad Wolf said . . . ?
55 Figure skater's jump
56 Rocklike
57 Clamor
59 Overhaul
62 What Noah Webster said . . . ?

64 Aftershock
65 Shepherd's locale
66 Nylons
67 High-school honey
68 Directional suffix
69 Ready for business

DOWN

1 Flows out
2 Request at a medical exam
3 Viewpoint
4 Put to good ___
5 Porch protector
6 "Rock of Ages" accompaniment
7 Hair colorers
8 Picasso output
9 Little piggy
10 Actress Jessica
11 Rated NC-17, e.g.
12 Fathers
13 Wee
18 Hand-wringer's words

24 Monk's home
25 Traffic noises
26 Merrie ___ England
27 Command to Rover
30 ___ Miguel, largest island of the Azores
31 Part of N.C.A.A.: Abbr.
32 Actor Robbins
33 Commercial prefix with phone
34 Row
35 "You're ___ talk!"
36 Rent out
37 Trio after K
38 "___-hoo!"
40 Slanted type: Abbr.
43 Sis or bro
44 Lightheaded
46 Novelist Melville
47 Witches' blemishes
48 Put forth, as effort
49 Flood stopper

50 Transporter across the Andes
51 Not cut up
52 HBO's "Real Time With Bill ___"
53 Lottery winner's yell
54 Convalescent home employee
58 Biblical place of innocence
60 Hip, in the '60s
61 Delve (into)
63 "Sez ___?"

by C. W. Stewart

ACROSS

1 MacDowell of "Groundhog Day"
6 #41 or #43
10 These may be coddled
14 Nickel and dime
15 Home to most Turks
16 Maul or awl
17 Providential
19 Mr. Peanut prop
20 Vogue competitor
21 Not 'neath
22 Walked like a tosspot
24 Disco ___ of "The Simpsons"
26 Conclude one's argument
27 Nary a penny
33 Gymgoer's pride
34 Portfolio contents
35 Carrot or radish
37 Ending with bed or farm
39 Mai ___
40 Cass and Michelle, in '60s pop
41 Does something
42 Like cows, to Hindus
44 Hieroglyphics serpent
45 In close pursuit
48 Double reed
49 One of two in "boxcars"
50 Never-before-seen
53 Be in hock
55 Follow closely
59 Pope from 440 to 461
60 Adds up . . . like this puzzle's theme?

63 "We try harder" company
64 Up to the task
65 Bracelet site
66 Thought before blowing out the candles
67 Tide type
68 Significant ___

DOWN

1 Ibuprofen target
2 Coward of the theater
3 "Don't touch that ___!"
4 Play the market
5 Suffix with Brooklyn
6 When stolen, it stays in place
7 Tech caller
8 Covet thy neighbor's wife, say
9 Dislikes, plus
10 "Yadda, yadda, yadda"
11 Slap shot success
12 Auctioneer's last word
13 Iditarod entry
18 Some are proper
23 Upper-left key
25 Wart cause, in folklore
26 Hit the hay
27 Gunslinger's mark
28 "___ a Nightingale"
29 Everything that's left
30 Get to
31 "___ is an island"
32 Done for, slangily

33 Org. with dens
36 Cough medicine amt.
38 Really wow
40 Early 17th-century year
42 One with a carrot nose, maybe
43 Tricky turns
46 U.K. honour
47 Full range
50 What "there oughta be"
51 Strauss of jeans
52 Cohort of Clark
53 State with a panhandle: Abbr.
54 Show grief
56 Hieroglyphics cross
57 Archipelago unit
58 Sly glance
61 "Honest" prez
62 ___ Paulo

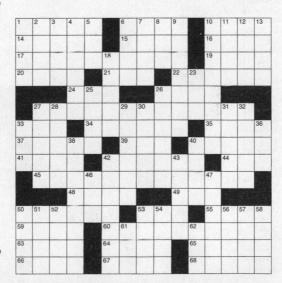

by David Pringle

150

ACROSS
1 Ooze
5 La ___, Milan opera house
10 One-spot cards
14 "Not guilty," e.g.
15 Jeopardy
16 Phileas ___, who went around the world in 80 days
17 Like 39-Across's fans on his induction day?
19 Plenty
20 Uses a stool
21 Spy Mata ___
23 Warmongers
26 H.S. junior's exam
28 Old horse
31 Away from the wind
32 Layers
34 Letter before omega
35 "___ Bitsy Spider"
36 Waved one's arms at, as a cab
37 Place to wager on the 28-Acrosses: Abbr.
38 Goes bad, as fruit
39 Notable Army inductee of 3/24/58
40 Military no-show
41 Part of a gearwheel
42 Flexible
43 Land of Lima and llamas
44 French "a"
45 Makes very happy
46 Balletic bend
47 ___ and feather
48 Simplicity
49 Legendary Chicago Bears coach George
50 Singer ___ Anthony
52 One who makes a good first impression?
54 Derrière

56 Last movie 39-Across made before his Army stint
62 Dunce cap, geometrically
63 1975–78 U.S. Open champ Chris
64 Finger's end
65 Novelist Seton
66 Artist who liked to paint dancers
67 Hard journey

DOWN
1 Place to refresh oneself
2 Building wing
3 Wriggly swimmer
4 Openers for all doors
5 Good name for a Dalmatian
6 Corporate V.I.P.'s
7 Noah's ___

8 "Ally McBeal" actress Lucy
9 Some computer software checks
10 Light years away
11 Army officer who met 39-Across in 25-Down
12 Self-esteem
13 Last Army rank of 39-Across: Abbr.
18 What the "H" of H.M.S. may be
22 Not too much
23 Much-photographed event after 39-Across's induction
24 City with a Penn State campus
25 Where 39-Across was stationed overseas
26 First Army rank of 39-Across

27 Like seawater
29 Waldorf-___ Hotel
30 First movie 39-Across made after his Army stint
32 Defeated soundly
33 Actresses Shire and Balsam
40 Clear to all
42 Word before group or pressure
49 What the "H" of H.M.S. may be
51 Neighborhood
52 Indian tourist city
53 Police hdqrs.
54 Record label of 39-Across
55 Long, long time
57 "___ had it!"
58 Photo image, briefly
59 Rowboat mover
60 Made-up story
61 Antlered animal

by David J. Kahn

The New York Times

SMART PUZZLES

PRESENTED WITH STYLE

Available at your local bookstore or online at www.nytimes.com/nytstore

🦋 St. Martin's Griffin

Answers

1

S	P	A	M		A	C	M	E		S	C	H	M	O
T	O	G	A		B	A	I	L		A	R	E	A	R
A	L	E	C		O	R	M	E		L	A	M	P	S
P	E	N	E	L	O	P	E	C	R	U	Z			
L	A	D		I	K	E		T	O	T	E	B	A	G
E	X	A	C	T		T	W	I	C	E		A	L	A
		A	H	A		O	O	O		C	L	A	M	
S	H	A	K	E	D	O	W	N	C	R	U	I	S	E
K	O	B	E		A	R	E		O	E	R			
A	P	E		E	G	A	D	S		L	E	A	R	Y
T	I	T	A	N	I	C		I	I	I		L	E	A
		G	R	O	U	N	D	S	C	R	E	W	S	
M	A	R	G	O		L	O	N	E		A	X	I	S
A	V	A	I	L		A	V	E	R		M	E	R	E
J	E	W	E	L		R	A	Y	E		P	I	E	R

2

A	D	O	R	E		S	H	H		T	R	O	O	P
M	O	T	E	L		M	I	A		E	A	R	L	E
F	L	I	P	F	L	O	P	S	A	N	D	A	L	S
M	E	S	A		O	R	P	H	A	N		N	I	T
		S	C	R	E	E		H	I	N	G	E	S	
R	A	P	T	O	R		S	A	S	S	Y			
E	U	R		W	I	D	T	H		S	E	D	G	E
F	R	E	E	B	E	E		A	S	H	T	R	A	Y
S	A	Y	S	O		M	E	T	O	O		E	E	R
		P	Y	L	O	N		M	E	D	D	L	E	
S	T	R	O	B	E		C	E	A	S	E			
A	R	I		O	N	C	A	L	L		L	P	G	A
B	E	D	R	O	O	M	S	L	I	P	P	E	R	S
L	E	G	I	T		D	E	A		C	H	E	E	K
E	D	E	N	S		R	D	S		S	I	N	G	S

3

N	E	S	T	S		B	O	S	S		E	G	A	D
O	N	T	A	P		A	L	T	O		N	O	D	E
A	D	E	L	A		Y	E	A	S		S	L	O	T
H	O	T	C	R	O	S	S	B	U	N		D	R	E
			S	R	O			S	E	E	D	I	E	R
N	E	B		O	N	U	S		M	A	I	L		
A	R	E		W	A	R	M	W	E	L	C	O	M	E
R	O	D	E			A	I	R			E	C	O	N
C	O	O	L	M	I	L	L	I	O	N		K	A	Y
	F	L	A	N		E	T	T	E		S	T	A	
C	A	N	A	S	T	A			T	W	A			
A	M	A		C	O	L	D	C	O	M	F	O	R	T
R	U	I	N		N	O	R	A		A	I	M	E	E
O	S	L	O		E	N	O	S		T	R	A	N	S
B	E	S	T		S	E	P	T		H	E	R	D	S

4

D	R	U	M		B	A	G			A	C	U	R	A
A	N	N	E		O	D	E	A		M	O	T	E	L
M	A	L	C	O	L	M	M	C	D	O	W	E	L	L
		A	C	E	D		M	O	A			R	I	O
	S	T	A	N	L	E	Y	K	U	B	R	I	C	K
T	L	C		O	Y	L		E	B	R	O			
O	O	H	S		G	E	T			A	B	I	E	S
B	E	E	T	H	O	V	E	N	S	N	I	N	T	H
E	S	S	A	Y		N	A	H		N	E	H	I	
			S	P	A	T		N	E	A		S	O	N
A	N	T	H	O	N	Y	B	U	R	G	E	S	S	
C	I	O			E	S	E		W	E	R	E		
C	L	O	C	K	W	O	R	K	O	R	A	N	G	E
R	E	T	R	O		N	E	R	O		S	C	O	T
A	S	S	T	S			T	A	D		E	E	O	C

5

6

7

C	L	A	S	P	■	I	C	O	N	■	F	L	A	B
H	A	I	T	I	■	R	O	M	A	■	L	U	L	L
I	D	T	A	G	■	A	M	A	T	■	U	R	G	E
■	■	L	S	D	■	P	H	I	L	■	C	A	N	■
S	E	D	A	T	E	■	L	A	V	I	S	H	E	D
T	R	I	C	Y	C	L	E	■	E	M	T	■	■	■
A	N	A	T	■	A	U	T	O	■	B	A	L	D	S
M	I	N	I	■	F	I	E	L	D	■	L	O	R	N
P	E	A	T	S	■	S	C	A	R	■	A	R	O	O
■	■	E	A	R	■	O	V	E	R	G	R	O	W	■
N	U	T	S	H	E	L	L	■	G	A	M	E	L	Y
E	N	E	■	L	U	A	U	■	S	R	I	■	■	■
A	L	A	N	■	B	U	M	P	■	E	T	T	A	S
R	I	S	E	■	E	R	N	E	■	S	E	W	E	R
S	T	E	T	■	N	A	S	A	■	T	S	A	R	S

8

M	A	I	M	■	A	L	T	O	■	A	B	A	C	I
A	L	D	A	■	L	E	A	P	■	B	A	S	I	C
N	E	O	N	■	O	G	L	E	■	E	L	I	T	E
■	C	L	O	S	E	S	C	R	U	T	I	N	Y	■
■	■	■	R	E	V	■	■	A	P	T	■	■	■	■
P	A	T	■	W	E	R	E	■	C	I	G	A	R	S
E	L	I	A	■	R	A	N	K	■	N	A	D	I	A
C	O	N	S	T	A	N	T	N	A	G	G	I	N	G
K	H	A	K	I	■	T	E	E	N	■	S	O	S	A
S	A	S	S	E	S	■	R	E	A	D	■	S	E	N
■	■	■	O	R	O	■	■	C	O	O	■	■	■	■
■	C	O	N	N	I	P	T	I	O	N	F	I	T	■
J	O	D	I	E	■	T	O	R	N	■	F	L	E	D
O	R	O	N	O	■	E	G	A	D	■	E	S	A	U
B	A	R	O	N	■	D	O	N	A	■	R	A	R	E

9

L	A	T	H		U	C	L	A		S	T	A	I	D
E	C	H	O		M	R	E	D		W	A	L	D	O
A	L	A	S		B	E	A	M		E	N	T	E	R
P	U	R	P	L	E	P	R	O	S	E		O	A	K
			E	R	E		N	A	P	S				
I	P	A	N	A		S	H	I	V		M	A	S	S
D	I	N	E	R	O		I	S	O		E	D	N	A
L	A	V	E	N	D	E	R	H	I	L	L	M	O	B
E	N	I	D		E	V	E		R	E	T	I	R	E
S	O	L	E		S	A	S	S		A	S	T	E	R
		D	I	S	C		T	A	S					
A	H	A		M	A	U	V	E	D	E	C	A	D	E
M	A	N	I	A		A	E	R	O		H	U	R	L
A	L	O	N	G		T	I	E	R		E	R	A	S
D	O	N	N	E		E	L	O	N		W	A	G	E

10

A	R	C	H	E	R		S	A	L	S		S	H	E
G	A	L	O	R	E		I	M	A	C		T	A	D
A	D	O	N	I	S		L	A	V	A	T	O	R	Y
T	I	S		E	A	V	E		A	M	A	N	A	S
H	O	E	D		W	I	N	G		A	L	E	S	
A	S	T	E	R		S	T	A	I	R	C	A	S	E
		N	E	O		L	E	S	T		G	E	L	
H	O	L	Y	C	O	W		A	B	I	D	E	R	S
A	R	I		E	R	R	S		N	S	A			
T	A	K	E	S	T	E	P	S		T	Y	P	E	S
	T	E	A	S		N	O	T	O		O	I	L	Y
T	O	N	S	I	L		O	D	O	R		N	A	S
A	R	E	Y	O	U	O	K		H	A	C	K	I	T
G	I	S		N	A	P	E		E	R	M	I	N	E
S	O	S		S	U	E	D		R	E	D	E	E	M

11

B	O	R	E	S		L	A	M	A		C	H	A	P
E	L	I	T	E		O	W	E	D		R	O	S	E
A	G	O	R	A		M	O	O	D		O	M	I	T
M	A	T	E	R	I	A	L	W	I	T	N	E	S	S
			E	R	N	S		T	H	Y				
P	A	R	A	D	E			L	I	O	N	E	S	S
A	M	O	S		S	W	O	O	N		A	P	E	
S	I	G	H	T	S	E	E	I	N	G	T	R	I	P
T	E	E		H	A	T	E	S		A	T	R	A	
E	S	T	E	E	M	S		R	A	C	H	E	L	
		R	I	O		A	M	E	N					
O	B	S	E	R	V	A	T	I	O	N	D	E	C	K
T	A	L	C		A	L	A	N		A	R	L	E	N
T	R	O	T		R	O	L	E		L	I	S	L	E
O	N	E	S		S	E	E	D		S	P	A	T	E

12

A	L	T	E	R		B	O	A	T		S	R	T	A
P	E	E	V	E		A	B	L	E		C	O	I	L
E	A	S	E	L		L	I	E	S		R	A	R	E
	T	R	I	C	K	S	C	H	R	O	D	E	R
O	T	S		E	P	A			A	L	I	S	T
T	R	I	P	V	A	N	W	I	N	K	L	E	
T	I	T	L	E			I	N	R	E			
O	B	E	Y		V	O	D	K	A		A	T	M	S
			C	I	A	O		A	R	R	A	Y	
	T	H	A	N	K	W	I	L	L	I	A	M	S
S	P	O	O	N		G	A	S		P	A	T	
T	R	U	S	S	F	E	I	N	G	O	L	D	
R	A	P	T		A	C	T	I		R	O	O	M	Y
A	T	E	E		C	H	E	T		A	V	O	I	D
W	E	E	D		T	O	M	E		N	E	R	D	S

13

O	D	D	S	■	S	P	O	K	E	S	■	B	A	R
L	I	E	U	■	E	L	A	I	N	E	■	E	M	U
G	E	M	M	Y	C	A	R	T	E	R	■	F	E	B
A	D	O	■	E	A	T	■	■	G	L	O	B	E	■
■	■	W	A	N	O	L	D	R	E	A	G	A	N	■
O	L	D	E	S	T	■	A	W	A	I	T	■	■	■
V	A	U	L	T	■	D	Y	E	R	■	H	A	L	E
A	C	O	L	Y	T	E	■	L	E	V	E	L	E	R
L	E	S	S	■	S	L	O	T	■	A	R	D	O	R
■	■	I	R	A	T	E	■	C	L	E	A	N	S	■
J	E	S	T	E	R	A	R	T	H	U	R	■	■	■
A	X	L	E	S	■	■	H	U	E	■	E	R	A	■
V	I	E	■	H	A	I	R	Y	T	R	U	M	A	N
A	L	P	■	I	N	C	O	M	E	■	S	I	G	N
N	E	T	■	P	A	Y	E	E	S	■	A	R	E	A

14

A	C	D	C	■	L	I	N	E	■	B	A	T	T	Y
A	R	E	A	■	I	T	E	M	■	A	L	O	H	A
H	E	N	R	Y	F	O	R	D	■	D	I	N	E	R
S	E	T	T	E	E	■	D	A	N	G	■	E	N	D
■	■	E	N	V	S	■	S	O	U	P	■	■	■	■
■	W	A	L	T	E	R	C	H	R	Y	S	L	E	R
V	I	D	■	A	S	T	A	■	■	S	I	E	G	E
E	L	I	S	■	T	A	I	N	T	■	S	O	Y	A
I	C	E	U	P	■	N	O	U	N	■	N	P	R	■
L	O	U	I	S	C	H	E	V	R	O	L	E	T	■
■	■	T	Y	P	O	■	A	N	T	I	■	■	■	■
L	A	D	■	C	A	T	T	■	A	C	T	S	A	S
E	P	O	C	H	■	B	I	G	W	H	E	E	L	S
A	E	I	O	U	■	E	L	I	A	■	R	E	I	N
F	S	T	O	P	■	D	E	N	Y	■	S	P	A	S

15

E	L	M	S		A	G	R	E	E		M	I	L	K
C	I	A	O		P	R	O	M	S		A	V	O	W
H	O	C	U	S	P	O	C	U	S		T	O	G	A
O	N	E		T	E	A	K			S	I	R	E	N
		H	E	N	N	Y	P	E	N	N	Y			
D	E	M	A	N	D			A	D	O	S			
A	G	E	S			M	A	N	G	O		S	P	A
D	O	T	H	E	H	O	K	E	Y	P	O	K	E	Y
E	S	E		B	A	N	A	L			N	Y	S	E
		B	O	R	E			I	S	L	E	T	S	
	H	A	N	K	Y	P	A	N	K	Y				
S	T	O	R	Y			A	N	T	I		A	O	K
P	A	G	E		H	O	D	G	E	P	O	D	G	E
A	R	A	L		M	A	R	I	N		V	A	L	E
M	A	N	Y		S	K	E	E	T		A	M	E	N

16

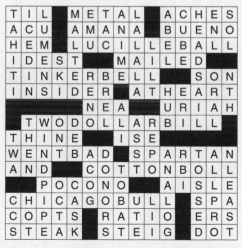

T	I	L		M	E	T	A	L		A	C	H	E	S
A	C	U		A	M	A	N	A		B	U	E	N	O
H	E	M		L	U	C	I	L	L	E	B	A	L	L
I	D	E	S	T		M	A	I	L	E	D			
T	I	N	K	E	R	B	E	L	L		S	O	N	
I	N	S	I	D	E	R		A	T	H	E	A	R	T
			N	E	A		U	R	I	A	H			
	T	W	O	D	O	L	L	A	R	B	I	L	L	
T	H	I	N	E		I	S	E						
W	E	N	T	B	A	D		S	P	A	R	T	A	N
A	N	D		C	O	T	T	O	N	B	O	L	L	
	P	O	C	O	N	O		A	I	S	L	E		
C	H	I	C	A	G	O	B	U	L	L		S	P	A
C	O	P	T	S		R	A	T	I	O		E	R	S
S	T	E	A	K		S	T	E	I	G		D	O	T

17

E	U	R	O		E	M	I	T		A	L	I	A	S
S	T	A	N		P	O	R	E		B	A	D	G	E
C	A	K	E	W	A	L	K	S		S	W	E	E	T
	H	E	R	O		A	S	T	O		C	A	S	H
		U	R	L	S		E	T	A	L				
	C	A	N	D	Y	S	T	R	I	P	E	R	S	
A	L	S		E	E	R		S	T	R	A	I	T	
D	I	T	C	H		S	U	P		S	K	I	L	L
S	M	I	L	E	S		C	A	P		T	A	C	
	B	R	O	W	N	I	E	P	O	I	N	T	S	
		I	S	O	N		A	L	T	O				
A	C	T	S		B	A	R	B		C	F	O	S	
T	O	O	T	H		P	I	E	C	H	A	R	T	S
V	I	D	E	O		E	G	A	D		I	S	E	E
S	N	O	R	E		T	A	R	S		R	O	M	A

18

O	L	A	V		E	R	A	S		A	C	H	E	D
J	A	P	E		X	O	U	T		B	O	O	T	Y
A	C	E	S		C	O	T	Y		D	U	R	A	N
Y	E	R	T	L	E	T	H	E	T	U	R	T	L	E
S	D	S		E	S	S	O		A	L	S	O		
	O	A	T	S		R	O	N		E	N	D	S	
D	I	N	G	S		S	E	G	A		H	O	I	
D	R	S	E	U	S	S		O	O	B	L	E	C	K
A	M	A		P	L	O	T		S	T	A	S	H	
Y	A	P	S		A	U	G		B	U	R	R		
	E	L	A	N		E	W	E	R		S	A	T	
S	P	R	I	N	G	F	I	E	L	D	M	A	S	S
H	O	S	E	D		A	S	I	A		Y	W	C	A
A	R	O	S	E		Z	E	S	T		T	H	O	R
G	E	N	T	S		E	L	S	E		H	O	T	S

19

20

21

S	W	A	M		R	A	S	H		D	A	I	S	Y
O	H	N	O		E	S	T	A		O	L	D	I	E
N	E	A	T		E	S	A	U		A	G	E	N	T
G	E	T	T	O	F	I	R	S	T	B	A	S	E	
			O	N	E	S			O	L	E			
E	S	S		T	R	I	R	E	M	E		F	I	T
L	O	T	T	O			A	L	E		H	I	D	E
B	A	L	L	P	A	R	K	F	I	G	U	R	E	S
O	P	E	C		S	U	E			C	H	E	A	T
W	Y	O		T	H	E	R	M	A	L		S	L	Y
		S	H	E			U	T	E	S				
	O	U	T	I	N	L	E	F	T	F	I	E	L	D
R	U	N	O	N		S	A	F	E		X	I	I	I
O	R	I	N	G		A	S	I	S		T	R	E	E
E	S	T	E	S		T	E	N	T		Y	E	N	S

22

I	B	E	R	I	A		J	A	I		S	T	A
D	A	N	A	N	G		C	U	T	S	H	O	R	T
O	N	E	D	G	E		A	L	L	E	Y	C	A	T
L	E	S	I	O	N		T	I	A		P	K	W	Y
		A	D	D		C	A	R	P	O	O	L	S
G	O	A	T		A	S	H		G	A	S		
A	C	C	E	S	S	C	O	D	E	S		F	A	B
L	H	A	S	A		A	F	R		T	A	L	I	A
S	O	D		F	O	R	T	U	N	A	T	E	L	Y
		F	E	R		H	M	O		L	E	S	S
C	A	M	I	S	O	L	E		N	S	A		
O	L	I	N		T	E	D		S	A	N	T	A	S
A	L	L	E	L	U	I	A		T	U	T	O	R	S
T	E	N	D	E	N	C	Y		O	N	A	P	A	R
S	S	E		I	D	A		P	A	N	E	L	S

23

A	P	T		C	H	I	L	I		G	O	R	E	N
D	A	Y		L	U	R	I	D		A	N	I	S	E
H	U	P	M	O	B	I	L	E		Z	A	P	P	A
O	L	E	I	N		S	Y	S	T	E	M			
C	A	S	S	I	S			A	B	A	S	E	D	
		O	N	E	L	U	M	P	O	R	T	W	O	
M	A	D		G	R	E	T	A		S	C	R	E	W
A	L	I	E		B	A	T	O	N		H	A	R	E
S	P	A	Y	S		P	E	R	I	L		Y	S	L
T	H	R	E	E	S	T	R	I	K	E	S			
S	A	Y	S	N	O			E	V	E	N	E	D	
		L	O	W	E	R	S		I	R	A	Q	I	
O	U	T	E	R		P	E	T	I	T	F	O	U	R
K	N	I	F	E		I	N	A	N	E		M	A	T
S	A	L	T	S		C	O	R	D	S		I	L	S

24

S	P	A	R	E		O	F	F	E	R		J	A	M
A	L	L	A	N		H	A	L	V	E		U	R	I
N	O	V	I	C	E	S	Q	U	A	D		N	I	L
S	W	A	N		M	U	S	E		T	O	K	E	N
		F	A	I	R			S	A	D	D	L	E	
N	O	T	A	B	L	E	H	O	P	P	E	R		
U	V	U	L	A		A	C	R	E		A	I	R	
D	A	N	L		P	A	R	T	Y		Y	W	C	A
E	L	I		T	E	M	P		C	O	E	U	R	
		N	O	Y	E	S	O	F	C	O	U	R	S	E
A	R	G	Y	L	L			R	A	N	G			
R	I	F	L	E		O	B	I	S		O	O	N	A
G	T	O		N	O	M	A	D	H	A	T	T	E	R
O	E	R		O	R	A	N	G		S	M	O	R	E
T	S	K		L	A	R	G	E		S	E	E	D	S

```
J E T S █ I M A █ A R E T O O
U P R O O T E D █ B A S I N S
T H U R G O O D █ A Z T E C S
█ █ B R O W N V B O A R D █
S P R E E █ █ E A R █
H U I T █ A N N E █ E E L E D
O L D █ A S E A █ O D D I T Y
P L E S S Y V F E R G U S O N
P I R A T E █ T R E E █ T I A
E N S O R █ E A R L █ T E L S
█ █ O P T █ B I N E T
█ O F E D U C A T I O N █
P A R L O R █ M A R S H A L L
A T E A M S █ P R E S A G E S
C H E N E Y █ S T S █ T O D D
```

```
L A Y S █ P H O N Y █ A W A Y
O R E O █ R A D I O █ R I M S
G O A L █ E L E G Y █ E T A L
J U S T A S I T H O U G H T █
A N T I C █ T O T █ H O M E R
M D S █ T E E █ C B S █ A U K
█ M I A █ W A R █ N Y R O
█ U P R I G H T P I A N O S █
A P E X █ E O S █ A W E █
B L T █ A R T █ S R A █ I F S
S I N A I █ C E L █ R A D I I
█ F A I R T O M I D D L I N G
A T M S █ I C I E R █ A D I N
R E E L █ L O T S A █ N I T E
M D S E █ T A S T Y █ S T E T
```

27

```
D I R E ■ T R A M P ■ C A S A
I D O L ■ R E C U R ■ A V O N
R E D S K Y A T M O R N I N G
T S E ■ H I P S ■ ■ A V A I L
■ ■ ■ B A N S ■ F I N A N C E
S P R A N G ■ S O A K S ■ ■ ■
I R A N ■ ■ K I N T E ■ T W O
D O G D A Y A F T E R N O O N
E W E ■ R E N T S ■ ■ O G R E
■ ■ ■ S N A G S ■ D R E A M S
T E M P E R A ■ H E A L ■ ■ ■
A L O E S ■ ■ S O L I ■ A C E
B L U E S I N T H E N I G H T
L E N D ■ B E A U T ■ R E I N
E N D S ■ N O T M E ■ E D N A
```

28

```
N O D ■ A F T E R ■ P O P U P
A L E ■ D O N N E ■ E L E N A
R E T ■ D U T C H T R E A T Y
C O H E I R ■ L E E S ■ C I E
■ ■ R A N T S ■ A N O T H E R
W R O U G H T I R O N Y ■ ■ ■
E O N ■ ■ S O S ■ R A R I N G
E V E R T ■ A S S ■ L O S E R
D E S I R E ■ U A R ■ V E E
■ ■ F U D G E F A C T O R Y ■
C O R T E G E ■ E C L A T ■ ■
E R O ■ P A T S ■ E O C E N E
C O L L A R S T U D Y ■ D O E
I N L E T ■ O L L I E ■ I L L
L O A T H ■ N O E N D ■ N O S
```

29

M	O	L	L		D	E	J	A		P	O	S	I	T
E	D	I	E		E	R	O	S		A	L	I	C	E
S	O	S	O		V	E	N	I		N	I	L	E	S
A	R	T	I	F	I	C	I	A	L	T	O	O	T	H
			V	A	S	T			I	R	S			
L	A	C		T	E	S	T	I	F	Y		G	T	O
A	R	U	B	A			A	R	E		W	R	A	P
P	O	P	U	L	A	R	C	A	R	D	G	A	M	E
E	M	I	T		R	F	K			U	N	D	E	R
L	A	D		R	E	D	S	T	A	R		E	R	A
		T	E	N			A	G	E	S				
H	I	G	H	W	A	Y	O	V	E	R	P	A	S	S
A	G	O	R	A		A	M	E	N		R	U	L	E
T	O	N	E	R		P	O	R	T		A	R	E	A
S	T	E	E	D		S	O	N	S		Y	A	W	N

30

S	A	H	I	B		O	P	E	R	A		B	A	R
A	M	I	N	O		W	A	L	T	S		O	N	O
P	I	C	K	Y	P	I	C	K	E	T		N	I	B
			C	E	N	T	S		A	U	N	T	Y	
R	A	P	S	O	N	G	S		L	I	B	Y	A	N
E	R	U	P	T	S			C	A	R	I	B		
S	T	P	A	T		B	O	O	Z	E		O	O	F
T	O	P	S		S	A	R	G	E		E	N	T	R
S	O	Y		B	A	R	B	S		P	E	N	T	A
		P	U	L	S	E			H	I	R	E	O	N
T	A	U	R	U	S		A	N	A	L	Y	T	I	C
A	P	P	L	E		E	R	O	D	E				
L	A	P		J	U	N	K	Y	J	U	N	K	E	T
I	R	E		A	N	G	I	E		P	I	A	N	O
A	T	T		Y	A	R	N	S		S	A	N	D	Y

31

W	A	L	K	S		A	B	E	L		N	A	T	S
I	N	E	R	T		C	L	I	O		I	N	I	T
S	T	E	A	L		C	A	N	O	P	E	N	E	R
P	I	C	K	U	P	T	H	E	P	A	C	E		
	S	H	A	K	E	S			L	E	M	O	N	
		T	E	N		B	A	W	L		E	R	E	
E	S	S	O		S	E	R	G	E	I		A	B	S
P	U	T	A	F	I	R	E	U	N	D	E	R	I	T
S	I	R		R	O	D	E	N	T		V	A	T	S
O	T	O		O	N	E	D		A	L	I			
M	E	N	D	S			A	P	O	L	L	O		
	G	E	T	T	H	E	L	E	A	D	O	U	T	
C	U	B	B	Y	H	O	L	E		T	O	R	T	E
S	P	O	T		O	M	A	R		H	E	A	R	S
I	N	X	S		R	E	N	T		E	R	N	E	S

32

O	A	H	U		G	O	O	P		D	A	R	N	S
O	L	A	N		A	C	R	E		E	L	I	O	T
M	I	D	D	L	E	E	A	R		P	L	A	T	A
P	B	S		A	L	A	N		L	O	O	S	E	N
H	I	T	C	H	I	N	G	P	O	S	T			
		L	O	C		L	Y	E	S	O	A	P		
A	D	E	E	R		S	H	E	A			M	N	O
C	O	F	F	E	E	T	A	B	L	E	B	O	O	K
E	S	T		L	A	T	E		L	O	O	N	Y	
D	E	S	P	A	I	R		A	D	S				
		E	N	T	R	A	N	C	E	H	A	L	L	
M	I	L	L	I	E		T	E	C	S		W	O	O
A	R	I	L	S		F	R	E	E	T	R	A	D	E
R	A	R	E	E		A	I	D	S		O	R	E	S
K	E	A	T	S		B	A	S	S		T	E	N	S

33

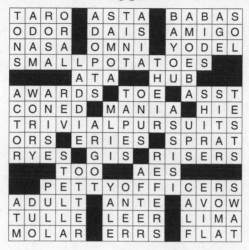

T	A	R	O		A	S	T	A		B	A	B	A	S
O	D	O	R		D	A	I	S		A	M	I	G	O
N	A	S	A		O	M	N	I		Y	O	D	E	L
S	M	A	L	L	P	O	T	A	T	O	E	S		
			A	T	A			H	U	B				
A	W	A	R	D	S		T	O	E		A	S	S	T
C	O	N	E	D		M	A	N	I	A		H	I	E
T	R	I	V	I	A	L	P	U	R	S	U	I	T	S
O	R	S		E	R	I	E	S		S	P	R	A	T
R	Y	E	S		G	I	S		R	I	S	E	R	S
		T	O	O			A	E	S					
	P	E	T	T	Y	O	F	F	I	C	E	R	S
A	D	U	L	T		A	N	T	E		A	V	O	W
T	U	L	L	E		L	E	E	R		L	I	M	A
M	O	L	A	R		E	R	R	S		F	L	A	T

34

E	R	I	C		L	I	L	A	C		A	M	E	N
D	A	D	O		A	B	O	I	L		P	I	L	E
T	H	O	M	A	S	M	O	R	E		A	S	I	S
		B	U	T	S			A	O	R	T	A	S	
O	B	L	I	G	E		D	O	N	A	T	E		
L	E	A	N	E	D		R	U	S	T		R	T	E
D	A	T	E	R		M	A	T	E	S		C	E	L
I	T	I	S		J	A	P	E	S		C	H	A	D
E	E	N		H	U	G	E	R		R	A	I	S	E
S	N	L		A	M	O	R		H	A	R	P	E	R
		O	L	D	B	O	Y		O	D	I	S	T	S
N	A	V	A	J	O			A	R	I	L			
A	L	E	C		J	O	H	N	M	I	L	T	O	N
S	E	R	E		E	L	A	T	E		O	K	I	E
H	E	S	S		T	A	M	I	L		N	O	L	O

35

B	E	E	C	H		S	A	L	T		I	S	A	K
A	D	L	A	I		O	R	E	O		A	C	R	E
Y	U	M	M	Y	Y	U	M	M	Y		G	R	A	D
			P	A	A	R				S	C	R	U	B	S
A	C	T	S		N	O	D	S		H	E	M	S	
T	H	A	I		K	N	E	E	D	E	E	P		
R	U	S	T	S		S	T	Y	E		T	I	A	
I	N	T	E	A	R	S		H	E	R	O	I	N	E
A	G	E		H	A	H	A			S	N	O	U	T
	S	T	A	G	E	M	O	M		T	U	R	N	
	A	G	A	R		A	S	I	A		A	S	E	A
A	O	R	T	A	S			L	A	I	R			
G	L	E	E		M	M	M	M	M	M	G	O	O	D
R	E	A	R		O	B	O	E		P	E	D	R	O
A	R	T	S		G	A	I	N		S	T	E	E	R

36

E	A	G	L	E		C	A	M	P		R	A	N	K
M	O	R	O	N		A	W	O	L		O	D	I	E
B	R	A	N	D	O	N	A	M	E		M	A	N	Y
E	T	S		G	R	E	Y		T	H	A	M	E	S
R	A	S	C	A	L	S		S	H	I	N			
			A	M	Y		P	H	O	T	O	O	P	S
P	A	S	T	E		H	A	I	R		F	L	A	T
A	U	T	O		B	E	R	R	A		O	G	L	E
C	R	A	B		E	A	S	T		G	R	A	S	P
T	A	B	U	L	A	T	E		S	O	U			
			R	I	C	H		C	L	A	M	S	U	P
L	E	N	G	T	H		G	O	A	L		P	R	O
I	D	O	L		B	O	N	O	V	O	Y	A	G	E
A	G	R	A		U	R	A	L		N	O	T	E	S
R	E	A	R		M	E	W	S		G	U	S	S	Y

37

H	A	U	L		I	R	I	S	H		C	H	I	A
A	S	T	A		T	A	B	O	O		L	O	O	N
S	T	I	C	K	S	H	I	F	T		U	P	T	O
N	I	C	E	L	Y		A	R	A	B	I	A	N	
T	R	A	D	E		A	C	R	O	S	S			
			E	C	R	U		D	I	O	N	N	E	
L	I	M	B		H	O	E	S		A	D	I	O	S
A	R	I	A		O	S	C	A	R		A	T	I	T
R	A	N	T	S		E	A	S	T		S	E	R	E
A	N	I	M	A	L		R	H	E	A				
			O	N	E	I	D	A		C	R	E	M	E
S	O	Y	B	E	A	N		S	N	A	R	E	S	
A	L	A	I		P	A	D	D	L	E	B	O	A	T
G	I	R	L		E	N	T	R	E		I	D	L	E
A	N	N	E		R	E	S	E	W		N	E	S	S

38

F	O	A	L		C	U	B	S		O	N	S	E	T
O	M	N	I		A	S	A	P		V	E	R	N	E
L	E	T	O		M	E	R	E		E	R	O	D	E
K	N	I	T	T	E	D	S	C	A	R	F			
			T	I	L			S	C	H		T	H	O
C	O	C	A	C	O	L	A		H	E	A	R	O	F
A	L	L			T	I	M	B	E	R	W	O	L	F
R	E	E	F	S		M	B	A		E	L	U	D	E
B	A	R	R	E	L	B	O	L	T			P	E	R
O	R	I	O	L	E		Y	I	E	L	D	E	R	S
N	Y	C		E	A	R			E	A	U			
			I	N	H	A	L	I	N	G	F	O	O	D
H	I	N	D	I		J	E	N	A		F	O	U	R
A	D	I	E	U		A	G	O	G		E	Z	R	A
S	A	L	E	M		H	O	N	E		L	E	S	T

39

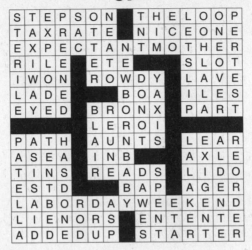

S	T	E	P	S	O	N		T	H	E	L	O	O	P
T	A	X	R	A	T	E		N	I	C	E	O	N	E
E	X	P	E	C	T	A	N	T	M	O	T	H	E	R
R	I	L	E		E	T	E		S	L	O	T		
I	W	O	N		R	O	W	D	Y		L	A	V	E
L	A	D	E			B	O	A		I	L	E	S	
E	Y	E	D		B	R	O	N	X		P	A	R	T
				L	E	R	O	I						
P	A	T	H		A	U	N	T	S		L	E	A	R
A	S	E	A		I	N	B			A	X	L	E	
T	I	N	S		R	E	A	D	S		L	I	D	O
E	S	T	D			B	A	P		A	G	E	R	
L	A	B	O	R	D	A	Y	W	E	E	K	E	N	D
L	I	E	N	O	R	S		E	N	T	E	N	T	E
A	D	D	E	D	U	P		S	T	A	R	T	E	R

40

S	O	N	I	C		H	O	L	M		I	R	E	S
E	R	I	C	H		E	R	I	E		N	O	A	H
W	A	K	E	I	S	L	A	N	D		N	A	V	E
O	R	E		S	C	I		T	A	P	E	R	E	D
N	E	S	T	E	A		T	Y	L	E	R			
		E	L	L	E	R		S	O	C	K	E	T	
D	O	W	N		D	R	A	W		N	I	N	A	S
I	R	O	N		S	O	F	A	S		R	O	S	A
S	C	R	I	P		O	F	A	N		C	B	E	R
K	A	N	S	A	S		I	C	A	L	L			
		C	Y	N	I	C		P	A	E	L	L	A
D	E	P	O	S	I	T		O	A	R		A	I	M
E	S	A	U		P	A	W	N	T	I	C	K	E	T
S	T	I	R		E	L	E	E		A	R	E	N	O
K	E	N	T		R	Y	E	S		T	O	R	S	O

41

42

43

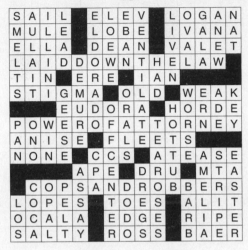

44

45

```
S T E M   ■   S T A B   ■   C E D A R
S O U R   ■   H E R O   ■   A L I V E
T E R M   ■   E R G O   ■   N A K E D
■   S O O N E R O R L A T E R   ■
■   ■   M O N O   ■   O R E   ■   ■
R A M   ■   V A R S I T Y   ■   G P A
A T O N E   ■   A N T   ■   F R A N
D O U B L E O R N O T H I N G
I L S A   ■   P O D   ■   O A T E R
O L E   ■   A C H I E S T   ■   S L Y
■   ■   G T O   ■   N E E D   ■   ■
■   F E A S T O R F A M I N E   ■
A L E U T   ■   P O O L   ■   T O B E
L O N G U   ■   E L L E   ■   S N A G
K E Y E D   ■   R E D D   ■   Y O Y O
```

46

```
S E L F   ■   C A C T I   ■   B R A T
E S A U   ■   A L I E N   ■   R A M A
A S I N   ■   T E A R S   ■   O D E S
L O D G E A C O M P L A I N T
■   ■   I L L   ■   ■   I O D I D E
A G O   ■   S O B   ■   O R B   ■   ■
C O T T A G E C H E E S E
E D I E   ■   A A A   ■   O M S K
■   C A B I N P R E S S U R E
■   ■   U S S   ■   A L A   ■   S I N
E T H I C S   ■   E G O   ■   ■
S H A C K U P T O G E T H E R
S I S I   ■   E L E N A   ■   T I D E
A N T E   ■   R E R A N   ■   E T T U
Y E A R   ■   S A I N T   ■   R S V P
```

47

S	W	E	P	T		A	J	A	R		S	I	P	S
P	A	T	I	O		N	O	P	E		T	N	U	T
A	D	A	G	E		E	K	E	D		R	A	R	A
				S	H	O	W	E	R	S	H	O	W	E	R
S	K	I	T	O	W					A	V	E	R	T
M	O	B	I	L	E	M	O	B	I	L	E		
E	A	S	E	D		I	M	O	F	F		C	P	R
A	L	E	S		P	A	N	T	S		S	H	O	O
R	A	N		C	O	M	I	C		C	O	A	S	T
			P	O	L	I	S	H	P	O	L	I	S	H
C	L	E	A	N			E	N	U	R	E	S		
A	U	G	U	S	T	A	U	G	U	S	T		
R	A	Y	S		E	X	P	O		O	I	L	E	D
D	U	P	E		A	L	T	O		L	O	T	T	O
S	S	T	S		L	E	O	N		E	N	R	O	N

48

B	L	A	B	S		F	A	R	E	D		A	B	C
A	U	D	I	T		I	M	B	R	O	G	L	I	O
S	N	I	D	E		L	O	I	N	C	L	O	T	H
I	C	E		A	C	L	U		S	O	T	T	O
C	H	U	C	K	B	E	R	R	Y		B	A	Y	S
		U	S	S		E	A	S	E	L	
R	O	I	L		A	I	S	L	E		I	Z	E
R	U	M	P	E	L	S	T	I	L	T	S	K	I	N
S	T	P		L	E	T	O	N		W	E	P	T
	R	E	F	E	R		A	L	A	
A	T	O	N		R	O	U	N	D	A	B	O	U	T
L	O	V	E	S		T	O	O	T		G	N	U
P	R	I	M	E	C	U	T	S		H	E	L	I	X
E	A	S	Y	T	O	S	E	E		A	R	E	T	E
S	H	E		H	E	A	R	D		M	A	R	E	S

49

50

51

O	N	R	Y	E		S	A	R	A	N		D	A	B
B	A	C	O	N		E	L	O	P	E		I	G	O
S	H	A	K	E	S	(P)	E	(A)	R	E		L	A	W
			E	M	O	T	E	D		S	M	A	Z	E
D	U	B	L	I	N		S	C	O	O	P	E	R	
O	S	U		E	Y	E	S		A	N	N	I		
G	U	L	F	S		A	T	M	S		I	D	E	A
M	A	L	L		F	R	U	I	T		C	(A)	R	T
A	L	(F)	A		O	L	D	S		N	A	(T)	A	L
		(I)	N	C	A		Y	O	G	A		(E)	S	A
B	I	(G)	G	A	M	E		A	S	I	D	E	S	
O	T	H	E	R		V	A	U	L	T	S			
R	A	T		H	A	I	R	(R)	(A)	(I)	(S)	(I)	(N)	G
O	L	E		O	R	L	O	N		E	U	R	O	S
N	O	R		P	E	S	O	S		R	E	A	T	A

52

K	E	E	L		R	A	M	P	S		A	F	A	R
N	Y	S	E		I	D	E	A	L		B	O	L	O
O	R	S	O	N	B	E	A	N	O		O	N	T	O
T	E	E	N	I	E	S	T			M	U	Z	A	K
			I	C	Y			A	T	I	T			
N	O	P		K	E	N	O	G	R	I	F	F	E	Y
A	M	A	S	S		O	R	E	O		A	L	E	E
B	A	L	I		S	T	O	N	Y		C	O	R	A
O	N	I	N		P	A	N	T		L	E	W	I	S
B	I	N	G	O	C	R	O	S	B	Y		N	E	T
			A	D	A	Y			A	S	K			
G	R	A	P	E			E	S	T	O	N	I	A	N
O	U	Z	O		T	R	E	N	T	L	O	T	T	O
O	D	O	R		A	U	R	A	L		W	C	T	U
N	E	V	E		G	R	O	P	E		S	H	U	N

53

| T | A | T | A | | O | N | U | S | | | P | R | A | D | O |

(crossword solution grid 53)

T A T A · O N U S · · P R A D O
O B I T · F E S T · · R E S I N
M E E T S F A C E T O F A C E
S T R I P · · G R A F · P E A
· · L A N E · E M I L · ·
· S T A N D S T O E T O T O E
A L I · K A T E · S N A R L
L E A N · K E E P S · G R A M
P E R O N · N E A L · D T S
S T A R E S E Y E T O E Y E ·
· · A M I N · R E G S · ·
A B E · E G G S · A C H O O
W A L K S H A N D I N H A N D
A D L A I · G O O D · E L I E
Y E A T S · E W E S · W E T S

54

W H O A · M O S A I C · U L E
H I N T · O P E N T O · H A T
I T E M · B A L D E R D A S H
G A S · K I L L S · S O U S A
· S E O U L · · R E V L O N
B L A T H E R S K I T E · ·
O U T I N · E P I C S · T I P
A M E S · R H I N O · C O N E
S P R · D E A L T · L A N C E
· · G O B B L E D Y G O O K
E R R A T A · · O N E A M ·
L O O S E · P E A C E · V E G
F L A P D O O D L E · M A T E
I F S · O R E G O N · G I A N
N E T · N O T Y E T · M L X X

```
P R I M | | G E R M | | T O A S T
O O N A | | E L I A | | O L L I E
O M A N | | T A L C | | P E S O S
L E T I T A L L H A N G O U T
| R A N G | | O N O | P X S
A S A | T R E S | S T P |
R U N S | I D L Y | C O N G A
K I C K U P Y O U R H E E L S
S T E I N | S E M I | T A U T
| N C O | S A P S | T E A
S C H | U P S | C O I F |
P A I N T T H E T O W N R E D
I D T A G | O D O R | T E A R
T E M P E | R E A D | R A V E
S T E A M | E N D S | O K E D
```

```
S H I V | A P P T | R E C A P
A E R O | C L U E | E R U P T
G N A T | C A N D I D A T E S
A R T I S T I C | R N S |
S I E N A | T H Y M E | A L I
| G N U | C O A C H M E N
A S I S | S O A K | K A B O B
D E L I | S P R E E | N E N E
D E L T A | I D L E | G R A D
T I G E R C U B | L E I |
O N O | M A M A S | A N G U S
| O R R | L A S T G A S P
A T T H E P O L L S | C L E O
L O U I S | L O S T | H A U T
B E G O T | E T A S | A S P S
D
```

57

L	Y	N	X		P	S	S	T		S	T	A	R	E
B	E	A	M		E	C	H	O		E	A	S	E	L
S	A	N	E		R	O	A	M		A	R	I	E	L
	H	A	N	D	O	N	H	A	N	D	O	F	F	S
			O	N	E		H	O	O	T				
D	E	C	A	Y	S		H	A	I	G		T	A	P
A	L	A	M	O		S	E	W	S		L	O	G	O
T	A	K	E	U	P	T	A	K	E	D	O	W	N	S
U	T	E	S		O	A	R	S		I	V	I	E	S
M	E	D		S	P	I	T		T	S	E	T	S	E
			S	T	I	R		T	A	C				
W	O	R	K	I	N	W	O	R	K	O	U	T	S	
A	L	I	E	N		A	L	E	E		C	O	O	L
S	L	E	E	T		Y	E	A	R		L	U	R	E
P	A	N	T	S		S	O	T	S		A	R	E	A

58

S	P	A	M		S	N	O	B		A	T	A	L	E
A	L	S	O		W	A	R	E		R	O	L	E	X
S	A	I	L		A	R	C	H		A	B	A	T	E
H	I	D	D	E	N	C	H	A	R	G	E	S		
A	D	E	S	T	E			R	O	O				
			H	E	A	D		K	N	O	W	E	R	
D	U	A	N	E		T	I	N	E		R	I	T	A
U	N	D	E	R	C	O	V	E	R	A	G	E	N	T
M	E	I	N		A	P	E	R		M	Y	N	A	S
A	S	T	E	R	N		R	O	B	O				
			E	S	Q			I	N	T	E	R	S	
	C	A	M	O	U	F	L	A	G	E	N	E	T	
J	O	Y	C	E		I	R	I	S		N	E	M	O
A	H	A	R	D		R	A	Z	E		T	R	I	O
M	O	N	E	Y		E	T	A	S		H	O	T	L

59

I	C	E	S		B	A	L	M		S	W	O	R	E
D	I	S	H		E	S	A	U		M	A	Y	O	R
E	N	T	R		A	C	D	C		O	G	L	E	R
A	C	E	I	N	T	H	E	H	O	L	E			
L	O	R	N	A				O	R	D		A	S	A
			K	I	N	G	O	F	B	E	A	S	T	S
I	F	S		L	A	I	R			R	O	S	E	S
R	O	O	F		M	A	D	A	M		L	E	N	A
A	C	R	E	S		E	D	A	M		T	O	Y	
Q	U	E	E	N	F	O	R	A	D	A	Y			
I	S	R		E	T	A			Y	E	A	S	T	
			J	A	C	K	B	E	N	I	M	B	L	E
N	O	V	A	K		L	A	M	E		E	B	A	N
O	X	I	D	E		E	L	M	S		N	E	T	S
D	O	Z	E	R		Y	E	A	S		I	S	E	E

60

B	E	S	T		O	N	E	N	D		C	E	D	E
A	R	N	O		R	U	M	O	R		O	M	A	R
Y	O	U	M	U	S	T	B	E	J	O	K	I	N	G
H	O	B	B	S		M	A	S		B	I	L	K	O
			O	P	E	S		F	E	E				
W	H	E	N	P	I	G	S	F	L	Y		P	L	O
H	A	R	D	E	R		Y	A	O		I	S	A	Y
A	L	M	A	N	A	C		T	R	A	S	H	T	V
L	E	A	K		N	O	D		I	N	T	A	K	E
E	S	S		T	H	E	R	E	S	N	O	W	A	Y
			A	H	A		A	N	T	I				
A	D	I	E	U		A	G	R		K	I	O	S	K
A	I	N	T	G	O	N	N	A	H	A	P	P	E	N
R	E	I	N		D	I	E	G	O		S	A	N	E
E	T	T	A		E	S	T	E	E		O	L	D	E

61

A	C	C	T	■	C	A	R	N	E	■	E	D	I	T
H	O	O	K	■	E	L	I	A	S	■	N	Y	S	E
S	O	L	O	F	L	I	G	H	T	■	A	N	O	N
O	L	D	■	L	E	S	S	■	R	O	M	A	N	S
■	■	H	A	R	T	■	S	A	L	E	M	■	■	■
W	A	T	E	R	Y	■	P	A	N	E	L	I	S	T
A	G	R	E	E	■	T	A	N	G	O	■	C	H	A
S	A	I	L	■	S	I	R	E	E	■	A	D	I	N
T	I	O	■	O	U	T	E	R	■	D	R	U	N	K
E	N	S	E	M	B	L	E	■	D	E	C	O	Y	S
■	■	O	L	I	V	E	■	P	O	L	O	■	■	■
D	O	N	A	T	E	■	A	I	N	T	■	A	H	A
A	H	A	T	■	R	A	J	Q	U	A	R	T	E	T
R	I	T	E	■	T	R	O	U	T	■	B	O	A	T
T	O	A	D	■	S	T	Y	E	S	■	I	N	D	Y

62

W	A	S	P	■	L	A	S	S	■	B	I	N	G	O
I	D	O	L	■	U	S	T	A	■	U	R	B	A	N
M	O	N	A	■	C	A	I	N	■	S	E	A	L	E
P	R	I	N	C	E	P	R	I	N	T	S	■	■	■
S	E	C	T	O	R	■	■	T	A	O	■	A	L	T
■	■	S	U	N	D	A	Y	S	U	N	D	A	E	■
P	E	A	■	P	E	A	L	■	A	T	E	A	S	E
L	A	M	B	■	■	D	O	G	■	■	O	P	E	N
A	S	P	E	C	T	■	N	E	A	P	■	T	R	Y
C	E	L	L	A	R	S	E	L	L	E	R	■	■	■
E	L	Y	■	P	E	I	■	■	A	R	I	S	E	S
■	■	M	U	S	S	E	L	M	U	S	C	L	E	■
P	A	P	A	L	■	T	R	I	O	■	K	A	L	E
A	G	A	Z	E	■	E	G	A	D	■	E	R	I	K
T	O	L	E	T	■	R	O	M	E	■	D	E	E	S

63

T	I	F	F	S		S	T	U	D		B	A	R	A
A	D	U	L	T		P	O	S	E		E	T	A	L
M	A	R	I	O		E	R	M	A		E	L	H	I
			G	L	A	C	I	A	L	S	T	A	R	E
M	U	S	H	E	R		I	T	T		S	A	N	
A	T	I	T		R	A	I	L		O	A	T	H	
R	A	S	P		A	I	D		G	M	C			
C	H	I	L	L	Y	R	E	C	E	P	T	I	O	N
		A	U	S		A	P	T		Y	O	G	A	
	C	O	N	S		S	L	A	M		O	N	L	Y
S	O	N		T	O	P		A	M	U	S	E	S	
C	O	L	D	S	H	O	U	L	D	E	R			
O	K	I	E		M	U	S	E		T	A	P	E	D
F	I	N	E		A	S	E	A		A	G	I	L	E
F	E	E	D		N	E	R	D		L	E	T	I	N

64

J	U	T	S		L	A	S	T		P	A	C	E	R
A	T	O	P		O	R	C	A		A	D	O	R	E
W	A	G	E		C	O	A	X		R	O	D	I	N
	H	O	W	V	A	S	T	I	S	S	P	A	C	E
			I	L	E		L	O	T					
M	A	S	O	N	S		F	L	A	N		P	A	N
A	L	L	A	N		Q	U	I	T		S	A	T	E
B	O	O	K	Y	O	U	R	S	E	A	T	N	O	W
E	N	T	S		K	I	L	T		M	A	I	N	E
L	E	S		S	A	P	S		D	A	N	C	E	R
		A	M	P		F	I	T						
S	P	A	C	E	I	S	L	I	M	I	T	E	D	
C	A	R	O	L		P	U	L	P		A	W	A	Y
O	V	E	R	T		A	X	E	L		L	A	Z	E
W	E	A	N	S		M	E	T	E		K	N	E	W

65

T	Y	R	O	■	B	E	A	M	■	T	U	B	A	S
R	O	A	R	■	U	C	L	A	■	U	S	U	R	P
I	D	L	E	■	G	R	I	D	■	R	O	M	E	O
B	E	L	L	Y	B	U	T	T	O	N	■	B	A	T
E	L	Y	S	E	E	■	■	V	I	T	A	L	■	■
■	■	■	E	G	A	D	S	■	L	O	V	E	I	N
J	E	B	■	G	R	I	T	T	Y	■	E	B	A	Y
A	M	A	S	S	■	S	I	R	■	F	R	E	T	S
D	I	L	L	■	S	C	R	I	B	E	■	E	E	E
E	L	L	I	O	T	■	S	O	I	L	S	■	■	■
■	■	O	P	R	A	H	■	■	G	L	E	A	M	S
A	G	T	■	B	R	E	A	D	B	A	S	K	E	T
R	A	B	B	I	■	E	L	L	A	■	T	I	D	E
A	B	O	U	T	■	D	O	I	N	■	E	R	I	N
T	E	X	T	S	■	S	W	I	G	■	T	A	C	O

66

C	A	N	C	A	N	■	■	■	T	U	T	T	U	T
E	P	A	U	L	E	T	■	S	A	N	R	E	M	O
C	O	M	R	A	D	E	■	W	I	S	E	M	A	N
I	R	E	S	■	■	S	T	E	L	E	S	■	■	■
L	T	D	■	O	U	T	W	A	I	T	■	B	B	B
■	■	■	O	S	B	O	R	N	■	B	O	R	O	■
N	O	S	■	M	E	A	T	■	G	O	O	G	O	O
E	S	T	O	P	■	N	I	M	■	U	N	I	O	N
C	H	I	C	H	I	■	M	E	S	S	■	E	K	E
K	E	N	T	■	R	E	E	D	I	T	■	■	■	■
S	A	G	■	M	I	D	R	I	B	S	■	Z	O	E
■	■	■	M	E	D	U	S	A	■	■	P	O	U	R
A	S	I	A	T	I	C	■	■	T	O	R	O	N	T	O
P	A	S	S	O	U	T	■	■	E	L	O	P	E	R	S
T	O	M	T	O	M	■	■	■	D	E	E	D	E	E

67

N	A	R	C		F	L	A	T	S		M	E	S	A
O	L	I	O		R	O	G	U	E		E	M	I	R
B	L	O	C		A	C	U	R	A		T	U	N	E
O	U	T	O	F	T	H	E	B	L	U	E			
D	R	E	A	R				O	U	T	R	A	G	E
Y	E	R		O	R	E	S		P	A	M	P	A	S
			S	T	O	R	E	S		A	I	N	T	
	W	I	T	H	N	O	W	A	R	N	I	N	G	
R	A	T	A			S	E	G	U	E	D			
I	N	B	R	E	D		R	O	T	H		E	A	T
B	E	E	G	E	E	S			R	A	N	G	E	
	A	L	L	O	F	A	S	U	D	D	E	N		
W	H	I	Z		E	D	I	C	T		D	E	N	S
H	A	T	E		T	A	R	R	Y		L	A	D	E
O	D	O	R		E	S	S	E	X		E	R	A	S

68

J	A	B		I	M	L	A	T	E		W	I	N	E
A	E	R		S	U	I	S	S	E		A	L	E	X
N	I	A		A	U	T	H	O	R	M	I	L	N	E
D	O	W	D		M	A	Y	S		O	K	I	E	S
J	U	N	E	A	U			B	R	I	C			
		B	L	U	E	S	M	A	N	K	I	N	G
S	E	P	T	A		P	H	I	L		I	T	E	R
O	U	R		R	E	S	E	A	L	S		L	I	E
U	R	I	S		D	O	R	M		S	L	Y	L	Y
P	O	E	T	C	U	M	M	I	N	G	S			
	D	A	R	C			E	T	A	L	I	I	
W	H	O	M	E		U	S	F	L		T	E	N	K
R	A	P	P	E	R	C	O	O	L	J		A	N	N
A	L	E	E		E	L	I	X	I	R		R	I	O
P	O	N	D		M	A	R	X	E	S		N	E	W

69

```
A M O R   A V I D   E J E C T
R O L E   D I N O   V A L O R
I T S D E J A V U   E Z I N E
A T E S T   L O B E   Z A N Y
S O N T A G   L L A M A
      A L L O V E R A G A I N
T S A R   A W E   T S E T S E
E L I   D S L   S H H   O A T
R A D I U S   E T D   I N N S
I T S D E J A V U A L L
      C L A R O   Y A L I E S
M E G A   W I L D   V E R V E
E X E R T   O V E R A G A I N
S P A D E   S E E D   A T A D
H O R S E   O D D S   L E N S
```

70

```
B A S E D   E G A D   P A R S
I R E N E   R I D E   T R O T
G E E N A D A V I S   A C M E
  S M I L E   E D I T   E E R
    S U S A N S A R A N D O N
O U T S I D E   S E R A
A P O   N O R D   T Y P E A
R O B S   N O E A R   S H A G
S N E A K   B R E T   O R E
      L A S S   O P E N E N D
J A C K N I C H O L S O N
E M U   E C H O   A T T I C
T U R K   K E V I N B A C O N
E S S O   O M E N   A T I L T
R E E D   F E R N   N E A T H
```

71

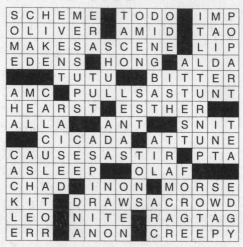

```
S C H E M E █ T O D O █ I M P
O L I V E R █ A M I D █ T A O
M A K E S A S C E N E █ L I P
E D E N S █ H O N G █ A L D A
█ █ T U T U █ B I T T E R
A M C █ P U L L S A S T U N T
H E A R S T █ E S T H E R █ █
A L L A █ █ A N T █ S N I T
█ C I C A D A █ A T T U N E
C A U S E S A S T I R █ P T A
A S L E E P █ █ O L A F █ █
C H A D █ I N O N █ M O R S E
K I T █ D R A W S A C R O W D
L E O █ N I T E █ R A G T A G
E R R █ A N O N █ C R E E P Y
```

72

```
A L A R █ H E E D █ S M E A R
S A D E █ A R C O █ W R E N S
S N O W █ T O R N █ A F L A T
H A R R Y H O U D I N I █ █
E I E I O █ █ I N E X A C T
█ █ T U T S I █ G E I G E R
H E L E N H U N T █ T O D O
E C O █ G E C K O E S █ N E V
W O M B █ █ H E N R Y H Y D E
E L A I N E █ D I A N E █ █
R I N G E R S █ C R A P S
█ █ H E R M A N N H E S S E
J I H A D █ E Q U I █ I T A L
A V A I L █ L U M P █ A R T E
G E N R E █ L A B S █ M O S S
```

73

```
A V E R . W O R S T . E D G E
W A R E . A N I T A . M O L T
A L U M . R E F I T . S U E T
C U P O F C O F F E E . G N U
S E T T E R . F R E S H .
. . E D I T S . S L I N G S
R E F S . M O O T . E X U L T
E A R . T E A C H E R . T O A
P R I M O . D I A L . E S P Y
S N E A K S . O D E T S . .
. D R Y E R . M A T M A N
A P E . O R A N G E J U I C E
H U G S . A C O R N . A N T E
E R G O . P E T I T . R E E D
M E S S . E D E N S . Y O D A
```

74

```
O C C A M . J O S H . M A R G
S H A M E . A X L E . C B E R
H A P P Y . B E E S . S A B U
A R I S E S . N E S T . L O M
P A T . R I D . P E A S O U P
E D A M . G R A Y . C A N N Y
D E L I . N E T . W I N E D .
. . S N O W W H I T E . .
. A B H O R . A O L . S W I T
S T A I R . S R O S . T I T O
E A S T M A N . D O C . R E L
N T H . S U E Y . N O T E R S
T U F T . D E A L . N O T A T
T R U E . E Z R A . E R A T O
O K L A . N Y N Y . D O P E Y
```

75

```
A W A R D S   ■ C O M P   ■ C C S
P O T I O N   ■ O B O E   ■ A R E
R O A D W A R R I O R   ■ M E N
■   ■ E N T E R   ■ T E N E T S
U S S R   ■ C D I V   ■ ■ E R I E
M A L   ■ R H O D E I S L A N D
P R I M A   ■ ■ A T O M S   ■
S I D E C A R   ■ S N O O K E R
■   ■ R E N E W   ■ ■ K N A V E
R O W E D A S H O R E   ■ T E N
O R A L   ■ ■ T I N A   ■ C E N T
T A N Y A S   ■ T E S L A   ■
T N T   ■ R O D E S H O T G U N
E G O   ■ C Y A N   ■ E S T A T E
D E N   ■ H A M S   ■ S T Y L E D
```

76

```
V I C E S   ■ C A S A S   ■ B A T
E C L A T   ■ H I P P O   ■ E P A
T E E T O T A L L E R   ■ D A B
■   ■ R I P E R   ■ A R T D E C O
L O I N   ■ E G O S   ■ ■ E C H O
A R C   ■ O N E W H O T A K E S
S C A R F   ■ ■ L E A R N   ■
S A L U T E D   ■ S T A N D B Y
■   ■ B E S O S   ■ ■ C A I R O
I N V E N T O R Y A T   ■ S A Y
N E I N   ■ ■ R I E L   ■ O C T O
T W O S T E P   ■ N E R V E   ■
A T L   ■ A G O L F C O U R S E
C O E   ■ P A S E O   ■ U L N A R
T N T   ■ E N T E R   ■ T E S L A
```

77

B	E	B	O	P		G	A	R	B	O		B	L	T
I	R	A	N	I		I	D	E	A	L		R	U	R
B	E	D	A	N	D	B	O	A	R	D		A	C	E
			H	U	E	S			T	A	C	K	Y	
B	A	B	O	O	N	S		S	M	I	L	E	Y	S
O	T	O	O	L	E		R	H	U	M	B	A		
A	T	O	N	E		L	E	A	S	E		N	A	T
R	A	M	A		V	O	I	D	S		E	D	N	A
S	R	A		F	O	G	G	Y		U	N	B	O	X
		N	O	R	T	O	N		I	N	C	I	S	E
C	A	D	D	I	E	S		P	S	A	L	T	E	R
R	U	B	E	S			A	L	I	I	I			
E	D	U		B	O	R	N	A	N	D	B	R	E	D
S	I	S		E	J	E	C	T		E	M	O	T	E
T	E	T		E	S	T	E	E		D	W	E	E	B

78

P	A	S	A		G	E	R	A	L	D		C	H	E
A	L	O	T		O	U	N	C	E	S		L	E	X
B	I	L	L	Y	G	R	A	H	A	M		O	R	A
L	O	V	E	M	E		S	E	R		I	C	B	M
O	N	E	A	C	T	S		S	N	A	C	K		
		S	A	T	I	E		S	L	E	W	E	D	
T	A	C	T		E	L	M	O		A	S	I	D	E
H	E	R		C	R	A	C	K	E	R		S	I	N
A	R	O	L	L		S	E	R	A		G	E	T	S
N	O	S	O	A	P		E	A	S	E	L			
		S	O	D	O	I		S	T	R	A	S	S	E
R	A	F	T		L	C	D		S	A	S	H	A	Y
A	L	I		P	L	A	Y	S	I	T	S	A	F	E
C	A	R		R	E	R	E	A	D		E	W	E	R
E	S	E		O	N	E	D	G	E		S	L	R	S

79

C	P	A	S		R	I	S	K	S		O	S	H	A
D	E	F	T		O	S	H	E	A		L	U	I	S
R	A	R	A		L	E	O	N	I		A	R	E	S
O	N	E	L	I	F	E	T	O	L	I	V	E		
M	U	S	E	D				B	O	N		F	I	B
	T	H	R	E	E	B	L	I	N	D	M	I	C	E
			A	M	M	O			O	A	R	E	D	
S	O	D	S		S	W	O	R	E		T	E	S	S
O	D	I	U	M		P	A	L	S					
F	I	V	E	E	A	S	Y	P	I	E	C	E	S	
A	N	I		R	N	A			A	L	L	O	R	
	S	E	V	E	N	Y	E	A	R	I	T	C	H	
S	H	I	V		M	E	A	T	S		P	O	K	Y
P	A	V	E		I	S	L	E	S		O	R	E	M
A	M	E	N		A	T	E	S	T		N	O	T	E

80

F	I	L	E		M	O	L	E		G	A	M	U	T
A	R	I	D		S	P	A	M		A	B	A	S	E
C	O	N	G	O	G	A	M	E		R	A	N	U	P
E	N	T	E	R		L	A	R	V	A		G	A	I
		S	A	S	S			A	G	E	O	L	D	
R	E	T	I	N	A		C	A	M	E	T	O		
S	L	A	N	G	Y		A	M	P		A	F	R	O
V	I	N		E	G	O	M	A	I	L		G	A	P
P	E	G	S		R	Y	E		R	E	M	O	T	E
		O	N	C	A	L	L		E	V	A	D	E	D
B	E	L	L	O	C		I	S	A	K				
A	R	I		L	E	A	R	N		N	E	R	T	S
C	I	N	C	O		G	O	B	E	T	W	E	E	N
O	C	E	A	N		A	M	E	N		A	B	R	A
N	A	S	T	Y		R	E	D	S		R	A	M	P

81

```
E D N A    B A A S    S M E L L
G R I T    U C L A    T A L I A
G A L E    G R A M    A L L E Y
  W E A T H E R B U R E A U
    M A O      A M T
L I U    R U T H    P R A I S E
E R S E    S E E R    E I D E R
H E A T H E R L O C K L E A R
A N I T A    M E S H    S A T E
R E R U N S    N E A R    L S D
    D C C      R E A
  L E A T H E R J A C K E T
S A Y S O    L A U D    I R A Q
O N E T O    L I N E    T I L E
P E D A L    O D E S    A C E D
```

82

```
R A B A T    G O S H    T B S P
I M A C S    E N T O    R A T A
B A N T U    N E A R    O R E S
    I N D I A N A J O N E S
A T H    A Y E    T U P E L O
T R A U M A    L A I D    Y E N
V I R G I N I A W O O L F
S O U L      M P H    I R I S
    M I N N E S O T A F A T S
I R S    I A T E    A R E N O T
N I C E L Y    C R T    K O S
S T A T E S P E O P L E
A U R A    A L E R    E R U P T
N A U T    Y E L P    S I N A I
E L M S    S A S S    S K I L L
```

83

E	M	M	A	■	■	R	O	T	O	R	■	P	A	L
L	O	I	N	S	■	E	V	A	D	E	■	E	L	I
C	U	T	T	H	E	C	A	R	D	S	■	R	O	E
I	N	T	E	R	V	A	L	■	■	E	A	S	E	D
D	D	S	■	O	I	L	■	S	P	A	C	E	■	■
■	■	■	P	U	L	L	T	H	E	L	E	V	E	R
S	C	A	L	D	■	■	H	E	R	S	■	E	M	U
E	A	S	Y	■	C	A	R	A	T	■	A	R	I	D
A	M	S	■	S	O	L	E	■	■	P	I	E	T	Y
S	P	I	N	T	H	E	W	H	E	E	L	■	■	■
■	■	S	E	I	N	E	■	U	T	E	■	N	A	T
L	I	T	E	R	■	■	I	N	C	R	E	A	S	E
A	D	A	■	R	O	L	L	T	H	E	D	I	C	E
M	E	N	■	E	R	A	S	E	■	D	E	V	O	N
B	A	T	■	D	E	B	A	R	■	■	N	E	T	S

84

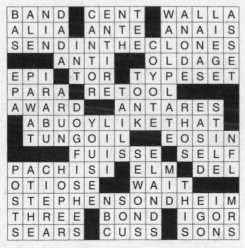

B	A	N	D	■	C	E	N	T	■	W	A	L	L	A
A	L	I	A	■	A	N	T	E	■	A	N	A	I	S
S	E	N	D	I	N	T	H	E	C	L	O	N	E	S
■	■	■	A	N	T	I	■	■	O	L	D	A	G	E
E	P	I	■	T	O	R	■	T	Y	P	E	S	E	T
P	A	R	A	■	R	E	T	O	O	L	■	■	■	■
A	W	A	R	D	■	■	A	N	T	A	R	E	S	■
■	A	B	U	O	Y	L	I	K	E	T	H	A	T	■
■	T	U	N	G	O	I	L	■	■	E	O	S	I	N
■	■	■	F	U	I	S	S	E	■	S	E	L	F	■
P	A	C	H	I	S	I	■	E	L	M	■	D	E	L
O	T	I	O	S	E	■	W	A	I	T	■	■	■	■
S	T	E	P	H	E	N	S	O	N	D	H	E	I	M
T	H	R	E	E	■	B	O	N	D	■	I	G	O	R
S	E	A	R	S	■	C	U	S	S	■	S	O	N	S

85

F	E	T	E		A	F	A	R		D	A	C	H	A
A	C	R	E		N	A	S	A		E	T	H	A	N
T	H	E	G	O	O	D	S	H	E	P	H	E	R	D
S	O	X		D	I	E	T		Q	U	O	T	E	S
			V	E	N	D		C	U	T	S			
P	A	L	E	S	T		G	R	A	Y		C	H	E
A	C	E	R	S		U	R	A	L		W	H	O	A
T	H	E	B	A	D	N	E	W	S	B	E	A	R	S
T	E	C	S		R	I	A	L		L	E	O	N	E
I	S	H		M	I	T	T		L	A	P	S	E	D
			P	A	V	E		H	A	Z	Y			
O	C	T	A	N	E		J	U	T	E		I	C	K
T	H	E	U	G	L	Y	A	M	E	R	I	C	A	N
T	E	R	S	E		A	V	O	N		D	O	M	O
O	W	N	E	R		M	A	R	T		A	N	E	W

86

C	A	S	H		S	A	T	I	N	Y		T	E	A
O	B	O	E		A	T	O	N	C	E		A	R	T
D	E	M	I		L	O	O	K	A	L	I	K	E	S
		B	R	E	A	M			A	P	I	E	C	E
F	I	R		S	M	I	T	E		I	O	T	A	
I	D	E	N	T	I	C	A	L	T	W	I	N	S	
T	E	R	I			N	I	N	A					
	D	O	P	P	E	L	G	A	N	G	E	R	S	
			I	D	E	E			V	E	T	S		
	S	P	I	T	T	I	N	G	I	M	A	G	E	S
S	P	U	D			S	T	O	R	E		U	T	E
A	R	M	O	R	S		V	I	T	A	L			
D	U	P	L	I	C	A	T	E	S		S	A	T	E
A	C	E		G	A	L	O	R	E		I	R	A	S
T	E	D		S	T	E	R	N	S		A	S	P	S

87

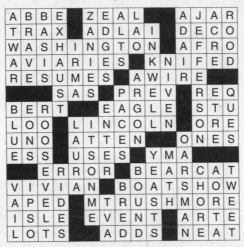

```
A B B E ■ Z E A L ■ ■ A J A R
T R A X ■ A D L A I ■ D E C O
W A S H I N G T O N ■ A F R O
A V I A R I E S ■ K N I F E D
R E S U M E S ■ A W I R E ■ ■
■ ■ ■ S A S ■ P R E V ■ R E Q
B E R T ■ ■ E A G L E ■ S T U
L O O ■ L I N C O L N ■ O R E
U N O ■ A T T E N ■ O N E S ■
E S S ■ U S E S ■ Y M A ■ ■ ■
■ ■ E R R O R ■ B E A R C A T
V I V I A N ■ B O A T S H O W
A P E D ■ M T R U S H M O R E
I S L E ■ E V E N T ■ A R T E
L O T S ■ ■ A D D S ■ N E A T
```

88

```
H A V E N S ■ S E C ■ S K I D
I D I D I T ■ T R Y ■ K E N O
M A R T H A D A N D R I D G E
O N T ■ ■ R U R ■ ■ A P S E S
M O U N T V E R N O N ■ ■ ■ ■
■ ■ ■ I R E ■ O M I C R O N
A M I G O ■ L O R N ■ R I P E
V I R G I N I A M I L I T I A
E L A L ■ A B R A ■ E S T E R
R O S E L L E ■ ■ M A T ■ ■ ■
■ ■ ■ V A L L E Y F O R G E
A L I B I ■ I A N ■ ■ A O L
C O N T I N E N T A L A R M Y
E R L E ■ B A T ■ H A B E A S
D E A N ■ C R Y ■ S T E R N E
```

89

P	E	P	S		P	H	O	T	O		A	W	E	S
A	L	E	E		A	A	R	O	N		M	A	R	T
P	A	T	A	N	S	W	E	R	S		A	S	E	A
A	T	A	L	O	S	S		T	E	E	T	H		
	E	L	I	S			P	E	T	P	E	E	V	E
		N	O	T	E	R			A	U	D	I	S	
G	T	S		A	R	R	E	S	T		R	O	S	S
R	O	T		P	I	T	S	T	O	P		U	T	E
A	N	A	T		B	E	L	U	G	A		T	A	X
S	T	R	A	P		E	N	A	C	T				
P	O	T	B	E	L	L	Y		K	I	S	S		
		A	L	C	O	A		I	C	E	D	T	E	A
A	C	N	E		P	U	T	O	P	T	I	O	N	S
P	O	E	T		E	R	A	T	O		E	L	S	A
T	O	W	S		S	A	G	A	S		D	E	E	P

90

M	A	Y	E	R		H	A	H	A		C	A	L	M
I	R	E	N	E		A	B	E	T		O	L	I	O
S	C	A	R	E	D	Y	C	A	T		A	S	E	A
S	H	R	O	V	E		S	T	A	R	T	O	U	T
		L	E	C	H		S	C	O	T				
L	E	O		S	L	O	P		K	O	A	L	A	S
A	T	M		A	R	E	A		M	I	A	T	A	
T	H	E	C	O	W	A	R	D	L	Y	L	I	O	N
T	E	N	O	R		S	O	L	E		N	N	E	
E	R	S	A	T	Z		N	A	S	H		E	E	R
		S	H	I	P		I	T	I	S				
I	S	O	T	O	P	E	S		E	N	C	O	D	E
B	A	L	I		P	A	P	E	R	T	I	G	E	R
E	V	E	N		E	C	C	E		A	F	L	E	A
G	E	O	G		R	E	A	L		T	I	E	R	S

91

G	A	Z	E		S	C	A	P	E		S	L	O	W
I	G	E	T		H	A	B	I	T		P	A	S	O
B	R	I	C		A	M	A	N	A		O	C	H	O
B	A	T	H	S	H	E	B	A		K	N	E	E	L
			A	S	T		F	L	A	G	D	A	Y	
P	A	T	T	Y		O	T	O	O	L	E			
A	U	G	U	S	T		A	R	R		C	E	N	T
C	R	I	B		O	C	H	E	R		A	M	A	H
T	A	F	T		R	O	O		E	S	K	I	M	O
		H	A	M	L	E	T		H	E	L	E	N	
R	E	F	U	G	E	E		E	S	O				
A	R	O	M	A		S	O	A	P	O	P	E	R	A
G	A	R	P		U	L	T	R	A		A	T	A	D
E	T	T	E		S	A	T	E	D		G	A	Z	A
D	O	E	R		S	W	O	R	E		E	L	E	M

92

M	A	T	T		S	T	E	A	L		S	A	I	L
A	R	I	A		T	E	S	L	A		E	T	T	U
D	E	E	R		I	N	T	E	L		N	E	A	L
	S	T	I	L	L	E	R	A	N	D	A	L	L	
S	L	O		N	E	B		L	O	A	M	Y		
M	I	N	C	E	S		S	W	A	N	K			
A	T	E	U	P		D	E	A	N		G	A	S	
S	H	O	R	T	E	R	A	N	D	S	W	E	E	T
H	E	N			G	I	L	D		P	A	T	S	Y
		L	O	O	P	Y		P	I	S	T	O	N	
	G	I	A	N	T		E	O	N		O	P	E	
H	U	N	T	E	R	A	N	D	P	E	C	K		
A	I	D	E		I	M	A	G	E		U	N	I	T
U	S	E	S		P	E	T	E	Y		T	O	R	O
T	E	X	T		S	N	O	R	E		S	W	A	P

93

```
A L E C   A C T U P   A D A M
T E R I   M O U S E   V I B E
N O T T O B E B E L I E V E D
O V E R R I D E   L A R V A E
      I C E   D E M   Y M A
H O W C A N T H A T B E
A P E   S C R A P   S T E A K
L E S S   E A R P S   C A T O
O N T A P   D E L T A   S R O
      G I V E M E A B R E A K
S T A   Q E D   R N A
A R M O U R   S E L E C T E E
Y O U R E N O T S E R I O U S
S O S A   A V A S T   N O R A
O P E L   L A G O S   E N O S
```

94

```
P A T S   M E C C A   S H U E
A C R E   A T A R I   K A R L
S H E R Y L C R O W   E R I E
T E A P O T     N A M E T A G
A D D E D   U N E   I T C H Y
    N A C H O S   S E R
P O E T   L O O   S T R A F E
R I D   J O H N J A Y   N O R
O L D H A T   D U N   S E E R
    Y O N   B A N G L E
C A R T E   E Y E   E A S Y A
I N A S T I R   F A M O U S
G I V E   P E T E R F I N C H
A S E A   S T A L E   L A C E
R E N T   O S S I E   E R A S
```

95

S	E	P	I	A		S	H	O	D		M	A	I	L
A	G	E	N	T		H	O	U	R		A	C	N	E
T	O	R	S	O		A	P	S	E		G	A	T	E
		O	N	E	H	I	T	W	O	N	D	E	R	
P	R	O	F	E	S	S			Z	A	I	R	E	
R	E	P	A	S	T		M	A	N	O		A	N	D
Y	E	A	R		P	A	C	I	N	O				
	F	L	A	S	H	I	N	T	H	E	P	A	N	
	S	H	A	P	E	S			E	R	A	T	
T	A	U		I	M	E	T		F	I	N	A	L	S
A	S	T	O	R		L	A	S	T	L	A	P	
S	H	O	O	T	I	N	G	S	T	A	R	
S	O	P	H		T	A	R	A		B	A	R	R	E
E	R	I	E		E	M	I	T		E	D	U	C	E
L	E	A	D		M	E	N	S		L	E	G	A	L

96

A	S	H		E	D	G	E	D		B	E	I	N	G
B	O	O		L	O	R	R	E		A	M	T	O	O
S	N	L		S	W	E	E	N	E	Y	T	O	D	D
C	O	M	P	A	N	Y		I	R	E				
A	M	E	R			I	M	A	R	O	U	N	D
M	A	S	O	N	J	A	R		A	L	O	E	
			T	O	N	K	A	S		T	E	T	E
S	T	E	P	H	E	N	S	O	N	D	H	E	I	M
H	O	A	R		S	O	O	N	E	R			
I	T	S	O		M	E	E	T	W	I	T	H
N	O	T	W	H	I	L	E		A	C	R	O
		E	L	I		F	O	L	L	I	E	S
I	M	S	T	I	L	L	H	E	R	E		N	A	T
R	E	C	O	N		T	I	T	A	N		G	T	E
A	L	I	V	E		S	M	E	L	T		S	Y	D

97

A	C	T	S	■	S	T	R	A	T	A	■	S	A	W
C	O	A	T	■	P	E	A	L	E	D	■	U	R	I
H	O	P	E	D	I	A	M	O	N	D	■	P	I	N
E	L	E	V	E	N	■	■	U	S	U	R	P	E	D
■	■	■	E	L	A	T	E	D	■	C	H	E	S	S
A	D	D	■	P	L	O	Y	■	S	E	E	R	■	■
Q	U	A	S	H	■	P	E	S	O	■	S	C	A	B
U	N	V	E	I	L	S	■	I	N	D	U	L	G	E
A	K	I	N	■	O	Y	E	Z	■	U	S	U	A	L
■	■	D	A	R	T	■	W	E	A	L	■	B	R	A
C	A	S	T	E	■	F	E	S	S	U	P	■	■	■
A	P	P	E	A	S	E	■	■	S	T	I	N	G	S
I	R	A	■	P	U	R	P	L	E	H	E	A	R	T
R	I	D	■	E	R	A	S	E	S	■	C	I	A	O
O	L	E	■	R	E	L	I	E	S	■	E	L	B	A

98

G	A	P	E	D	■	W	A	T	T	S	■	H	O	N
A	B	A	C	I	■	I	D	A	H	O	■	A	P	E
S	E	L	L	S	O	L	D	I	E	R	■	V	E	X
■	■	A	N	D	E	S	■	D	E	C	E	N	T	
R	E	L	I	E	D	■	■	B	A	S	E	H	I	T
H	A	I	R	Y	■	B	R	A	■	P	L	A	T	O
E	R	G	S	■	F	O	O	T	H	O	L	D	■	■
A	S	H	■	P	O	T	S	H	O	T	■	D	N	A
■	■	T	O	U	G	H	I	E	S	■	C	O	U	P
S	P	L	A	T	■	E	N	D	■	G	E	C	K	O
T	R	I	S	T	A	R	■	■	B	O	N	K	E	D
R	E	T	T	O	N	■	A	G	E	N	T	■	■	■
O	F	T	■	S	I	T	S	A	T	U	R	D	A	Y
D	E	E	■	E	M	I	T	S	■	T	A	U	P	E
E	R	R	■	A	E	S	O	P	■	S	L	O	T	S

99

C	H	I	E	F		C	O	L	A		C	A	S	H
R	O	D	E	O		A	L	A	R		L	I	P	O
A	L	L	E	N		R	E	S	T		O	S	L	O
B	Y	E		D	E	P	O	S	I	T	S	L	I	P
			S	U	R	E			S	H	E	E	T	S
T	E	E	T	E	R	T	O	T	T	E	R			
Y	I	K	E	S		F	O	R	E		N	A	B	
P	R	E	P		D	I	T	T	Y		A	O	N	E
O	E	D		R	I	D	E			U	N	I	T	E
			B	U	S	I	N	E	S	S	T	R	I	P
P	E	O	R	I	A			N	O	E	S			
U	R	B	A	N	S	P	R	A	W	L		R	E	F
T	O	O	K		T	E	A	M		E	V	I	T	A
I	D	E	E		E	T	T	E		S	A	G	A	L
N	E	S	S		R	E	E	L		S	T	A	L	L

100

F	R	O	G		B	L	O	B		V	A	D	I	S
L	I	M	O		R	O	M	A		I	W	O	N	T
A	C	N	E		O	B	I	T		N	E	W	E	R
T	H	I	S	I	N	S	T	A	N	T		N	R	A
			A	N	C			A	A	A		S	T	Y
T	H	A	T	G	O	O	D	N	I	G	H	T		
R	E	L		E	S	A	I		L	E	H	R	E	R
I	R	E	S			S	T	A			H	E	D	Y
B	O	X	C	A	R		C	L	I	O		A	N	A
		T	H	E	O	T	H	E	R	W	O	M	A	N
P	A	R		R	O	O			O	E	D			
O	D	E		O	D	D	S	A	N	D	E	N	D	S
B	A	B	E	S		A	H	S	O		S	E	E	M
O	N	E	N	O		T	U	T	U		S	A	F	E
Y	O	K	E	L		E	T	A	T		A	R	T	E

101

B	A	A	L		R	A	S	H		F	L	O	E	S
E	D	G	Y		A	D	A	M		L	A	U	R	A
A	M	I	N		B	O	L	O		A	S	T	R	O
M	I	L	D	A	B	R	A	S	I	V	E			
S	T	E	A	D	I	E	S		N	O	R	M	A	N
			I	T	S		H	E	R		A	L	E	
A	B	B	I	E			G	A	P		A	V	O	W
G	R	A	D	U	A	T	E	S	T	U	D	E	N	T
L	I	L	O		M	U	M			P	A	N	G	S
O	D	S		D	O	G		C	O	S				
W	E	A	P	O	N		C	A	R	E	S	S	E	S
			A	N	G	R	Y	P	A	T	I	E	N	T
S	P	A	R	K		U	N	I	T		M	E	T	E
A	L	I	K	E		T	I	T	O		O	M	E	N
T	O	D	A	Y		S	C	A	R		N	E	R	O

102

F	R	O	T	H		E	D	N	A		A	S	T	O
R	O	D	E	O		V	E	A	L		S	T	I	R
I	M	E	A	N		E	E	R	O		P	A	N	T
	P	A	R	D	O	N	M	Y	F	R	E	N	C	H
			D	A	H	L		T	E	N	D	T	O	
A	M	O	R		D	Y	E	D		N	S	A		
R	E	P	O	S	E		R	O	U	E		S	A	P
U	S	E	P	L	A	I	N	E	N	G	L	I	S	H
T	A	N		U	R	L	S		H	E	E	D	E	D
		S	A	M		O	T	T	O		T	E	A	S
S	T	E	P	P	E		W	O	O	L				
T	H	A	T	S	G	R	E	E	K	T	O	M	E	
E	A	S	E		B	A	R	R		T	O	U	R	S
E	N	O	S		D	R	I	P		E	S	S	A	Y
R	E	N	T		F	E	E	S		R	E	S	T	S

103

A	G	N	E	W	■	A	F	A	R	■	T	E	S	T
C	R	I	E	R	■	D	I	R	E	■	A	T	M	O
T	A	K	E	I	T	O	N	T	H	E	C	H	I	N
S	S	E	■	T	O	B	E	■	E	S	T	A	T	E
■	■	S	E	R	E	■	P	A	T	■	N	E	D	■
L	I	S	T	O	N	■	B	A	R	E	S	■	■	■
A	G	E	O	F	■	W	E	T	S	■	T	H	I	S
D	O	W	N	F	O	R	T	H	E	C	O	U	N	T
E	R	N	E	■	V	E	T	O	■	A	R	E	N	A
■	■	■	S	C	E	N	E	■	D	R	E	S	S	Y
O	N	E	■	H	R	S	■	M	A	P	S	■	■	■
T	E	N	D	E	R	■	E	A	V	E	■	S	T	E
T	H	R	O	W	I	N	T	H	E	T	O	W	E	L
E	R	O	S	■	D	O	T	E	■	E	V	A	N	S
R	U	N	E	■	E	V	E	R	■	D	A	N	T	E

104

C	A	B	L	E	■	B	A	B	A	R	■	B	R	A
A	L	I	E	N	■	S	I	E	V	E	■	R	A	H
R	E	D	S	Q	U	I	R	R	E	L	■	O	J	O
O	R	O	T	U	N	D	■	T	R	A	M	W	A	Y
M	T	N	■	I	T	E	M	■	S	P	I	N	■	■
■	■	■	F	R	O	■	A	M	I	■	A	B	E	T
A	M	B	L	E	■	C	I	A	O	■	S	E	R	E
C	O	L	O	R	F	U	L	A	N	I	M	A	L	S
C	P	U	S	■	R	E	B	S	■	M	I	R	E	S
T	E	E	S	■	E	R	A	■	A	M	C	■	■	■
■	■	W	I	R	E	■	G	O	G	O	■	R	D	A
R	E	H	E	E	L	S	■	D	I	D	G	O	O	D
I	R	A	■	G	O	L	D	E	N	E	A	G	L	E
T	I	L	■	A	V	A	I	L	■	S	T	E	E	L
Z	E	E	■	L	E	V	E	L	■	T	E	R	S	E

105

```
G A R P . M E L B A . E A R L
I C E R . I D E A S . A R I A
R U N E . M E D I C . R A M P
D R E S S I N G R O O M . . .
S A W T O . . E N T R A N C E
. . . O A F S . . B R A Y S
A C T . P O O D L E S K I R T
P R E P . A F O O T . S L U E
T O A S T M A S T E R . S S E
T O K Y O . . . I S O F . . .
O N S C R E E N . I R E S T
. . H O R N O F P L E N T Y
G O B I . R U L E R . N O O K
E X E C . E R A S E . C L U E
E Y E S . D E N T S . H A T S
```

106

```
H E E L . I B E A M . A T M S
E S A I . L Y N D E . P E E P
S Q U A R E R O O T . O R N O
. . . R O T O . . A F L C I O
E A R L Y . T A B L E L E A F
E R E I . H E I R . D O L L S
N O B A K E . R E N O . . . .
. W A R D R O B E T R U N K .
. . . L O C A . W A N I N G
T A N Y A . A S S T . D A I S
B R A I N S T E M . M E S T A
O R T E G A . . O M A R . . .
N A T L . B A N K B R A N C H
D Y E D . E N N E A . G O R E
S S R S . R E E D S . E R T E
```

107

```
I S L E T █ T R I A L █ F O G
R H I N O █ H A N O I █ E V A
K I N D O F R I F L E █ E A R
E R G █ K R O N E █ A L L Y
D E O █ T A W █ R O A R S █
█ █ C O U R T S U M M O N S
B A S H █ D U O █ R O B R O Y
M E T E S █ G N P █ K A R E N
O R I E N T █ E R S █ N Y S E
C O R R O B O R A T E D █ █
█ C U B A N █ T A P █ B U S
W A R P █ █ L O T T O █ O N E
E T A █ T R I P L E C R O W N
B I Z █ R A N E E █ H A Z E D
S T Y █ A M E N D █ S H E D S
```

108

```
A L O H A █ R A C E R █ S Y D
W I D O W █ E D D I E █ H O E
N E E D L E P O I N T █ E S S
I N S █ S T E P █ A P R E S
N O S E █ D A T I N G G A M E
G R A S P █ L E N O █ S T I R
█ █ P U P █ E C O L █ O T T
█ T E N N I S █ A N Y O N E █
S E X █ T A C O █ E L M █ █
P A P A █ N A B S █ E I D E R
E R E C T O R S E T █ T A X I
C I R C A █ █ C A R T █ L A C
I N T █ S A F E T Y M A T C H
A T L █ K L I N E █ E M O T E
L O Y █ S I X E D █ N I N A S
```

109

110

111

T	U	B	A		P	A	T	R	O	L		B	O	P
A	T	O	P		E	R	R	A	T	A		I	D	E
L	A	R	A		S	E	A	S	O	N		G	O	T
C	H	E	C	K	O	N	C	H	E	C	K	O	U	T
			H	E	S	A			E	N	T	R	Y	
H	O	M	E	Y			P	L	A	T	O			
A	C	E		E	I	L	E	E	N		W	I	T	S
S	T	A	N	D	F	O	R	S	T	A	N	D	U	P
P	O	L	O		F	O	S	S	I	L		O	N	E
			T	H	Y	M	E		E	S	S	E	X	
A	L	A	M	O			A	C	C	T				
T	A	K	E	O	V	E	R	T	A	K	E	O	F	F
B	R	R		T	I	N	I	E	R		W	O	O	L
A	G	O		E	L	I	C	I	T		E	Z	R	A
Y	E	N		R	E	D	O	N	E		D	E	E	P

112

W	A	R	D		A	D	D	S		V	E	R	G	E
A	X	O	N		P	E	R	T		O	D	O	U	L
D	I	S	A	P	P	E	A	R	I	N	G	I	N	K
E	S	E		L	A	P	T	O	P		E	L	S	E
			R	U	R		S	P	A	Y		E	H	S
A	B	D	O	M	E	N		N	E	E	D	Y		
D	R	I	B	B	L	E	G	L	A	S	S			
Z	A	S	U		H	R	E		C	O	E	D		
			S	Q	U	I	R	T	F	L	O	W	E	R
	D	A	T	U	M		S	O	A	R	E	R	S	
S	A	P		O	I	S	E		R	S	T			
A	P	I	A		A	N	D	R	E	S		T	L	C
T	H	E	J	O	K	E	W	A	S	O	N	Y	O	U
U	N	C	A	P		A	I	R	E		U	R	G	E
P	E	E	R	S		K	N	E	E		B	O	O	S

113

C	I	G	A	R		A	L	A	M	O		T	R	A
E	C	O	L	E		B	E	B	O	P		W	I	Z
D	O	U	B	L	E	A	G	E	N	T		I	C	U
E	N	T	A	I	L	S		S	K	I	N	N	E	R
			E	L	E	C			M	E	E	S	E	
E	N	D	I	V	E		O	B	T	A	I	N		
S	E	E	M	E		S	A	R	A		T	G	I	F
S	O	U	P		F	A	X	E	D		H	I	R	E
O	N	C	E		B	L	E	D		P	E	N	A	L
	E	D	G	I	E	R		R	E	R	E	N	T	
A	T	S	E	A		S	E	E	R					
D	O	W	D	I	E	R		D	E	F	T	E	S	T
A	L	I		T	A	B	L	E	F	O	R	T	W	O
G	E	L		E	V	I	A	N		R	E	R	A	N
E	T	D		R	E	S	T	S		M	E	E	T	S

114

D	A	F	T		S	H	A	R	K		T	K	T	S
A	C	R	E		N	O	W	A	Y		R	A	R	A
W	H	E	N	H	E	L	L	F	R	E	E	Z	E	S
N	Y	T	I	M	E	S		T	A	X	B	A	S	E
			N	O	R	T	H			C	L	A	S	S
S	I	L	O	S			O	S	S	I	E			
P	A	I	N		E	S	T	O	P	S		W	H	O
O	N	C	E	I	N	A	B	L	U	E	M	O	O	N
T	S	K		G	O	N	E	O	N		A	L	O	E
		B	O	W	E	D			R	I	F	F	S	
L	A	P	A	T		S	P	A	I	N				
E	M	E	R	I	T	A		R	U	M	M	A	G	E
T	W	E	N	T	Y	F	O	U	R	S	E	V	E	N
H	A	V	E		P	A	N	D	A		N	E	R	D
E	Y	E	S		E	R	T	E	S		U	S	E	S

115

A	B	Y	S	S				S	O	D		A	L	G	A
S	O	O	T	H	E			U	N	O		V	I	E	D
P	I	G	O	U	T			D	U	C	K	I	N	T	O
S	L	A	P		H	I	S	S		N	A	D	I	R	
				S	P	E	C			A	E	R	A	T	E
S	Q	U	I	R	R	E	L	A	W	A	Y				
P	U	R	G	E		R	I	L	E	D		Z	I	G	
R	A	I	N		F	I	E	L	D		E	U	R	O	
Y	D	S		B	I	N	G	E		I	G	L	O	O	
			M	O	N	K	E	Y	A	R	O	U	N	D	
A	S	P	I	R	E			E	D	A	M				
T	H	E	S	E		W	I	S	E		A	G	R	A	
W	O	L	F	D	O	W	N		P	O	N	Y	U	P	
A	N	T	I		P	I	N		T	R	I	P	L	E	
R	E	S	T		T	I	S		B	A	S	E	S		

116

I	C	B	M		T	A	M	E	S	T		S	A	O	
M	O	R	E		O	P	E	N	T	O		T	A	D	
P	L	A	Y	A	D	E	L	R	E	Y		A	L	Y	
L	O	V	E	T	O		R	A	E		B	R	A	S	
I	N	E	R	T		T	O	P	L	A	Y	E	R	S	
E	E	L	S		L	O	S	T		S	A	R	G	E	
S	L	Y		G	A	L	E		K	I	N	S	E	Y	
			W	O	R	D		P	L	A	Y				
M	E	L	I	N	A		P	E	E	N		R	A	G	
A	L	O	N	E		R	E	N	E		C	A	R	L	
N	E	W	O	R	D	E	R	S		P	A	T	I	O	
A	G	E	S		A	S	U		A	O	R	T	A	S	
T	A	R		C	R	O	S	S	S	W	O	R	D	S	
E	N	E		P	I	L	E	U	P		L	A	N	E	
E	T	D		A	N	D	R	E	S		S	P	E	D	

117

C	A	D	■	N	I	C	K	E	L	■	S	R	T	A
U	T	E	■	E	V	O	N	N	E	■	H	E	R	S
B	A	L	L	R	E	T	U	R	N	■	E	M	I	T
I	L	I	A	D	■	■	R	O	A	D	R	A	C	E
C	L	A	W	■	B	E	L	L	P	E	P	P	E	R
■	■	F	E	E	L	■	■	E	R	A	■	■	■	■
F	R	A	U	L	E	I	N	S	■	■	A	S	A	■
B	I	L	L	O	F	A	T	T	A	I	N	D	E	R
I	M	P	■	■	S	H	O	W	P	I	E	C	E	■
■	■	S	O	B	■	■	L	O	O	P	■	■	■	■
B	O	L	L	W	E	E	V	I	L	■	P	O	S	H
A	X	H	A	N	D	L	E	■	■	L	E	T	H	E
L	E	A	N	■	B	U	L	L	D	U	R	H	A	M
M	Y	S	T	■	U	D	D	E	R	S	■	E	V	A
Y	E	A	S	■	G	E	T	S	E	T	■	R	E	N

118

S	P	L	A	T	■	A	M	F	M	■	G	E	L	S
G	R	E	C	O	■	V	I	D	A	■	O	R	A	L
T	E	D	D	Y	B	E	A	R	S	■	G	A	L	A
■	■	■	C	E	O	■	■	H	O	O	T	A	T	■
R	A	W	■	D	O	W	N	P	I	L	L	O	W	S
E	Z	I	O	■	B	O	A	T	E	D	■	■	■	■
M	U	S	H	R	O	O	M	S	■	P	U	N	C	H
A	R	E	T	O	O	■	■	S	A	H	A	R	A	
P	E	S	O	S	■	E	N	V	E	L	O	P	E	S
■	■	■	C	A	R	E	E	R	■	H	E	A	T	■
B	A	L	L	O	T	B	O	X	E	S	■	S	K	Y
I	N	A	S	E	C	■	■	N	E	A	■	■	■	■
Z	I	M	A	■	O	V	E	R	E	A	T	E	R	S
E	T	A	T	■	S	O	L	O	■	L	O	S	E	R
T	A	S	S	■	T	W	I	N	■	Y	M	C	A	S

119

C	A	P	S		C	E	D	A	R		B	A	B	A
A	L	O	E		O	R	A	T	E		E	D	A	M
S	P	I	T		W	O	R	L	D	P	E	A	C	E
H	O	N		P	E	S	T		H	A	N	G	O	N
		T	S	A	R		B	O	T		E	N	D	
S	E	L	T	Z	E	R	W	A	T	E	R			
O	R	E	O		D	A	H	L		N	E	P	A	L
L	I	S	P	S		T	E	T		S	T	A	L	E
E	N	S	U	E		I	R	I	S		A	R	E	A
		P	E	R	F	E	C	T	P	I	T	C	H	
M	I	C		S	H	Y		A	B	L	Y			
A	D	A	G	I	O		M	A	Y	S		L	A	B
S	E	C	O	N	D	W	I	N	D		P	I	P	E
T	A	T	A		E	A	S	E	R		O	N	E	S
S	L	I	T		S	H	O	W	Y		T	E	X	T

120

D	U	O	S		N	Y	S	E		A	L	D	A	S
O	T	R	O		A	U	E	L		M	E	E	T	S
L	A	F	F		U	C	L	A		O	A	T	E	R
T	H	E	T	U	S	C	A	N	S	U	N			
S	N	O	W	P	E	A		A	R	E	N	A	S	
		A	H	A		U	R	N		D	I	V	A	
O	H	A	R	E		A	N	D	E	S		C	A	L
C	O	V	E	R	O	F	D	A	R	K	N	E	S	S
O	V	I		E	R	T	E	S		A	O	R	T	A
M	E	O	W		A	A	R		A	T	T			
E	R	N	E	S	T		I	D	E	A	T	E	S	
		T	H	E	B	O	A	R	D	W	A	L	K	
F	O	A	M	Y		A	M	M	O		A	R	I	A
E	R	R	O	L		B	I	B	I		K	O	O	L
W	E	E	P	Y		A	T	I	T		E	S	T	D

121

P	E	S	T	S		S	E	A	R		N	O	V	A
R	A	T	O	N		M	L	L	E		A	R	E	S
O	R	I	G	I	N	O	F	S	P	E	C	I	E	S
	L	O	T	T	O			S	P	H	E	R	E	
A	C	E			H	T	T	P		H	O	N	E	S
H	O	T	E	L		H	A	U	T	E		T	D	S
A	R	T	G	U	M		B	R	O	M	O			
	R	O	O	T	O	F	A	L	L	E	V	I	L	
		S	H	O	E	S		D	R	U	M	U	P	
I	D	S		E	D	I	C	T		A	M	P	L	E
S	I	T	A	R		N	O	I	R		E	U	R	
A	R	O	M	A	S			N	I	C	E	R		
B	E	G	I	N	N	I	N	G	O	F	T	I	M	E
E	L	I	S		O	B	O	E		O	N	A	I	R
L	Y	E	S		B	M	W	S		S	A	L	T	S

122

S	C	R	A	P		S	H	A	G		L	A	M	B
K	O	A	L	A		P	U	R	R		E	W	E	R
Y	O	G	I	S		A	N	T	I		A	F	R	O
			S	I	T	T	I	N	G	D	U	C	K	
I	S	R	A	E	L		E	G	O		L	Y	E	
S	T	A	N	D	I	N	G	R	O	O	M			
L	O	R	D		E	Y	E			D	E	N	E	B
A	V	E	R		D	U	N	E	D		R	U	L	E
M	E	R	E	S			I	I	I		I	D	E	A
		W	A	L	K	I	N	G	S	T	I	C	K	
A	G	E		K	A	I		I	N	S	E	T	S	
R	U	N	N	I	N	G	M	A	T	E				
I	N	T	O		D	A	U	B		A	E	S	O	P
E	K	E	S		E	L	S	E		K	R	A	F	T
L	Y	R	E		D	I	E	T		Y	E	N	T	A

123

G	R	I	N		L	A	G	O		F	E	D	E	X
R	E	N	O		A	B	U	T		A	D	E	L	E
A	S	S	T		S	O	L	E		R	I	L	E	S
P	A	P	E	R	O	R	P	L	A	S	T	I	C	
E	W	E		A	R	T		L	I	I				
		C	R	E	D	I	T	O	R	D	E	B	I	T
	S	T	U		A	V	A		S	E	N	A	T	E
N	E	I	L			E	K	E			G	R	A	D
A	M	O	E	B	A		E	N	D		E	L	L	
W	I	N	D	O	W	O	R	A	I	S	L	E		
			N	O	R		M	A	I		Y	M	A	
	R	E	G	U	L	A	R	O	R	D	E	C	A	F
L	O	P	E	S		T	E	R	I		L	O	N	I
A	L	I	N	E		E	P	E	E		B	R	E	R
S	E	C	T	S		S	O	D	S		A	N	T	E

124

O	T	B	S		B	E	A	D		A	L	C	O	A
N	O	O	N		A	L	L	I		G	I	R	L	S
T	W	O	E	G	G	S	O	V	E	R	E	A	S	Y
A	N	E	A	R			T	O	T	E		Z	E	E
P	E	R	K	I	N	S		T	H	E	R	E	N	T
			E	L	E	N	A		E	T	E			
F	O	U	R	L	E	A	F	C	L	O	V	E	R	S
G	U	S			F	O	O				G	U	T	
S	I	X	F	I	G	U	R	E	I	N	C	O	M	E
			U	N	O		E	U	B	I	E			
T	O	R	N	A	D	O		R	E	C	R	O	O	M
E	L	I		S	O	P	S			H	E	N	N	A
E	I	G	H	T	T	R	A	C	K	T	A	P	E	S
M	V	I	I	I		A	L	A	I		L	O	G	O
S	E	D	E	R		H	E	R	D		S	T	A	N

125

A	D	A	M	S		S	O	F	A		I	N	G	E
B	A	D	A	T		A	W	E	S		N	E	O	N
A	N	D	C	R	O	W	N	T	H	Y	G	O	O	D
S	I	S		I	L	O		A	T	O	M			
E	S	T		D	E	F	S		R	R	A	T	E	D
	H	O	M	E	O	F	T	H	E	B	R	A	V	E
		A	S	S		R	H	E	A		D	E	B	
B	A	A	S		H	A	H			P	A	N	T	
A	R	T		O	L	I	N		I	P	O			
L	E	T	F	R	E	E	D	O	M	R	I	N	G	
M	A	N	I	A	C		S	U	M	O		A	A	S
		S	L	A	B		G	I	G		B	T	U	
W	I	T	H	B	R	O	T	H	E	R	H	O	O	D
O	D	I	E		R	A	N	T		A	B	B	R	S
W	A	N	D		E	T	T	A		M	O	S	S	Y

126

T	R	E	K	S		T	A	C	K		S	E	C	T
E	A	G	L	E		O	B	O	E		I	N	R	E
A	N	G	E	R		U	L	N	A		X	D	I	N
	S	E	A	N	P	E	N	N	S	P	E	N	S	
N	A	H		T	E	R	I		I	M	A	G	E	
B	R	E	A	T	H	E		V	I	M		R	E	D
C	E	L	L	O		D	E	N	I	M				
	A	L	A	N	L	A	D	D	S	L	A	D	S	
		S	E	E	D	S			A	R	R	A	Y	
D	A	D		D	I	M		P	E	R	S	O	N	A
A	E	I	O	U		I	M	A	X		P	E	W	
B	R	A	D	P	I	T	T	S	P	I	T	S		
S	A	L	E		B	O	W	S		T	A	H	O	E
A	T	I	T		A	N	T	E		S	T	O	R	M
T	E	N	S		R	E	F	S		Y	A	T	E	S

127

A	B	B	A		D	R	I	V	E		L	O	A	N
C	O	E	N		E	A	T	E	N		O	P	I	E
H	E	A	D	I	N	T	H	E	C	L	O	U	D	S
E	R	N		R	I	S	E	R		A	S	S	E	T
			T	A	R			O	N	E				
H	E	A	R	T	O	F	D	A	R	K	N	E	S	S
A	L	B	E	E		L	A	I	T	Y		N	A	T
R	E	O	S		F	O	U	R	H		A	N	T	I
S	N	O		T	O	W	N	E		B	R	U	I	N
H	A	N	D	S	O	N	T	R	A	I	N	I	N	G
			O	L	D			T	K	O				
C	A	R	G	O		S	U	I	T	E		A	S	K
H	E	A	L	T	H	I	N	S	U	R	A	N	C	E
E	R	I	E		A	D	D	O	N		S	T	A	G
W	O	N	G		L	E	O	N	E		H	E	R	S

128

P	A	R	E	R	S			B	Y	E		C	B	S
A	B	I	L	E	N	E		O	A	K	T	R	E	E
P	O	P	F	O	U	L		O	P	E	R	A	T	E
E	D	U		B	A	L	M	S		I	S	A	N	
R	E	P	E	L		N	E	T		R	A	H		
			S	A	I	D	N	O		A	D	D	E	D
D	O	C	T	O	R		S	W	A	N		I	D	O
E	R	R	A	T	I	C		N	E	S	T	E	G	G
A	L	A		I	S	L	E		R	O	U	T	E	S
L	Y	C	R	A		A	P	L	O	M	B			
	K	I	N		P	E	A		S	E	E	M	S	
B	A	S	S		S	T	E	M	S		V	I	I	
A	C	H	E	F	O	R		B	I	G	B	A	N	G
D	I	O	R	A	M	A		S	P	I	E	D	O	N
E	D	T		R	E	P			S	N	E	E	R	S

129

```
I C O N   S C T V   O C C A M
C U B A   C R U E   R H E T T
B R I M   O U S T   W O O L S
M E T E O R S H O W E R
        T A C O     E L A P S E
  W E A T H E R B A L L O O N
R I D G E     A E R   E C U A
E M I   S H U T E Y E   O R C
A P T S   U S E     A M N O T
C L O U D F O R M A T I O N
T E R R I F     A S S N
        F L Y I N G S A U C E R
C I L I A   M U N I   S I Z E
A R E N T   A D E S   E T R E
B A D G E   Y E T I   S E A L
```

130

```
U M A S S   P L U M S   J A W
T E N T H   H O S E A   U S E
E N D R O A D W O R K   S S E
    A V I S     L E N T E N
W A F T E D   V I I   O M N I
A B R A D E   A N N O T A T E
D U E     S P C A   O R R
S T E P S   L A P   H E R B S
    K E Y   A N T S     I R A
T R I A S S I C   U P B E A T
E A T S   A N Y   S L E D G E
A T T E S T     T H U S
S T E   P R I Z E I N S I D E
E E N   A A R O N   K I L O S
T D S   S P E E D   S E E M S
```

131

G	A	L	A	S		V	O	C	A	L		I	R	S
A	L	A	N	A		A	I	S	L	E		V	I	C
Z	E	S	T	F	O	R	L	I	F	E		O	V	A
A	C	H	I	E	V	E			A	S	T	R	A	L
			R	A	S	C	A	L		K	Y	L	E	
T	A	C	O		L	E	A	D	F	O	O	T		
E	X	O	D	U	S		M	O	A	T		O	R	C
C	L	A	S	S		L	E	S		R	A	W	E	R
H	E	S		E	Z	I	O		G	A	Z	E	B	O
		T	O	D	I	E	F	O	R		T	R	A	P
O	L	G	A		P	U	F	F	I	N				
C	O	U	R	I	C			N	E	O	N	G	A	S
T	R	A		T	O	N	E	O	F	V	O	I	C	E
E	R	R		A	D	E	P	T		A	L	L	O	W
T	E	D		R	E	T	I	E		S	O	A	P	S

132

L	E	W	D		D	W	A	R	F		J	E	S	T
A	R	E	A		R	A	R	E	R		U	T	A	H
W	I	N	B	Y	A	N	O	S	E		M	A	U	I
N	E	T		A	M	E	S		E	B	B	I	N	G
		F	A	C	A	D	E	S		A	L	L	A	H
S	M	I	R	K	S			T	U	B	E			
T	O	R	T		R	E	U	S	E		U	S	N	
L	O	S	E	O	N	E	S	B	A	L	A	N	C	E
O	T	T		C	O	N	E	S		A	D	O	S	
		N	E	W	T		C	A	R	E	T	S		
S	A	M	O	A		S	O	B	E	R	E	R		
A	L	U	M	N	I		C	O	D	A		O	U	I
V	I	S	A		D	R	A	W	A	B	L	A	N	K
E	K	E	D		O	I	L	E	R		E	T	T	E
R	E	D	S		L	O	A	D	S		W	H	O	A

133

S	E	E	P	■	O	K	L	A	■	C	H	A	S	E
H	U	L	A	■	N	A	I	L	■	L	O	G	I	N
O	B	I	T	■	E	R	N	E	■	E	R	O	D	E
W	I	Z	■	L	A	N	E	C	H	A	N	G	E	S
S	E	A	■	A	L	A	■	■	O	N	E	■	■	■
■	■	B	E	T	■	K	E	N	T	S	T	A	T	E
C	R	E	P	E	S	■	L	O	D	E	■	D	A	B
R	A	T	A	■	C	H	I	N	O	■	D	A	T	A
A	S	H	■	R	H	O	S	■	G	E	R	M	A	N
W	H	I	T	E	L	I	E	S	■	R	E	A	■	■
■	■	■	U	T	E	■	■	E	R	A	■	N	A	P
D	A	I	L	Y	P	L	A	N	E	T	■	D	I	E
A	S	C	A	P	■	A	L	A	S	■	M	E	M	O
S	T	O	N	E	■	D	O	T	E	■	O	V	E	N
H	O	N	E	D	■	S	T	E	T	■	W	E	D	S

134

M	A	M	M	A	■	A	D	S	■	A	B	U	T	S
A	B	E	A	T	■	L	E	T	■	N	E	P	A	L
T	E	R	R	A	■	T	A	I	■	T	A	S	T	Y
A	L	V	I	N	T	O	F	F	L	E	R	■	■	■
■	■	■	N	E	O	■	■	F	E	N	■	T	L	C
S	I	M	O	N	W	I	E	S	E	N	T	H	A	L
E	M	O	■	D	I	V	A	■	■	A	R	O	M	A
D	I	O	R	■	T	E	R	M	S	■	I	M	A	M
A	G	R	E	E	■	■	L	O	T	T	■	A	Z	O
T	H	E	O	D	O	R	E	D	R	E	I	S	E	R
E	T	D	■	W	W	I	■	■	E	R	N	■	■	■
■	■	■	T	H	E	C	H	I	P	M	U	N	K	S
A	T	A	R	I	■	H	A	N	■	I	R	E	N	E
R	O	G	E	T	■	E	S	T	■	T	E	H	E	E
M	O	O	S	E	■	R	H	O	■	E	D	I	E	S

135

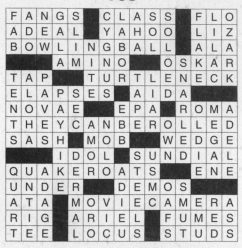

F	A	N	G	S		C	L	A	S	S		F	L	O
A	D	E	A	L		Y	A	H	O	O		L	I	Z
B	O	W	L	I	N	G	B	A	L	L		A	L	A
		A	M	I	N	O			O	S	K	A	R	
T	A	P			T	U	R	T	L	E	N	E	C	K
E	L	A	P	S	E	S		A	I	D	A			
N	O	V	A	E			E	P	A		R	O	M	A
T	H	E	Y	C	A	N	B	E	R	O	L	L	E	D
S	A	S	H		M	O	B			W	E	D	G	E
			I	D	O	L		S	U	N	D	I	A	L
Q	U	A	K	E	R	O	A	T	S			E	N	E
U	N	D	E	R		D	E	M	O	S				
A	T	A		M	O	V	I	E	C	A	M	E	R	A
R	I	G		A	R	I	E	L		F	U	M	E	S
T	E	E		L	O	C	U	S		S	T	U	D	S

136

O	N	C	E		I	D	E	A	L		F	A	S	T
L	E	I	A		R	E	T	R	O		O	N	T	O
D	O	N	T	B	E	A	S	T	R	A	N	G	E	R
		M	U	D	D		E	N	D	Z	O	N	E	
P	A	V	E	S		E	S	S	E	S		L	O	U
A	T	E		B	N	A	I			R	A	S	P	
C	A	E	S	A	R		R	A	D	I	O			
	D	R	O	P	I	N	A	N	Y	T	I	M	E	
		L	T	C	O	L		A	O	L	E	R	S	
L	O	G	O		B	E	I	N			N	A	P	
A	L	A		T	I	L	E	S		B	O	S	S	Y
W	E	L	F	A	R	E		O	D	I	N			
Y	A	L	L	C	O	M	E	B	A	C	K	N	O	W
E	R	O	O		N	A	V	A	L		E	A	R	P
R	Y	N	E		S	N	A	R	E		Y	M	C	A

137

P	A	L	E		O	G	E	E		A	M	B	E	R
E	L	E	E		R	U	L	E		L	O	O	S	E
P	A	R	K	E	D	I	L	L	E	G	A	L	L	Y
S	R	O		N	E	D			L	I	T			
I	M	I	N	T	R	O	U	B	L	E		H	E	P
		O	R	S		N	A	I	R		O	X	O	
E	M	O	R	Y		D	R	E	S	C	H	E	R	
M	A	R	M		H	E	R	B	S		H	O	C	K
C	R	E	A	T	U	R	E			B	O	S	S	Y
E	C	O		I	R	I	S		P	E	R			
E	O	S		P	R	E	S	S	A	G	E	N	T	S
		U	S	A		P	R	E		I	I	I		
L	E	N	G	T	H	Y	M	E	E	T	I	N	G	S
O	V	U	L	E		E	B	A	N		M	E	R	S
S	A	T	Y	R		P	A	R	T		P	R	E	Y

138

O	B	I	T		H	E	C	H	E		D	R	A	B
W	I	F	I		E	C	L	A	T		R	E	P	O
N	O	S	E	A	R	O	U	N	D		A	C	R	O
			T	B	O	N	E			T	W	A	I	N
S	M	E	A	R		O	D	D	C	O	U	P	L	E
T	A	L	C	U	M		E	A	R	P				
E	D	S		P	A	C	M	A	N		O	F	F	
P	A	I	N	T	T	H	E	T	O	W	N	R	E	D
	T	E	E		Z	I	T	H	E	R		I	D	O
		T	O	O	L			D	I	C	T	U	M	
S	N	O	W	W	H	I	T	E		T	R	O	P	E
M	U	R	A	L		O	M	A	H	A				
I	D	I	G		J	O	B	O	P	E	N	I	N	G
L	I	N	E		I	R	A	T	E		N	C	A	A
E	E	G	S		M	E	T	E	D		Y	E	G	G

139

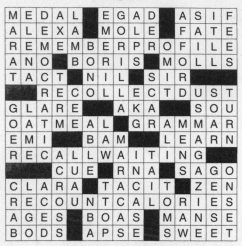

M	E	D	A	L		E	G	A	D		A	S	I	F
A	L	E	X	A		M	O	L	E		F	A	T	E
R	E	M	E	M	B	E	R	P	R	O	F	I	L	E
A	N	O		B	O	R	I	S		M	O	L	L	S
T	A	C	T		N	I	L		S	I	R			
	R	E	C	O	L	L	E	C	T	D	U	S	T
G	L	A	R	E		A	K	A		S	O	U
O	A	T	M	E	A	L		G	R	A	M	M	A	R
E	M	I		B	A	M		L	E	A	R	N
R	E	C	A	L	L	W	A	I	T	I	N	G
	C	U	E		R	N	A		S	A	G	O
C	L	A	R	A		T	A	C	I	T		Z	E	N
R	E	C	O	U	N	T	C	A	L	O	R	I	E	S
A	G	E	S		B	O	A	S		M	A	N	S	E
B	O	D	S		A	P	S	E		S	W	E	E	T

140

B	O	B	U	P		F	L	U	B		G	E	A	R
A	B	A	S	E		I	O	T	A		O	M	N	I
L	I	B	E	R	A	L	B	E	N	E	F	I	T	S
K	E	Y		F	L	I	E	S		V	E	R	S	E
		L	E	I	A		P	E	R					
R	A	D	I	C	A	L	S	I	G	N		A	L	T
A	L	E	R	T	S		M	E	A	T	S	T	E	W
I	L	I	A		O	A	R		L	A	N	A
N	O	T	S	O	F	A	R		P	O	U	R	I	N
S	T	Y		L	E	F	T	H	A	N	G	I	N	G
	A	D	Z		A	Y	E	S
S	T	Y	L	E		P	A	T	T	Y		H	A	T
P	R	O	G	R	E	S	S	I	V	E	L	E	N	S
I	O	W	A		L	A	I	N		A	O	R	T	A
N	Y	S	E		S	T	A	G		R	Y	D	E	R

141

Y	I	P	S		L	E	E	J		G	L	A	R	E
A	R	I	A		O	B	L	A		O	O	Z	E	S
K	A	T	Y		G	R	A	F		S	Q	U	A	T
O	N	T	H	E	G	O	L	F	C	O	U	R	S	E
V	I	S	I	N	E			A	L	F	A			
			L	R	O	N		A	T	C	O	S	T	
S	E	L	M	A		L	O	R	N		I	N	T	O
P	L	A	Y	I	N	G	E	I	G	H	T	E	E	N
A	L	U	M		Y	A	N	G		E	Y	I	N	G
R	A	D	I	A	L		D	A	W	G				
			S	L	O	E			R	E	V	I	S	E
H	I	T	T	I	N	G	T	H	E	L	I	N	K	S
A	S	I	A	N		R	A	I	N		L	O	I	S
S	T	A	K	E		E	X	E	C		L	I	L	A
H	O	S	E	D		T	I	S	H		A	L	L	Y

142

P	O	P	S		C	O	A	S	T		H	A	L	F
A	N	E	W		A	L	L	A	H		O	L	I	O
S	T	R	I	P	T	E	A	S	E		M	E	S	A
T	O	U	P	E	E		S	H	E		E	X	A	M
		E	A	R	L			N	R	A				
S	K	A		S	A	N	D	D	O	L	L	A	R	
C	I	T	E	D		R	E	O		B	O	O	Z	E
A	T	A	L	E		E	G	G		I	N	C	U	R
M	E	R	I	T		D	E	L		N	E	H	R	U
P	R	I	M	E	M	O	V	E	R			S	E	N
		I	R	A		G	O	B	S					
W	O	O	D		G	O	T		T	A	P	O	U	T
A	L	V	A		P	A	I	N	T	H	O	R	S	E
S	E	A	T		I	R	E	N	E		T	E	S	S
H	O	L	E		E	S	S	E	N		S	O	R	T

143

T	O	A	D		P	O	P	S		S	N	O	R	E
A	R	G	O		U	P	O	N		W	O	M	B	S
L	E	A	N		L	A	T	E		E	T	A	I	L
C	O	R	N	E	L	L	S	A	N	D	E	R	S	
		E	M	T		K	E	E	P					
P	I	S		M	A	T	E		E	N	A	C	T	S
E	M	O	R	Y	B	O	A	R	D		P	A	R	E
C	O	D	A	S		F	R	O		R	E	N	E	E
A	N	O	N		T	U	L	A	N	E	R	O	A	D
N	A	M	A	T	H		S	N	A	P		E	T	S
		C	O	R	K		M	O	P					
	M	A	R	Q	U	E	T	T	E	S	H	A	R	E
A	E	I	O	U		P	O	E	T		O	R	A	L
P	A	R	S	E		I	D	E	A		N	I	T	S
B	L	E	S	S		S	O	N	G		E	A	S	E

144

M	A	R	I	E		A	D	D	S		A	C	T	
A	M	A	N	D	A		N	U	D	E		R	H	O
T	O	N	S	I	L		G	E	T	A	G	R	I	P
E	N	G		T	E	A	L			E	O	N	S	
G	E	T	O	U	T	O	F	T	H	E	W	A	Y	
		E	R	T	E		R	E	A					
U	R	S	A			H	E	A	D	G	E	A	R	
G	E	T	T	H	I	S	S	T	R	A	I	G	H	T
H	O	U	S	E	S	A	T			R	O	S	E	
			L	A	G		M	A	S	T				
G	E	T	A	L	O	A	D	O	F	T	H	A	T	
A	N	O	N			Y	O	U	R		F	U	N	
G	E	T	A	L	I	F	E		S	O	N	A	T	A
O	R	E		O	V	E	R		E	N	A	C	T	S
N	O	D		B	Y	E	S			G	E	T	I	T

145

G	O	L	F		A	C	I	D	S		S	C	A	R
A	R	E	A		C	U	M	I	N		M	E	M	O
F	E	A	T	H	E	R	B	O	A		A	L	B	A
F	O	R	C	E		B	U	R	P		S	L	E	D
		A	R	I	S	E		A	B	H	O	R	S	
D	E	B	T	O	R		S	T	R	E	P			
R	U	E	S		A	C	M	E		A	S	H	E	N
A	R	E		U	N	L	O	A	D	S		A	X	E
G	O	F	A	R		A	M	M	O		A	N	E	W
	F	E	I	G	N		D	E	T	E	C	T	
S	P	A	R	S	E		B	O	O	Z	E			
M	O	J	O		N	A	R	C		R	A	T	E	S
I	S	I	S		T	H	A	T	S	A	W	R	A	P
T	I	T	O		L	E	V	E	E		A	U	R	A
E	T	A	L		E	M	O	T	E		Y	E	N	S

146

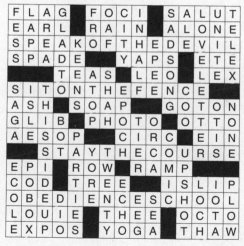

F	L	A	G		F	O	C	I		S	A	L	U	T
E	A	R	L		R	A	I	N		A	L	O	N	E
S	P	E	A	K	O	F	T	H	E	D	E	V	I	L
S	P	A	D	E		Y	A	P	S		E	T	E	
		T	E	A	S		L	E	O		L	E	X	
S	I	T	O	N	T	H	E	F	E	N	C	E		
A	S	H		S	O	A	P			G	O	T	O	N
G	L	I	B		P	H	O	T	O		O	T	T	O
A	E	S	O	P		C	I	R	C		E	I	N	
	S	T	A	Y	T	H	E	C	O	U	R	S	E	
E	P	I		R	O	W		R	A	M	P			
C	O	D		T	R	E	E			I	S	L	I	P
O	B	E	D	I	E	N	C	E	S	C	H	O	O	L
L	O	U	I	E		T	H	E	E		O	C	T	O
E	X	P	O	S		Y	O	G	A		T	H	A	W

147

A	L	T	A	R		I	R	I	S		S	M	E	E
G	U	A	V	A		S	U	C	H		L	Y	N	N
E	X	P	E	C	T	S	T	H	E	W	O	R	S	T
S	E	A	S	C	O	U	T		S	O	T	R	U	E
			O	B	E	Y	S		U	S	H	E	R	
C	A	T	T	O	Y			A	U	K				
A	L	I	E	N		F	E	N	G		E	T	A	S
H	O	P	E	S	F	O	R	T	H	E	B	E	S	T
N	E	S	S		A	G	R	A		X	A	C	T	O
			G	N	U			S	P	Y	H	O	P	
W	A	S	T	E		P	L	U	T	O				
A	V	A	I	L	S		O	N	A	S	P	R	E	E
C	O	U	L	D	N	T	C	A	R	E	L	E	S	S
K	I	T	E		A	S	A	P		R	O	M	P	S
O	D	E	S		P	E	L	T		S	T	O	N	E

148

E	S	A	U		S	O	D		A	T	L	A	S	T
B	A	N	S		C	R	Y		R	O	A	D	I	E
B	Y	G	E	O	R	G	E		T	E	N	U	R	E
S	A	L		Y	E	A	R			G	L	E	N	
	H	E	A	V	E	N	S	T	O	B	E	T	S	Y
			B	E	N		O	L	E					
S	A	T	B	Y		G	O	O	D	G	O	L	L	Y
A	T	I	E		I	R	A	T	E		N	E	M	O
O	H	M	Y	S	T	A	R	S		G	E	T	N	O
			I	A	M			H	I	T				
W	E	L	L	B	L	O	W	M	E	D	O	W	N	
A	X	E	L		H	A	R	D		H	U	E		
R	E	V	A	M	P		O	H	M	Y	W	O	R	D
T	R	E	M	O	R		L	E	A		H	O	S	E
S	T	E	A	D	Y		E	R	N		O	P	E	N

149

150

The New York Times

Crossword Puzzles

The #1 Name in Crosswords

Available at your local bookstore or online at nytimes.com/nytstore